Indian Renaissance & Rabindranath Tagore

Indian Renaissance & Rabindranath Tagore

Indra Nath Choudhuri

Vani Book Company

Vani Book Company

Head Office

4695, 21-A, Daryaganj, New Delhi 110 002, India
Phone +91 11 23273167 Fax : +91 11 23275710

Registered Bookstores and Offices

Ashok Rajpath, Patna 800 004, Bihar
Coffee House Campus, Mahatma Gandhi Marg, Allahabad 211 001, Uttar Pradesh
Mahatma Gandhi International Hindi University, Wardha 442 001, Maharashtra
Sultania Road, Moti Park, Bhopal 462 001, Madhya Pradesh
Goripur Taliya Para, 313, R.B.C. Road 24- Parganas (North) Kolkata 743 166, West Bengal

www.vaniprakashan.in
marketing@vaniprakashan.in
sales@vaniprakashan.in

Indian Renaissance and Rabindranath Tagore
by Indra Nath Choudhuri

ISBN : 978-93-89012-58-3
Poetry/Criticism

First Edition 2019
Price : ₹ 695

Printed and bound in India at City Press, Delhi-110 095
Vani Prakashan's signature motif is created by Artist Maqbool Fida Husain

Dedication

To my old student, Shri Arun Maheshwari,
a very distinguished entrepreneur of the
Publishing World.

7 May 1861 - 7 August 1941

"Deliverance is not for me in renunciation.
I feel the embrace of freedom
in a thousand bonds of delight."

Books by Indra Nath Choudhuri

- Aravachin Bangla Sahitya
- "The Genesis of Imagination : Selected Essays on Literature. Theory, Religion and Culture", 2001
- "Sparks Fly Upward : Three Essays on Aesthetics", 1999
- Tulanatmak Sahitya Ki Bhumika, (2004)
- Tulanatmak Sahitya : Bharatiya Paripreksha (2015, Punar Mudran),
- Hinduism : A way of Life and a Mode of Thought 2012, (Niyogi Books), Nirala Kavya Per Bangla Ka Prabhav, 2019
- Bharatiya Navajagaran : Rabindranath Tagore. Gandhi and Swami Vivekananda
- 'Babu Gulab Rai', 2011
- 'Medieval Indian Legacy : Linguistic and Literary' 2012 in English, Published by IGNCA

Introduction

These articles are mostly lectures delivered in the past many years on Tagore in different forums within India and abroad and also during my stay at Edinburgh Napier University as First Tagore Chair. There is some repetition in some lectures but it occurs without disturbing the flow of these papers. These lectures on different aspects on Tagore are mostly concerned with his time and his multifaceted creativity, a discussion on myth, orality and folklore with reference to Tagore, intellectual conflict and companionship between Tagore and Gandhi.

There is a lighter side in both Tagore and Gandhi which always refreshed their lives. Once Gandhi asked Tagore to spin the charkha Tagore immediately replied , "you write a poem and I will spin the wheel."

There are similarly articles on Tagore and his intellectual cum logical and reasoned relationship with Jagadish Chandra Bose, Mahalanobis and Ramananda Chattopadhyay and their idea about India. This idea of India was further elaborated with reference to Swami Vivekananda and also with reference to post colonialism.

One will also find how Tagore could renounce his long time friendship with Kakuzo (Tenshin) Okakura for the sake of establishing peace against war in the world. The book also relates the story of Gitanjali and people's false publicity that W. B. Yeats corrected English of the poems of Gitanjali. With reference to Gitanjali there is a long discussion on Medieval Indian Bhakti Poetry of Conversion and Subversion and Continuity of a Tradition .

Contrary to the ideas of Martha Nussbaum and Isaiah Berlin on cosmopolitanism there is a lengthy analysis on Tagore's independent strong view on the issue that one cannot be a cosmopolitan without rooted to one's heritage and culture and it is also endorsed later by Amartya Sen. Tagore also gave his considered views on universality, universal man and related it with his idea of other modernity.

Besides Gitanjali this book adds another interpretation of one of his novel as at home in the world.

One should not forget that he followed activism all through his life and did not hesitate to relinquish his knighthood in 1919 against the barbaric killing of people at Jallianwala Bagh. One can find his activist traces while discussing his concept of Community Development, Village Reconstruction and Community College Movement.

The star paper of this book is the formation of Tagore's spirituality and the evidence of it in his artistic endeavour.

Tagore was one of the most distinguished writers of children literature. His children writings are discussed in a paper with reference to the children writing of the noble prize winner Spanish writer Juan Ramon Jimenez.

One of Tagore's late age interests was painting and his paintings are interpreted by the connoisseurs of art in different ways and hailed him as a pioneer in the field of modern painting.

This book deals with the life and his much splendored creativity under the big sun umbrella of Indian Renaissance whose reality was for the first time was brought into focus of public domain.

I thank Rashmi of Vani Prakashan for editing these papers to the best of her ability and also deeply thank Shri Arun Maheswari, the publisher and Managing Director of Vani Prakashan for his all out help and cooperation in bringing these lectures/papers into light. God bless him.

Indra Nath Choudhuri

Guru Purnima

16 July 2019

Contents

Chapter One

The Various Streams of Indian Renaissance

The word Renaissance came to India during the colonial period in the 19th century. In the West it meant the cultural rebirth that occurred in Europe from roughly the fourteenth through the middle of the seventeenth centuries, based on the rediscovery of the literature of Greece and Rome and hence Renaissance meant "rebirth" or "reawakening."

With the passage of time Renaissance came to be known as new birth, new dawn, or new beginning and as a result the impact of western civilization, the rise of political consciousness, and the change in society could be seen in what was written during that time.

K N Pannikar in an insightful article on "Was there a renaissance?" in Feb 2011 issue of Frontline, raised certain issues such as

(i) The movements of reform in the pre-colonial period, which were an attempt to reform prevalent socio-religious practices, is quite common in all civilizations; it is a part of the reformers' efforts to refine and refurbish the inner resources of their civilizations.

(ii) Most of these reforms which goes back to the intellectual efflorescence of the 5th to 18thcentury are identified as Indian version of renaissance which overlooked the historical specificities of these movements. Buddhism, Shankaracharya's Advaita Vedanta, Sufism and Bhakti, he further said, did not lead to powerful social churning even if they challenged the existing power relations in society.

(iii) K N Pannikar also said that these socio cum religious movements were unable to break out of the feudal ethos and serve as the ideological harbingers of a progressive transition.

My contention is that K N failed to go deep into the historical reasons to understand the pre colonial India's various ancient streams of renaissance.

I strongly feel that first Indian renaissance took place during the period of Upanishads between 800 BCE and 500 BCE, during a time when Indian society started to questioning, interrogating the traditional Vedic religious order.

The most extraordinary thing about Upanishads is that young students like Svetaketu, or Satyakama, or Nachiketa or Bhrgu, the young boy or a young Brahmachari beggar, or that band of six youthful seekers after truth, Sukesha, Satyakama, Gargya, Aswalayana, Bhargava and Kabandhi or the young women like Gargi or Maitreyi or common man like a cart driver Raikwa are found to be seeking answers or raising questions or even explaining the concept of the eternal or pure consciousness and how that acts as a source of truth and joy. When such kind of awareness is found in youth and common man it stirs a nation and leads to a movement and a renaissance takes place.

In a passage in the Chandogya Upanishad from the seventh millennium BCE, young Svetaketu's father, UddalakAruni, tells young Svetaketu about the manifestation of God in all beings including Svetaketu himself. He says : It is the Self (atman), and thou, O Svetaketu, art thou (Tat tvamasi).

This idea turns into a revolution, an upheaval in the traditional mode of thinking; it was a new idea, a new thinking which shook the psyco- physico entity of human beings. This was the first renaissance in India that took place in the Upanishadic times during 800 BC when the human beings had this thrilling experience in the realization of the message of the Upanishads that the self or atman and Brahman or the Supreme Consciousness are not two distinct realities but two different levels for one and the same reality.

In the Vrihadaranyaka Upanishad it is said, "Let the Universal Soul give us the intellect to have access to His nature." Hence it is not something transcendental but realizing the truth through a complex cognitive process : perception, communication and reasoning.

The extension of this stream of renaissance was to be found in 8th century in Shankaracharya's notion of Advaita Vedanta.

Shankaracharya or Shankara (8th Century A.D.), one of the greatest minds of Indian philosophy, stated that the empirical self realizes itself as pure Consciousness which is to be understood both as Cartesian duality** as well as Vedantic oneness of the empirical self and the Supreme Self. Shankaracharya uses the term *prajna* knowledge also for consciousness.

It is *prajna* or in fact *samyakprajna* or comprehensive knowledge which reveals this meaning of self as (Self/*Atman)* Brahman or pure consciousness. Nothing is mystical or transcendental in the realization of the self as Brahman as in this realization knowledge or reason plays a major role which develops into a new idea , a new thought, a new vision of life.

Bimal Krishna Matilal, one of the very distinguished philosophers of the modern times, also was Spalding professor of philosophy at Oxford said that Indian thought even in its most metaphysical and soteriological (theology of salvation) concerns, was rigorously analytical, logical and discursive. One can strongly argue about the seriousness and professionalism of Indian mystical philosophy. Using Nagarjun's "vigrahavyavartini" and Sri Harsha's "khandanakhandakhadya", one can bring out the logic behind the so-called mystical positions.

This concept of Vedanta was picked up by two important

** Descartes' famous saying epitomizes the dualism concept. He said, "cogito ergo sum," "I reflect therefore I am." Descartes held that the immaterial mind and the material body are two completely different types of substances and that they interact with each other. He reasoned that the body could be divided up by removing a leg or arm, but the mind or soul were indivisible.

figures of the 19th century Indian renaissance : Raja Rammohan Roy and Swami Vivekananda. Both were keen to regenerate India and its people through reforms, and reappraisal of India's ancient faith, particularly Vedanta and bring a new awakening in the light of Western science and knowledge. If Raja Rammohan Roy created Brahmo Samaj Vivekananda developed a man-making religion based on Advaita Vedanta. Rammohun Roy intended to transform the pure philosophy of *Advaita* into a philosophy of life. Through his syncretism, it became a living faith. Vivekananda accentuated this process further by reinterpreting Vedanta as practical Vedanta which according to Vivekananda, rejects exclusiveness in matters of belief and all claims to monopoly of truth and fortifies his understanding of *dharma* as a social construct.

It is therefore not religion but a social construct and hence *sarvodaya,* the keyword of Mahatma Gandhi, the good of everyone, the development of all. *Dharma*, if properly practiced, is the surest means to universal welfare, *sarvabhutahita* and is the goal of all cosmic processes. This is a goal not of an individual to be realized in isolation but it is a cosmic goal to be experienced collectively. This was Vivekananda's ideal which is expressed in the motto of the Order of Ramakrishna, *atmanomokshartham, jagaddhitaya cha* : for the spiritual liberation of oneself and for the welfare of the world. Bamkim Chandra Chattopadhyay because of his strong view against institutional religion in favour of dharma as humanity *(manushvata)* and harmony (*samanjasya*) became a great champion of religio-cultural renaissance of the 19th century India.

K N Pannikar's statement that the social and religious reforms witnessed in 19th century India were neither a continuation of past efforts nor their reinvocations to face contemporary challenges can easily be contested.

Firstly, the historical reasons can be found in various rebellions that took place in different parts of India which fired the imagination of middle class to create a politics based nationalism or religious cum organized national movement and the harbinger of that were Rammohan Roy and Vivekananda.

The 18 century Sannyasi revolt of Hindu Sadhus and of Muslim Fakirs in later part of 18th century which continued for around half century. They raided government treasuries, killed British officers and caused acute chaos and misery. The rebellion continued for around half a century and later got weakened.

Similarly the revolts of Puli Thevar of Tirunevalli of late 18th Century, of Syed Mir Nisar Ali Titumir of Bengal in the beginning of the 19th century, of Kerala Varma of Malabar in 18th Century, of Rani VeluNachiyar of Shivaganga and her women's army in 18th Century, of Veerapandiya Kattabomman of Tamil Nadu in 18th Century and the war of independence raised a rebellious consciousness in the mind of the Indian people and created a historical situation for Raja Rammohan Roy to become the father of modern Indian political thought and Vivekananda to offer a clarion call to Indians for social justice which was almost an indianize Marxian call :

Swami Vivekananda while talking of depressed classes of India first castigates the rich and says, "You, the upper classes of India, do you think you are alive? You are but mummies ten thousand years old and it is you who are the real walking corpses.... of India! You represent the past tense, with all its varieties of form jumbled into one. You are the void, the unsubstantial nonentities of the future. You merge yourselves in the void and disappear, and let New India arise in your place. Let her arise – out of the peasant's cottage, grasping the plough; out of the huts of the fisherman, the cobbler and the sweeper. Let her spring from the grocer's shop. Let her emanate from the factory, from marts and from markets. Let her emerge from groves and forests, from hills and mountains. These common people have suffered oppression for thousands of years – suffered it without murmur, and as a result have got wonderful fortitude. They have suffered eternal misery, which has given them unflinching vitality." Mind you all these were said long before the 1917 Soviet revolution.

It was not only Vivekananda but much much before in Indian history there appeared one of the greatest scholars of India Patanjali, who in his introductory chapter of Mahabhasya written about 2500 years ago, clearly pronounced, *prayukta Lokarthah* and accordingly, *loka* i.e. folk, tribals, depressed class or the comman man, is the authority of word, and its meaning and their relationship, and not the classical brahmanical rules. *Loka* is one of the important guides of human behaviour and *lokamata* or the views of common people constitute a significant part of polity (*nripanaya*) of a country and even the essence of Veda (*nigamanichoda*) and the views of the wise (*prajnavana*). Before Patanjali in the Atharva Veda (XI.7), it is said that in the left over, *ucchaste*, resides Brahman. It is a clever and powerful indictment of the higher class in favour of the lower class.

It is beyond my imagination as how these kinds of words of profound justification for loka could not continue in the long social history of India. The only possible reason one can forward is that due to Brahmanical decadence and degeneration followed by lust for power created a social hierarchy resulting in the creation of depressed classes of India.

It was Buddhism that brought a renaissance by raising the position of humanity. By the time it was 6th century BC the second urbanization took place in India and slowly because of religious renaissance of Buddhism the societal change created a revolution among the excluded section of Indian society and our humanity was revived which was lost during the post Brahmanical-Vedic period when the cast of a person was determined not by his profession (*karmana*) but by his birth (*janmana*). The existence of humanity is the most basic philosophical doctrine of religious cum cultural cum social renaissance. The Buddha introduced the idea of placing a higher value on morality and the equality of people instead of on family or caste a person is born into. This was also the first attempt to abolish discrimination and slavery in the history of mankind.

A prince of Shakya republic Siddartha was born in 563BC. He rejected his life of riches and embraced a lifestyle of asceticism, or extreme self-discipline. After long days of meditation in a forest under a pupil tree (now known as bodhi tree) he received *sambodhi*(enlightenment) and came to beknown as Buddha, or "enlightened one". He went to the nearby village where people spoke in Pali and gave his sermons to them in Pali and the most marvelous extraordinary thing happened in the history of the world that Buddha's sermons given in Pali became a world religion. How did it happen is a wonder of the world.

The existence of humanity is the most basic philosophical doctrine of religious cum cultural cum social renaissance.

This renaissance effect could be seen in the modern times in Tagore and Ambedkar. The issue of the depressed class, the untouchables and the caste spirit, are great setbacks in all round development of India and in realizing the idea of India. Annanya Mukherjee Reed in her perceptive article in 'Outlook' in May 2011 issue says that on the question of inequality and democracy, the parallels between Ambedkar and Tagore go very far : both viewed India's development from the perspective of inequality and saw 'chauvinistic nationalism' as a disaster; both wished for the 'annihilation' of caste rather than its reform; and both hoped to see resistance of the oppressed. Tagore wrote :

> *He more durbhagadeshjaderkarechoapaman*
> *Apamanehotehabethahadersabarsaman*
> Your breathern you have treated with disrespect,
> You have denied them their simple human rights.
> You have made them stand and wait before you,
> And not given them a place in your affection.
> You must share with them all, their ignominy.

To both Tagore and Ambedkar, the primary questions for India were those of inequality and social justice; the primary contradiction between the façade of formal democracy and the reality of structural injustice and the equal position for the comman man.

In Bangla story telling formula, says Nabaneeta DevSen, a tale begins, *Ek je chhilo raja,* ("There was a king"). In one of his last pieces written in 1941, just before his death, Tagore begins his tale with this formulaic expression *Ek je ache manush* ("There is a man"). He makes two enormously important changes in the formula, he changes its tense from the past to the present, and changes its subject from a king to a common man. Instead of *there was* he writes *there is,* and instead of *a king* he writes *a man,* meaning a common *human being* and along with Swamiji, thus, Tagore exalts the position of a common man in the making of the idea of India. He is a comman man not a renaissance man like Leonardo da vinci, Michael Angelo, Raphael, Botticelli .The Indian common man may not be a polymath but he lives with dignity and self esteemthat what Indian renaissance has bestowed on him.

In Tagore's Gora untouchability is the main issue which could be resolved by universal humanism. Ramananda Chattopadhyay, the most celebrated editor of "Modern Review" from 1908 to 1947 is very candid in this respect and says that to do away with untouchability to the extent that Mr. Gandhi wants though that itself would be to pullout one much of a remedy, it is the caste spirit which must be exorcised.

But it is sad that caste spirit is slowly getting entrenched more deeply because of the fundamental defect in our form of democracy which is based on the vote of the individual which can be easily manipulated by muscle and money power and which has given rise to criminalization of politics. It is the atomization of society that is responsible for this kind of political system. The state cannot be an arithmetical sum of individuals. The people, the nation, the community can never be equated with the sum of individual voters. There is no doubt that electoral democracy is one of India's greatest political achievements and affirmation of human political freedom. But that is not all particularly when we have been watching over the years how the voters are manipulated particularly in the name of cast and as the things are dalits will remain dalits for the next hundreds and hundreds of years in this system of vote of one individual. No doubt our democracy has given momentum to the politics of poor but without the communitarian polity** things can not have a smooth sailing.

All these variety of thoughts, diversity of ideas vividly display the existence of a nation of thinking minds and a knowledge society otherwise Pattanjali's statement in praise of *loka* or Buddha's social renaissance of which the pall bearers in the modern times were Tagore, Nayayana Guru, Bhimrao Ambedkar, 'Periyar' E.V. Ramasamy, Ayyankali, Ayothee Das, Mahadev Govind Renade, Ramabai Renade and many more could not have started their social movements which impacted the society rather so deeply. They came in the forefront with their new ideas; new vision which are the basic ethos of a knowledge society. It is only lack of interpretation

** As a visionary and an idealist, JP came out with a bold formulation at the conceptual and practical level in terms of his concepts of Communitarian Polity ot Partyless Democracy and understanding that scholars say that the cultural creativity and intellectual efflorescence that were the hallmarks of the European Renaissance were conspicuous by their absence in the Indian situation.

More than the social renaissance Buddhism ushered a renaissance in the field of art, architecture and culture. Encyclopedia Britannica says that the term renaissance was first used by French art historians of the late 18th century in reference to the reappearance of antique architectural forms on Italian buildings of the early 16th century. The term was later expanded to include the whole of the 15th and 16th centuries and, by extension, to include sculpture, painting, and the decorative arts. The term indicates a phenomenon that had its origins in Italy and then spread through Western Europe.

Indian renaissance in art, architecture and sculptor influenced by Buddhism was ushered in by Mauryan dynasty in 269 BC. When king Ashoka after the Kalinga war became a pacifist and decided to have stone monuments as a symbol of the message of peace, brotherhood and cultural unity. Traditions say, he created several *stupas* or dome-shaped monuments as well as erected monolithic pillars or *lat* which have defied the ravages of time and have set an example as the most magnificent artistic record of Indian renaissance of the Buddhist times. Asokan pillars are a triumph of engineering, architecture and sculpture. The capital of the Sarnath Pillar is undoubtedly the most magnificent and has been declared the finest piece of sculpture.

The famous art historian, Dr. V.A. Smith, says "it would be difficult to find in any country an example of ancient sculpture or even equal to this beautiful work of art, which successfully combines realistic modeling with ideal dignity and is finished in every detail with perfect accuracy".

The Mauryan Emperous were succeeded in Magadha by the Sunga(184-22 BCA) and Kanva rules, while the Greeks(327 BCA), the Parthians, the Sakas (139BCA) and the Kushanas (80-144 BCA) ruled the north-west frontier. In the trans-Vindhyan India the Satavahana (200 BCA) ruled. During this time, almost for four hundred years, there was an outburst of activity in the realms of religion, literature and art.

The alien rulers in India, the Greeks, the Sakas and the Kushanas were indianised. The famous Greek ruler Menander embraced Buddhism while Saka rulers embraced the vedic religion.

Under the liberal patronage of Kushan rulers, specially, Kanishka, Buddhism spread far and wide especially in Central Asia and China. They were instrumental in developing Mahayana Buddhism and the Gandhara and Mathura schools of art.

The rise of the Gandhara School of art testifies to the prevalence of foreign influence on the art of the country. The Indian art underwent a rapid development in this period. It is said that the artists took considerable pain in carving and evolved perfect techniques of sculpture. This was probably on account of the natural growth of an aesthetic progress.

The main theme of the Gandhara School of Sculpture was the form of Buddhism, and its most important contribution was the evolution of an image of the Buddha. The votaries of Western renaissance would not discover in it the birth of a man in full perfection rather they would locate in the Renaissance paintings the celebration of human body and call it a reflection of the rebirth of man.

The base reliefs of Bharhut, Sanchi, Amravati and other places serve the purpose of an illuminating commentary on the life of the age. They reflect spontaneous joy, emotions and movements of the life of the masses. For the first time Indian art became conscious of the socio-economic structure of the society.

In the south during the rules of Pallavas and Cholas (600-650) there took place a religious revival that aimed to synthesize Hinduism and Islam to ensure communal goodwill and unity and to create an environment of toleration and cooperation. Through this mingling a new type of Indo-Islamic architecture was developed. The Muslims added to the Hindu architecture the special characteristics of spaciousness, massiveness, majesty and width. They introduced mehrab or arch, dome, minar and tomb in the indigenous architecture. Patterns of subtle curves, intricate and geometrical designs were used for rich decorative treatment. The Hindu schemes of profuse ornamentation were applied to decorate the arches or mehrabs.

Besides, Pallavas are most noted for their patronage of architecture, the finest example being the Shore Temple, a UNESCO World Heritage Site in Mahabalipuram and built series of temples which still today speak highly of a renaissance period of art and architecture.

Gupta period of Indian history (600 BCA), is known as the golden age of Indian creative, artistic and scientific advancement. Architecture, sculpture, painting, terracotta, metallurgy, music dancing, literary advancement etc. - all attained unprecedented progress under the Guptas.

Great progress was made in the domain of scientific studies during the Gupta period. The formulation of the theory of zero and consequent evolution of the decimal system are to be credited to the thinkers of this age. Aryabhatta, Varahamihira and Brahmagupta were in their own days, "the foremost astronomers and mathematicians of the world". In his famous work Surya Siddhanta Aryabhatta examines and explains the true causes of solar and lunar eclipses. His calculation of the size of the earth is very near that estimated by modern astronomers.

The art of casting metals reached a degree of perfection which may well be regarded as exceptional. It is sad that by ignoring this aspect of Indian renaissance, people would like to make such unjust statements that the cultural creativity and intellectual efflorescence that were the hallmarks of the European Renaissance were conspicuous by their absence in the Indian situation and the period of renaissance was not particularly known for creativity.

Another stream of Indian renaissance was medieval bhakti movement. During the rules of Pallavas and Cholas in the south, the Tamil Alwar saints in the 6th and 7th century AD, preached the simple religion of love and complete surrender to an immanent being and the idea spread from Tamilnad to Andhra (though there was no Andhra that time) and then to Karnataka, and Maharashtra and Gujarat and by the time it was 13-14 century, it spread in Rajasthan and went up to Kashmir where two women saints Lalded and Abba Khatun surprised everybody with their mystical love poetry. From there it spread in mid-India and another stream of devotion came through Chaitanya Mahaprabhu and brought Manipur, Bengal,

Assam and Odessa in its fold. With the advent of Sufis and their philosophy bhakti movement touched the soul of the people and ultimately became a pan Indian movement. It was a revolution that took the imagination of people by storm. In spite of diversity of this literature written in different Indian languages they are connected by common belief, faith, myths and legends.

Medieval devotional i.e. bhakti poetry is poetry of conversion of the total India into an alternative way of showing love for the divine and also of subversion and interrogation.

Bhakti literature questions the social and religious norms, and brings gods (Vishnu, Shiva, Rama, Krishna) from the temples to make them members of the human family by crossing and subverting the boundaries of hierarchies. It was domestication of Godhead.

The medieval *bhakti* movement was in fact initiated by the common people, mostly belonging to lower caste, poor, involved in low professions but always ecstatic in their love for God. Just to cite one example from the Kannada *vachana* texts of Basavanna (1134-1196), the leader of the Virasaiva religious movement of medieval Karnataka :

> The rich/will make temples for Siva/What shall
> I/a poor, do?
> My legs are pillars/the body the shrine/the head a
> cupola/of gold.
> Listen, O lord of the meeting rivers/things standing
> shall fall/but the moving ever shall stay.

Indian temples are traditionally built, as explained by A.K. Ramanujan, in the image of human body. The temple in brick and stone carries the primordial blueprint of the human body but in time the human metaphor faded and temple became a static standing thing of brick, stone and mortar and its moving originals were forgotten. The Virsaiva movement was a social upheaval by and for the poor, the low-caste and the outcaste against the rich and the privileged.

If it is not a social churning and breaking out of the feudal ethos, what it is then? It was a rising of the unlettered against the literate pundit and demonstration of the common man's perception of the mundane world as something real and concrete not as illusory or transient. *Bhakti*, is the last of the great Hindu anti-contextual notions. It defies all contextual structures, caste, ritual, temples, sacred space, sacred time, the Vedas and the *Sastras* (systematized knowledge). And within this movement, women defy more structures : gender, and all that goes with it (notions of modesty, marriage, dependence on men). Once again *bhakti* shows us how close the independent, defiant women of the oral tales are to women in the *bhakti* movement. Akkamahadevi of Karnataka and Lal Ded of Kashmir, both gave up family life, wandered about without clothes and the necked body covered only with their tresses, defying social norms of the male governed society and spread the gospel of *Jnana*(knowledge) and worship of Siva. In one of her vachanas Akkamahadevi says :

> To the shameless girl
> Wearing the white Jasmine Lord's
> Light of morning;
> You fool,
> Where is the need for cover and jewel?

Akkamahadevi uses the mystic symbolism of the Virsaivas and Lal Ded employs the old Buddhist symbolism of river and ferry in her many songs. They were all socially ostracized but they cared less and established themselves as the precursor of a social movement of great magnitude by intertwining sacred with the love for life.

There are two more streams of Indian renaissance to be discussed : nationalism and modernity and thereafter I am done with my presentation.

As in ancient India there was no concept of a nation-state, no concept of a boundary of a country, it lived in an open pace with an open mind and welcomed people to come and stay. Hence people of different races came and settled here. One can find examples of love for the country, regional patriotism but not the concept of *rashtra* or a nation. The notion of nationalism is a contribution of 19th century Indian renaissance.

Freedom Struggle brought into focus the notion of Nationalism. Initially during the renaissance period the religio-cultural nationalism, as propagated by Bankim Chandra Chattopadhyay and Vivekanada and many others flourished but it was quite broad in its conception and embraced the whole humanity. This religio-cultural nationalism as said by the famous historian, K.M.Panikkar, was responsible in uniting the people of India into one nation. He said, "What gave Indian nationalism its dynamism and ultimately enabled it to weld at least the major part of India into one state was the creation of a sense of community among the Hindus to which the credit should, to a very large extent, go to Swami Vivekananda." Initially in every Indian language the idea of renaissance nationalism was to glorify one's own kshetra, land e.g. in Malayalam the first and foremost of the poets expressing this sentiment was Vallattol Narayana Menon. Having whole- heartedly accepted Mahatma Gandhi as his guiding star in 1920 wrote his famous poem, '*Entegurunathan*', My Master that made him an eloquent champion of the nationalist movement. At the same time Vallattol also wrote poems like '*Matrivandanam*' extolling not Bharatbarsha but his motherland Kerala.

This is the ambivalence of the whole issue of renaissance nationalism in Indian context. Here both nation (*desa*) and region (*kshetra*) are of equal importance and for the West it was difficult to understand because of the notion of exclusive nationalism of nation- State. India is a combination of many regions or kshetras and it is obvious that from kshetra one moves into desha and therefore regional nationalism is essential for a federal India which develops progressively into pan Indian nationalism. After all in Indian nationalism there is a harmonious relationship between kshetra and desha and Tagore spoke strongly about this federal structure of India. In consequence, India does not have just not one main stream but several main streams which remain together in perfect harmony without losing their identities. This is what is popularly known as unity in diversity. India's political arrangement there is no way for any person to be only Indian and nothing else; you can be a good Malayalee, a good Hindu or Muslim and a good Indian all at once and there is no hierarchy in these identities. They remain harmoniously blended together.

Both Tagore and Gandhi created a moral universe and made it a part of politics and gave a bigger lofty meaning to nationalism. The foundation stones of nationalism, for them, were the idea of plurality and the sense of communality which are the bases of the inclusive plural notion of nationalism that seeks for human unity or universal nationalism. Tagore and Gandhi both say that people are greater than the nation and this message of humanism is the core ethos of India.

Colonialism, as says K N Panikar, led to the emergence of a new breed of Indians who idealized the West, adopted a Western-modern way of life and subjected tradition to critical inquiry. The relationship between the traditional and the "colonial-modern" was not dialogical but mainly one of domination. There is nothing to contest here but when KNP says that the period of renaissance was not particularly known for creativity, which received an impetus only when renaissance and reformation merged with nationalism and tried to usher in an alternative modernity can very strongly be contested.

KNP's premises are all western and he tries to analyze Indian categories in the light of western premises and the whole thing becomes probalametic.

No concept comes from thin air, it grows in a certain socio-cultural context and hence the notion of renaissance, reformation or western nationalism or western modernity can't be applied to understand our idea of new dawn, new birth or reawakening,

Rajiv Malhotra's well founded proposal for a reversal of gaze from West to East to Eastern gaze upon the West is primarily to contest the western categories and its de facto status of an arbiter of what is considered universally true. In simple terms it is a challenge to Western universalism and an effort to understand the West on Indian terms or socio-cultural categories.

Sharing the theory of savageology, the Indologists attempted to wash out India's cultural memory by popularizing the so called notion that 'westernization is modernization' This view encouraged a debate in India between the advocates of 'tradition' (*purana*) and the advocates of 'modernity' (*nutana*) throughout the 19th century and many great writers discovered the universal, everlasting values in our ancient texts, Vedas and Upanishads and in the medieval devotional poets like Kabir, Nanak, Dadu, Meera,Vasavanna and Vaishnava poets and also a message of humanism in the Indian folk songs and folk religious expressions like Bauls of Bengal. On top of it the continuity of a tradition exposed the obvious fault lines of modernity that could be easily detected in the notion of the Whiteman's burden and their understanding of orientalism as exposed by Edward Said.

In India, modernism as a phenomenon or value is not an absolutely unrelated one without reference to the past or the future. It absorbs in it traditional values as well as new innovations and is indicated by the term 'continuity'. It is essential to do that because the spirit of India, as says Tagore or as the writers have observed over the ages, is not to reject anything. Everything has a place here as an alternative. India lives with many alternatives which become part of the continuity of thought and creativity and hence the choice which Gandhi or Tagore offered to us was not tradition versus modernism, but the choice of both versus the forced acceptance of one. This is the Indian way of thinking. Indian thinking is not logo-centric and exclusive, but symbolic or inclusive and hence India has no problem to live with many life choices and this is possible because as said by Tagore, one has the freedom of mind and boldly explained that "true modernism is freedom of mind, not slavery of taste. It is in dependence of thought and action, not tutelage under European school masters" [9]. He further mentioned in his essay on "Modern Poetry" that the joy of natural and detached way of looking at things belongs to no particular age; it belongs to every one whose eyes know how to wander over the naked earth. [10] It is over a thousand years since the Chinese poet Li-Po wrote his verses, but he was a modern, he looked upon the universe with freshly opened eyes :

> Why do I live among these green hills?
> The question makes me laugh, I don't answer.
> My mind is still.
> I live under another sky and on another earth—
> In a world that belongs to no man.
> The peach tree blossoms, the stream flows by [11]

In the unity of beings one realizes the spirit, *atma.* Hence, while defining modernity in his own terms, he had no hesitation to declare in Beijing in 1924 that 'The impertinence of material things is extremely old. The revelation of spirit in man is modern. I am in its side, I am modern.'

In this way Tagore created his other modernity by stressing on freedom, objectivity, continuity of a tradition particularly bhakti and spirituality and prepared the basis for his Nobel prize winning book of poetry, Gitanjali.

In India, modernism as a phenomenon or value is not an absolutely unrelated one without reference to the past or the future. It absorbs in it traditional values as well as new innovations and is indicated by the term "continuity". To give an example, however innovative the classical singer Bhimsen Joshi might be with the introduction of new ways of singing or the sarod player Amjad Alli khan be they would never be called modern singers or musical instrument players like Jazz and rock singers but only a part of the continuity of a musical tradition of India.

Tradition is defined as the handling down of knowledge or the passing on of a doctrine or a technique.

We often assume that a form is handed down in an unchanging fashion and that what comes to us is its pristine form.

However, the sheer act of handling on a tradition introduces change, and not every tradition is meticulously bonded by mnemonic or other devices to prevent interpolations or change. A tradition, therefore, has to be seen in its various phases.

Even the concept *parampara* (tradition), which at one level appears to be frozen knowledge, reveals, on investigation, variations and change.

In other words, what we regard as tradition may well turn out to be our contemporary requirements fashioned by the way we wish to interpret the past.

This is explained by two important terms :

Kula and *shila*.
Kula is heredity, inheritance, tradition.

Shila is the making of man , his demeanour and personality of man which, however, are conditioned by his *kula*. *Shila* in his own given time and space goes on discarding elements of *kula* which have lost their potency and in the process generates new mode of thought enriches and invigorates the shila making tradition dynamic and not static. There is a wonderful story which I heard from A. K. Ramanujan which endorses this view of tradition. There was a philosopher who went to a village in Karnataka where a village showed him a dagger and said, it is our family dagger about three hundred years old. In these three hundred years its wooden handle or butt has been changed several times and also the blade of the dagger which got rusted many times in these three hundred years times was also changed several times. But it is the same dagger.

Is there any way to historically reconstruct the tradition?

There is always a normative code of tradition but at the same time there exists numerous deviations from the norm. It is therefore possible to project a variety of traditions as dominant in Indian culture none of which is more or less authentic than the rest.

The Indian tradition has given to every sensitive Indian the ability to internalize a multiplicity of traditions.

Western historiography of literature is based on literary histories which do not have multiple parallel traditions.

The term parallel can be applied to popular or folk traditions in European contexts.

In India the parallel traditions are really alternative traditions rather than low value traditions.

Tagore was not adamantly opposed to the lessons and practices of the West and even said, it was providential that the West had come to India. What needed to be resisted, however, was the imposition of Western standards as imperial edict; for India was not beggar of the West and must find her own path toward modernity, thus making a distinctive contribution to human thought in general.

❑❑

Chapter Two

Remembering Tagore : His Times and his Multifaceted Creativity

Rabindranath Tagore in his autography, "My Reminiscences" (*Jibansmriti,* 1912) and "My Boyhood Days" (Chhelebela, 1940) speaks about his birth in 1861 at a great period of history when the currents of three movements had met in the life of our country :

(i) The first movement was a religious movement introduced by Raja Ram Mohan Roy, a great hearted man of gigantic intelligence, who fought against orthodoxy to reopen the age old channel of spiritual life. Tagore's father Maharshi Debendranath Thakur joined this movement and was ostracized by the society. He became an ascetic early in his life and remained deeply involved in spiritual pursuits and came to be known as Maharshi, a great seer. He impacted Tagore in a big way to the path of Upanishads and spirituality and provided him one of the fundamental metaphors in his poetic creativity.

What distinguishes Tagore from other great poetical genius of his time is the unity of inspiration described so insightfully in his poetry :

> The Infinite wants the finite's intimate comradeship
> And the finite wishes to lose itself in the Infinite.

But the father and the son had a big difference of approach

to life. Maharshi Debendranath Tagore would never like spiritual puritan ethics to be intertwined with joy of life whereas Tagore would by referring to the first mantra of Isopanishad would always say, rejoice and renounce. W.B. Yeats, therefore, made a comment about Tagore that he is the only saint who did not refuse to live. This is also diametrically opposite to what Gandhi said to an English journalist when asked to give in five words, the meaning of life, Gandhi said, why five I will give you in three words, renounce and rejoice. However the father, according to two autobiographical account suggests, never seriously interfered with Rabindranath's autonomy except in only one thing the father was uncompromising about taking bath in cold water; Rabindranath says that even at Dalhousie, in the Himalayas, he had to bathe in icy cold water.

(ii) Second movement was a literary movement initiated by Bankim Chandra Chatterjee, who brought freedom in literary style, created new forms and took our literature to new heights in strength and grace. Tagore's inherent poetic creativity automatically moved towards the world of literature. Jyotirindranath Tagore was the first person to offer young Rabindranath a model of patriotic zeal and fervour and intense capacity for artistic expression together with a style of creativity which borrowed uninhibitedly from both the East and the West. It was Jyoti who introduced Rabindranath to the world of politics and the arts and it is his wife Kadambari Devi who was the first to recognise Rabindranath's immense creative talent and give Rabindranath, deeply unsure of his writing, confidence to himself.

She introduced Rabi to Biharilal, the most popular poet of Bengal those days whom even Rabi liked both as a man and a poet. Chitra Dev in her fascinating narration of 'Women of the Tagore Household' says that Kadambari not only nurtured the lamp of Rabi's genius but lit up the wick and disappeared into the darkness. How did it happen? She committed suicide within four months of Tagore's marriage to a 10 year girl Bhabatarini, quite thin, not good looking and almost illiterate whose name was changed to Mrinalini by Tagore's elder brother Dwijendranath.

Maharshi Debendranath was quite radical in his religious beliefs but rarely so in matters of social behaviour.

Why Kadambari, his sister-in-law committed suicide? There

are various answers which I would not like to discuss in this paper except what Tagore said about her with a deep tinge of sorrow and tenderness, "I was very fond of her. She also loved me a lot. It is this love that has attuned my heart to the Bengali women." He wrote :

> *Nayano samukhe tumi nai*
> *Nayanero majkhane niyechho je thnai*
> 'You are no longer before my eyes
> You have taken up abode in the midst of my eyes.'

In the course of time Tagore developed deep love for his wife, whom he called "chhoto bau" (little bride), "chuti" (holiday) and "my little wife" and wrote in a letter in 1890 from Europe, "I became restless thinking of seeing you again." In another letter in 1898 he said, "May the two of us remain to the very end sure refuges for each other's world-weary heart' and in another letter in 1900," if you sweeten my life with your love and care...your efforts will be precious to me.'

The Metaphor of Death

She gave birth to Bela, the first child of them at the age of 13 and subsequently four more children and died at the age of 29 within 19 years of their marriage. Tagore's family life was, for the most part, tragic.

After the death of his wife his daughter, Renuka, died in1903. Later he lost his youngest son, Shamindranath, his eldest daughter Bela, and his only grandson.

In all these deaths particularly in his wife's death Tagore saw death as conjoined with life which triumphs so beautifully (amrita se-mritu hote daao tumi ani).

This notion of death is so poignantly but beautifully described in his most popular play "The Post Office" (Dakghar), which is staged and being staged all over the world even today. When Hitler's Nazi army attacked Paris in the beginning of the 2nd World war, the Radio Paris was that time broadcasting the French translation of Andre Gide's "The Post Office" and in Hitler's Jewish ghetto in Poland, a well known doctor, writer and director Korczak, directed and staged this play with the help of some of the 200 orphan children, who were under his care, knowing well that very soon his and their life would end in gas chamber. When Korczak was asked by someone, why did he select this play, his reply was that he wanted to give the message to the children as how to accept the angel of death in peace.

(iii) The third movement was national movement which was not political in its initial form but mostly an assertion of our identity and a voice of indignation at the humiliation heaped upon us by the colonial rulers by desecrating our culture and disdainfully rejecting our works of art, literary creativity and knowledge as creation of an inferior culture and bringing a divide between our people as irrational primitive and enlightened western oriented modern. The leaders of this movement or revolt belong to Tagore's own family, his brothers and cousins who discovered the universal, everlasting values in our ancient texts, Vedas and Upanishads and in the medieval devotional poets like Kabir, Nanak, Dadu,Vasavanna and Vaishnava poets and also a message of humanism in the Indian folk songs and folk religious expressions like Bauls of Bengal. This national movement, on one side, induced Tagore's family to establish a patriotic Hindu mela in 1860, a fair to promote indigenous goods, ideas and infuse love for the Indian products and sale of those and Hindu-Muslim unity. On the other side, on the analogy of Italy's guru of unification and freedom, Giuseppe Mazzini (1805 -1872) and his associate, Giuseppe Garibaldi (1807-1882) Jyotindranath, the elder brother of Tagore and his young friends and cousins established a secret society *"Sanjivini Sabha"* and under the auspicious of that Rabindranath Tagore wrote fiery songs to raise the passion of the people against the 1905 Bengal partition.

Rabindranath : The Lonely Boy

Before I further elaborate this issue let us recapitulate his younger days as a boy he grew up by reciting the mantras of the Upanishads and when he became a little older he showed his genuine deep love for English literature particularly Shakespeare, Walter Scott and the English Romantics but his adoration for Indian literature particularly Kalidasa and Vaishnava poets, Vidyapati, Kabir, Vasavanna and Dadu was in no way eclipsed by his interest in English literature..

Being the youngest of the fourteen children of his parents he had to spend his days mostly in the company and under the strict vigilance of servants and felt extremely lonely and forsaken. On Tagore's centenary celebrations in 1961, Satyajit Ray made a feature film on Tagore. In that there was a scene of young Tagore standing at the back of a window covered with iron bars as if he was imprisoned in a jail and young Tagore was looking restless and eager to be freed from this enclosed environment so that he could be one with the earth, its flowing river and the wind, in fact with nature. Tagore loved nature and always desired to absorb the loneliness of the vast pulsating nature with its growing trees, dark forest and flying birds.

Tagore gave his acceptance speech for the Nobel prize award for his slim book of songs, Gitanjali or "Song Offerings" on 26 May 1921 after a gap of 8 years in Stockholm. Tagore in fact received the award in Calcutta in a function on 29th Jan 1914 from Lord Carmichael, Governor of Bengal as he could not attend the Nobel Award Ceremony on 10 Dec 1913 at Stockholm but sent a telegram accepting the prize which was declared on 13 Nov 1913. In his acceptance speech Tagore said,

"On that day at night when the telegraphic message came about the award of the Nobel Prize to me, I sat upon the terrace alone and asked myself the question :

What could be the reason of my poems being accepted by the West in spite of my belonging to a different race, parted and separated by seas and mountains from the children of the West?"

Tagore then attempted to trace out the source of his creativity and also the reasons for his acceptance by the West. He said,

"His life in his young days was spent in absolute seclusion in the company of wild ducks, flowing river, sunshine and starry nights."

Infinite Peace and Feeling of the Eternal

Tagore thought that no poet of the West could have spent his days in such seclusion because seclusion itself has no place in the Western world. He further thought that West in their overactive life had a thirst for the infinite peace and feeling of the eternal and that what they had found out in his poetry.

Then he decided to come out from seclusion and do some work for his fellow beings by teaching their children. His love for nature opened up his love for children. His objective was to give freedom and joy to children and men. He created a school in 1903 and named it Shantiniketan, 'an abode of peace' where the world meets in one nest :

Yatra viswam bhavet eka nidam.

During his stay there working for the school which later turned into an university and named it Visva-Bharati, Tagore found peace in the silence of the afternoon watching the trees of the shadowing avenue, in the chats and songs of the children filling the air with a spirit of delight, in the bosom of the infinite sky, under the glorious stars of the silent night, he wrote the poems of Gitanjali and the west accepted him. He was hailed by W. B. Yeats, Ezra Pound and others as a great poet from the East and others found in him the imprint of god. They found in his poetry offerings from finite to infinite.

Struge Moor, after hearing Tagore's reading of his poems at Rothenstein's residence had remarked to W.B. Yeats that the poems are preposterously optimistic. To this Yeats replied,

Ah! You see he is absorbed in God.

This peace and the feeling of the eternal is possible if one tries to understand the unity of mankind- an idea which was so much needed for people to realize during that time in the war ravage Europe and even today in the world.

Tagore said in his acceptance speech that the spirit of unity of all races is the message of the East to the West and quoted Upanishads to establish his point :

> He who sees all beings in his self, and his self in all the beings does not hate any one, and knows the truth

In the unity of beings one realizes the spirit, *atma.* Hence, while defining modernity in his own terms, he had no hesitation to declare in Beijing in 1924 that :

"The impertinence of material things is extremely old. The revelation of spirit in man is modern. I am in its side, I am modern."

Revelation of Spirit in man is the core philosophy of Tagore. Tagore's was not the lone voice during those days. Jose Ortega Y Gasset, considered to be the greatest Spanish philosopher of the modern time, developed a philosophical system known as "ratiovitalism" had said clearly that modernity brought two common elements.

Disorientation and Dehumanization in poetry and then affirmed that artisans are recognized by their tools. The poetical tools of the Bengali poet Tagore resembled the universal propositions of philosophy. Rabindranath is not in need of anything historical and sumptuary, particular to his time or his land :

With a little of sun,
With sky and clouds,
With mountain and thirst,
With storms and river banks,
With a door and frame of window from
which to look out,
and above all, with all a loving favour
for God,
He produces his songs.

This lyric poetry thus consists of universal things which are and have been everywhere and transforms it into a bird eager to sing from every branch. Then Ortega includes a sentence of Tagore, 'In the creation of God, nothing has an end. All which is true remains.'

Unity of Mankind

In 1922 in Pune in the Kirlosker Theatre he gave a lecture on Indian Renaissance, elaborating the same idea as was mentioned in his acceptance speech, the Bengali version of that is titled : "shikkhar milan", he said that a man who is alone or one is meaningless because there is no unity in one. The one with many is truly one because in that one can see the unity and this unity gives the message of truth.

In his receiving the noble prize tremendous exuberance was shown during that time and Tagore was accepted as the messenger of peace, unity of mankind and transcendentalism who found God in nature- a messenger from the orient belonging to a culture of the other.

But very soon the exuberance faded away. In the words of Professor Dimock, Tagore, after receiving the Nobel Prize in 1913 and thereafter for about two decades, flashed across the Western skies like a comet and like a comet he disappeared and again like a comet he made his appearance in the 1960s of the last century when the children of the neo romantics like Aane Akhmatova and Donald S. Harrington and others found in him a sympathetic voice of :

(i) anti-materialism,

(ii) adored his vision of the spiritual, and

(iii) his search for beauty in man and nature

which were very much familiar to them and also his late poetry which became less and less poetry, more and more unadorned human voice and his journey towards greater and greater honesty attracted them.

Like a comet he appears again though a little dimmed with time. Today, it seems to me that Tagore's effort in raising in us the consciousness of the Asian identity is bearing fruit. Asian soil has mastered the trick of trapping eternity somewhere, somehow. The Asian identity is just not poverty and suffering but an endless quest for inner peace and spiritual freedom that binds mankind together.

This idea of human unity goes against any kind of violence to human beings and also the western notion of the other and rejection of freedom of man. Tagore posited the idea that the history of the growth of freedom is the history of the perfection of human relationship. In fact i) freedom and ii) unity of mankind are the two voices of Tagore which are two very important aspects of India's civilizational values.

The East and the West

Tagore never had any narrow approach related to humanity. In his novel 'Home and the World' Tagore justified this view :

"I do not think that it is the spirit of India to reject anything, reject any race, and reject any culture. The spirit of India has always proclaimed the ideal of unity... We must discover the most profound unity, the spiritual unity between the different races. We must go deeper down to the spirit of man and find out the great bond of unity, which is to be found in all human races... Man is not to fight with other human races, other human individuals, but his work is to bring about reconciliation and peace and restore the bonds of friendship and love."

And so he could "In creative Unity" end his essay with a rebuttal of the imperialist notions of incompatibility voiced by Rudyard Kipling.

"It is true that they (East & West) are not showing any real sign of meeting. But the reason is because the West has not sent out its humanity to meet the man in the East but only its machine. Therefore, the poet's line has to be changed into something like this : Man is man, Machine is Machine and never the twain shall wed".

The Other

The idea of the East as some shadowy, threatening 'other' with which the West is in sharp conflict, and the essentialising of East and West into two simple and contrastive categories has a long history and can be traced back to the time of Herodotus but that history is now a past history. Sartre's famous statement 'hell is the other' carries a strong echo of Hegel, who always defines one's identity as identity against the other either to be appropriated or to be destroyed.

But the Western mind knows well that if he succeeds in completely subjugating the 'other', the identity of his own self becomes dubious. He wants to become whole by destroying the other but without the other, he becomes nothing. For Tagore the 'other' was never a source of reference to define one's own identity as it was for the Europeans. The self was always accepted as self referential, the other was never a threat to their identity, nor a source of confirmation of their uniqueness.

The concept of human unity so assiduously nurtured by Tagore is now at the centre of philosophical discussion in the West.

Emmanuel Levinas and Jacques Derrida, the most celebrated philosophers of the contemporary world, discuss this issue of the self and the other in detail. Levinas says, "The foundation of ethics consists in the obligation to respond to the other.' 'In being for the other only the sense of responsibility (goodness, mercy, charity) calls forth."

For Derrida, the foundation of ethics is hospitality, the readiness and the inclination to welcome the other into one's home.

Levinas's and Derrida's theories of ethics – responsibility and hospitality- no doubt, reveal a new consciousness emerging in the West about its relationship with the East but the view of the West is still just a broad view of particularism and is still linear and binary and so Huntington writes about the clash of civilizations between Western and Muslim civilizations each forcefully confronting the other and hence they are confused by Tagore's own description of his Bengali family as the product of a confluence of three cultures : Hindu, Mohammedan and British.

The spirit of India believes in the ideal of unity – it does not reject – comprehends all with love and sympathy.

Let us not forget that just three years before he wrote "Gitanjali"; he had written the famous novel "Gora" which gives a most vivid account of the most anguished debates which were raging within the Hindu society at the beginning of the 20th century, no less passionate and self searching than what Thomas Mann was to depict later in his famous novel "The Magic Mountain" concerning the dark and troubled state of European civilization. Two novels about two destinies.

Thomas Mann broods over the threatened collapse of the civilized values, which constitute the identity of Europe. Tagore, on the other hand, reflecting over the crisis of Hindu identity which is being threatened precisely by those "civilized values" of Europe which were being forced on a society that had no choice but to accept or reject them. This is the message of Gora and Tagore's approach to Western civilization and the realization of India's identity.

Gora in his journey from communalism, sectarianism, religious conservatism to the ideals of humanism says at the end of the novel;

"For me there is nothing bigger than my country- I am not beyond the pain and happiness, knowledge and ignorance of the total India. In me exists both Hindu and Muslim- All the casts of India are my cast."

Here the spirit is to acknowledge the whole world as one's family as conceived in the Vedic discourse : *vasudhaiva kutumbukam*. This is definitely different from what the Greek philosopher Diagenes of Sinope, said in 412 BC, 'I am a citizen of the world' because it does not in any prove one's identity as a member of a family. This is India's all-embracing age old vision of human unity or universal humanity.

A belief was created during the colonial time and still continuing in the post-colonial time that progressive West is universal and the regressive East is particular. This kind of a notion of cultural uniqueness goes against the concept of human unity so assiduously nurtured by Tagore by introducing the notion of universal humanity in his poem, 'Bharattirtha' :

> Oh my mind, awake heroically on the shores of the ocean of universal humanity.'
>
> Tagore's opinion was clear that first try to understand what is good in others and that would help in regaining one's selfhood and hence in his lecture *'purba o paschim'*
>
> he said,

"At every turn - in her laws and customs, in her religions and social institutions - India today deceives and insults herself. Meeting of East and West on our soils will succeed when there will be inner harmony between the two is achieved.

In Indian history, the meeting of the Muscleman and the Hindu produced Akbar, the object of whose dream was the unification of hearts and ideals."

Violance

Tagore's one of the central preoccupations in his writings was to raise his voice against violence which he thought was a crime committed against humanity.

The best example of his description of violence with full of pain and suffering is to be seen in his letter to the viceroy in 1919 while relinquishing his knighthood or in his travelogue "*Parashya*" in which he relates the penchant description of a Christian chaplain, attached to a British air force division stationed at Bhagdad, as how extremely easy to kill so many people dwelling in the desert by ferocious aerial bombing without any fear of repercussion. When asked for a message by the Christian chaplain he wrote :

"Man has accepted this dust-laden earth for his dwelling place, for the enacting of the drama of his tangled life ever waiting for a call of perfection from the boundless depth of purity surrounding him a translucent atmosphere. If in an evil moment man's cruel history should spread its black wings to invade that realm of divine dreams with its cannibalistic greed and fratricidal ferocity then God's curse will certainly descend upon us for that hideous desecration and the last curtain will be rung down upon the world of Man for whom God feels ashamed."

It is his complete apathy towards violence that he was so much against nationalism based on the concept of a nation-state which does not hesitate to kill in the name of sovereignty of a nation and rather goes for universal humanism. In the 1905 Bengal Partition Movement Tagore initially had a radical approach and a song composed by him during that time had a tremendous impact on the minds of the participants of the movement :

> In the dry river the water in flood has entered,
> just call the name of mother and row your boat.
> The famous Bengali essayists Rajendra Sunder Trivedi said about the song that what to talk of rowing the boat one felt like jumping in the river Ganges singing this very song.

In the year 1906 the middle-aged Bipin Chandra Pal of the Pal-Bal-Lal trio of our freedom struggle movement singing this very song held the rein of the horse of police superintendent Kemp, who with a baton in his hand was leading a police force to stop a street procession of the nationalist Indians.

During these days the poet read a paper "Avastha and byavastha" (problem and solution) in the Calcutta town hall in which he advocated the policy of establishing a parallel govt and said,

The terrifying image of the protector may protect us. We don't want charity – strike.

He wrote many songs during that time betraying similar ideas. There could be two reasons for the manifestation of this kind of militant nationalism. One was of course Jyotirindranath Tagore, his elder brother, who organised secret meetings for spreading the message of nationalistic militancy in which Tagore also participated but more than that, and it is my hunch, that Tagore was influenced by another, one of the greatest figures of his time, Swami Vivevekananda, who sang Tagore songs in Brahmasamaj gatherings such as "I have made you the polestar of my life" (tomarai koreachi jibaner dhrubatara) or "The sky is the platter and the sun and moon are the lighted lamps" (gaganer thale rabi-chandra-deepak jwale). Tagore met Narendranath Dutta turned Vivekananda in a tea party arranged by sister Nibedita on 27th Jan1899 but must have exchanged glances then conversing with each because Tagore knew about Vivekananda's firm belief that the literary creativity of the house of Tagors is not conducive for the development of masculinity in man. Swamiji would always say, in the present Indian condition forgetting the soft, sweet taste of poetry would not do us any harm. The hard truth is like the death image of Mother kali and not the happy love image of Krishna with flute in his hand. Then Swamiji made the most powerful statement, "Yes! The older I grow, the more everything seems to me to lie in manliness. That is my new gospel."

Tagore was totally against idol worship and hence he was not favourable towards Swami Vivekananda but he had personally noticed the tremendous revolutionary impact of Swamiji on the youth of India and after the death of Swami Vivekananda in 1902 Tagore spoke in high terms to Dilip Kumar Roy about Swamiji's acute sense of self respect. Tagore also recognised the great impact which Swamiji had on the awakening of the fighting spirit among the enslaved Indians and himself started writing poetry of militancy during the Bengal partition agitation (see Vivekananda o Samakaleen Bharatbarsha, Shankari Prasad Basu, vols iv, v, vi and vii.).

Tagore, an ardent advocate of the Bengal partition movement however withdrew his active participation because of disillusionment over the political exploitation of the Hindu-Muslim conflict and the realization about the movement turning violent.

In fact his love for the country, on one side

(i) called for the acceptance of a radical social programme as described in his essay 'byadhi o pratikar' (Malady and Cure,1907) against the divisive forces of caste, creed, poverty, and alienation between the elite and the masses and thus moved towards a more abiding freedom than what the political movement could attain and

(ii) on the other side his approach to nation and nationalism was very different. He remained anti-imperialist all through his life but went against any kind of violent or narrow nationalism and spoke about a world-embracing and inclusive nationalism which became the basis of Pt. Nehru's vision of India's future as a liberal secular democracy.

For Tagore India's unity was a social reality. It was not a political agenda. At the back of his participation in the Hindu mela from the age of 14 to his renouncing the knighthood after the Jalianwala Bagh massacre at the age of 58 and even after that his anti-imperialist viewpoints forcefully displayed in his last stirring lecture 'The Crisis in Civilization' at the age of 80 in which he mentioned the impertinent challenge by the imperial ruler to our conscience there was no politics. His anti-imperial disposition was a universal struggle for political justice and cultural dignity and a protest against violence.

In his classic autobiography, "Errata : An Examined Life", George Steiner, one of the foremost philosophers of the 20th century, wrote :

It is possible to suppose that the period since August 1914 has been, notably in Europe and Russia, from Madrid to Moscow, from Sicily to the Arctic Circle, the most bestial in recorded history (Steiner, 1997 :103).

Steiner's epitaph to the essential tragedy of the 20th century may well serve as a postscript to Rabindranath's critique of nationalism. Indeed, it would be logical to infer that much of the cause for the human grief, pain and humiliation in the 20th Century, can be attributed to the conflicting claims of Nation States. Far from acting as an instrument for realizing collective or communitarian aspirations and welfare, nationalism has tragically led to collective despair.

Tagore undoubtedly was a powerful critic of worshipping the Nation as God and was horrified by the crimes committed by modern nation-states. Yet he loved the land that had nurtured him and never abandoned a basic anti-colonial or anti-imperialistic stance and even gave up his knighthood for the heinous crime committed by the

British in 1919 by killing the 12unarmed peaceful people in Jalianbala Bagh in Amritsar, India. However he simply did not want Indian patriots to imitate European nationalists. It is not without reason that Mahatma Gandhi in his obituary comment on Rabindranath Tagore 1941 lauded the poet as "an ardent nationalist".

Today the new reading of nationalism by Tagore looks so relevant because of disastrous consequences of the prevalent notion of nationalism which we witnessed in the world :

(i) In the name of nationalism in the West ethnic nationalism unfolded itself resulting in two world wars;

(ii) In India nationalism has turned into ethnic politics which is creating all kind of problems for India;

(iii) Nationalism is spreading terrorism;

(iv) In the name of nationalism one finds deaths and conflicts in the 3rd world countries of Asia and Africa;

(v) The countries of Africa fought against colonialism and racialism to regain their freedom and the spirit of nationalism but now the net result of that is that these countries have become dens of corruption, cruelty and insolence;

The West is now seriously thinking has nation-state failed? Post colonial critics such as Ernest Gallner, Benedict Andrson, Tom Nairn or Frantz Fanon have pointed out how nationalism cultivates the sentiments of irrationality, prejudice and hatred in people.

The detailed analysis of cosmopolitanism by Isaiah Berlin and Ashis Nandy and also Martha Nussbaum and Amartya Sen indicates that the world view is strongly in favour of how to break boundaries by rejecting exclusive nationalism and establish universal nationalism which is very much possible as says Tagore that "a culture could reflect universal ideas, without a loss of national identity".

Though globalization tends to go for one homogenized culture by appropriation, co-option and homogenization even then a fierce debate is continuing for the last 30 years to speak in favour of particularism and exceptionalism. Amartya Sen by quoting Tagore says that Tagore's everlasting credit is that his great cosmopolitan vision never sacrificed the richest possible sense of tradition. His actual words are :

"The main point of cosmopolitanism, which is taken to be world-citizenship claim, need not militate against valuing elements in one's own tradition. It is particular cultural traditions that can provide the bases for understanding and morally relating to others and ultimately a vision of universality is developed."

Both Gandhi and Tagore were nationalist with a difference. Gandhi accepted nationalism because he wanted to use it as a way to internationalism and hence he would say our battle for freedom is to bring peace in the world. Tagore did not accept nationalism which is bound with the concept of nation state. If one understands Tagore's view that India's unity is a social fact, not a political agenda then it becomes easy to understand that for Tagore universal nationalism is an inclusive plural concept of a nation which goes beyond the idea of exclusive nationalism and where the whole earth is a family.

The dialogue between Gandhi and Tagore was the most important aspect of Tagore's time. Both had admiration, love and regard for each other but differed on issues like, non-cooperation movement or charkha or burning of foreign goods or use of English or rejection of science and technology or the Bihar earthquake which according to Gandhi was due to our sin for following the practice of untouchability..

Tagore was apprehensive that passive resistance will turn violent; spinning of the wheel would not generate ideas and that our poverty was not due to our lack of sufficient thread but due to our lack of vitality, our lack of unity; and burning of clothes will hurt our economy. Tagore was disturbed not so much for Gandhi's opposition to English as for calling Raja Rammohan Roy, a champion of English education, a pygmy though Gandhi retracted from his original statement available in the collected works of Mahatma Gandhi,Vol.xix, pp.476-78 and published a revised version in Young India now collected in Vol. xx, pp. 42-43 by deleting the derogatory word 'Pygmy' but without shifting from his original stand against English education. Tagore in a letter to C.F. Andrews from Zurich on May 10, 1921 said, The Mahatma believed Rammohan Roy was limited by his excessive familiarity with English but on the contrary he "had the comprehensiveness of mind to be able to realise the fundamental unity of spirit in the Hindu, Muhammadan and Christian cultures. Therefore he represented India in the fullness of truth, and this truth is based, not upon rejection, but on perfect comprehension. Rammohan Roy could be perfectly natural in his acceptance of the West, not only because his education had been perfectly Eastern—he had the full inheritance of the Indian wisdom. He was never a school boy of the West, and therefore he had the dignity to be the friend of the West." Stung by the criticism Gandhi immediately published his reply in "Young India" and made that famous oft quoted statement, "I hope I am as great a believer in free air as the great Poet. I do not want my house to be walled in on all sides and my windows to be stuffed. I want the cultures of all the lands to be blown about my house as freely as possible. But I refuse to be blown off my feet by any".

But the most interesting dialogue that took place between them, when Gandhi called Tagore in an article in "Young India" of 27 April 1921, "The Great Sentinel" but defended non-cooperation movement and charka, as a means of livelihood to many poor people and said in the end, "I found it impossible to soothe suffering patients with a song from Kabir. The hungry millions ask for one poem invigorating food."

Tagore In his speech on "Call of Truth" at the University Institute in Calcutta spoke against it. He said, "When the early bird awakens, its awakening is not merely for the purpose of looking for food. Its two untiring wings accept the call of the sky. The joy of seeing the light makes him burst out into song. The consciousness of the universal man of today calls out to our consciousness."

Mahatma Gandhi in his reply in "Young India" chose to point only to that bird which flies in the sky early in the morning and said," But I have had the pain of watching birds that for want of strength could not be coaxed into a flutter of their wings."

But both had the decency to oppose each other with dignity and respect. Tagore would call Gandhi, 'Mahatma' and Gandhi called the poet 'Gurudev'. In the only poem which Tagore wrote on Gandhi, a little over six months before his death, he called himself one of those who had the mark of Gandhi on their brow. On Tagore's death on 7th August 1941, Gandhi said in his message of condolence that there was hardly any public incident that took place without the impact of Tagore's strong personality. The unfortunate tendency among the modern historians to reduce the Gandhi-Tagore debate, which according to Nehru were the great debates of the 20th century, into a very simplistic version of a debate between superstitions versus rational thinking or the darkness of tradition versus the enlightenment of modernity or East versus West.

In spite of their differences on issues like non-cooperation movement Tagore created a prototype of Gandhi, Dhanjaya Bairagi, expressing his profound faith in the Gandhian ideal of a non- violent passive resistance movement. Similarly on the irrational statement made by Gandhi on the Bihar earthquake Tagore was very critical but when he found people are unnecessarily rubbing this point and criticizing him Tagore out of pain and anger issued a statement :

> "To one really great, the real adulation as well as the cheap sneers of the mob mean very little and I know Mahatmaji carries that greatness with him.'

There were no debates to prove one's superiority but only dialogues more to understand each other. Their differences were fundamental but their tributes to each other were unreserved. After all both were spiritual associates in their common task of regenerating their people. Both wore their differences rather lightly and showed their love and admiration more deeply, Once Gandhi requested Tagore to spin the charkha, Tagore immediately responded, you write a poem, I shall spin the wheel.

Tagore never ceased to remind us that he was first and foremost a poet. The French noble laureate, St. John Perse spoke about Tagore that he lived his poem and lived it integrally with all the integrity of man and of life.

Tagore once wrote to his young niece Indira, "In my life I may have done many things that were unworthy, with or without knowing, but in my poetry I have never uttered anything false; it is the sanctuary for the deepest truths I know." He had kept his promise to himself.

He also told her : "How I cherish light and space! Goethe on his death-bed wanted 'more light'. If I am capable of expressing my desire, my dream, my vision then, it will be for more light and more space."

Chapter Three

Tagore and Gandhi : Their intellectual Conflict and Companionship

It is always a rewarding choice for a Bengali brought up on a staple diet of Tagore to bring Gandhi into discussion and speak about their central philosophical questions that have defined Indian public life and contemporary world ideas about a desirable society and a concrete and universal humanism.

These two great thinkers of modern India had their strong differences, intellectual conflicts but at the same time both realized their deep affection for each other.

The ideas of Tagore are a part of my life. For many years I thought of Gandhi as a strange phenomenon, vending ideas that looked terribly eighteen century talking against British parliament, law courts and even railways but in due course I realized that Gandhi took an extreme position in his book "Hind Swaraj" written in 1909, which a great poet or a visionary is capable of taking. Poet William Blake once said that all extremes open the gates of heaven. Truth is not revealed with liberal views, but with extreme views. As a critique of the planned agenda of the British of civilizing Indians and modernizing India, Gandhi decided to deglamorize his opponents by criticizing all the icons of Western civilization and said that India is in danger of losing her soul. She must resist it for her own sake and that of the world.

Gandhi's approach was not to create a tussle between indigenous and foreign but to warn us about the danger of developing a colonial mentality or mental colonization. Tagore also said in those days that true modernism is freedom of mind, not slavery of taste; it is independence of thought and action, not tutelage under European school masters. Today I see the ideas of Mahatma as well as of Tagore a true bridge to the future.

Emotionally, I live in Tagore's world but intellectually, I recognize that twenty-first century belongs to Gandhi. Tagore is for all time, cannot be limited within the ambit of a century. After he received the noble prize and for two decades thereafter he flashed across the Western sky like a comet. It was the second decade of the last century and Rabindranath Tagore was already beginning to be ubiquitous, omnipresent. The works of Tagore were translated to the French by Andre Gide, and to the Russian by Boris Pasternak, both Nobel prize winners, and W.B. Yeats, another Nobel laureate, had written the preface to the first edition of Tagore's own translation of the Gitanjali in 1912 and Ezra Pound in a revised edition in 1913 compared him to Dante. Meanwhile twenty two of Tagore's titles had already been translated in 1917 to an immaculate Spanish, mainly through the pen of the Spanish poet Juan Ramon Jiminez, who later won the Nobel Prize in 1956 and his wife, Zenobia Camprubi who was an American. The French nobel laureate, St. John Perse spoke about Tagore that he lived his poem and lived it integrally with all the integrity of man and of life.

In due course like a comet he disappeared and again made his appearance in the 1960s of the last century when the children of the neo romantics like Aane Akhmatova and Donald S. Harrington and others found in him a sympathetic voice of :

(i) anti- materialism, and
(ii) adored his vision of the spiritual, and
(iii) his search for beauty in man and nature

which were very much familiar to them and also were attracted by his late poetry which became less and less poetry, and more and more unadorned human voice and his journey towards greater and greater honesty.

The comet disappeared for a short while to be brought back on the sky by a young English modernist poet, William Radice, who translated Tagore's poetry from original Bengali and broke the myth about Tagore as a mystical poet of the East. Radice's work marked a new initiative in the European understanding of Tagore. Not only lovers of literature but social and political scientists and thinkers from different fields of human knowledge took great interest in Tagore's ideas of nationalism, cosmopolitanism, new education and the changing nature of violence, and its bureaucratization and the unity of mankind.

Let me quote two distinguished thinkers, one a social and political theorist Isaiah Berlin, who believed in counter-Enlightenment and advocated an irreducibly pluralist ethical ontology, saw the value in Tagore's unique position and said many years ago in his well known book "Sense of Reality" that Indians ought to be proud of the rarest of all gifts of nature, a poet of genius, who even in moment of acute crisis... unwaveringly told them only what he saw, only the truth.

Second was from all together a different field, Chemistry. Ilya Prigogine, a 1984 Chemistry Nobel Laureate, went so far to say in the same year that curiously enough, the present evolution of science is running in the direction stated by the great Indian poet, Tagore.

Gandhi was different. It was Ashis Nandi, who once remarked, now recorded in the book, "Talking India" that there are four Gandhis who survived after Gandhi's death in 1948 : The first Gandhi is that of the Indian State and the second of the Gandhians. The third Gandhi is of the eccentrics and the fourth is the Gandhi who is basically not read but only heard of almost as a rumour.

Ashis Nandi says that this Gandhi survives in odd places – in people like Dalai Lama or Aung San Su Kyi or Nelson Mandela or even survives in movements of various kinds, in say, anti-nuclear or environmental movements, and or, this is my addition, in Bolywood films to the utter discomfiture and chagrin of the Indian elite.

Mohandas Karamchand Gandhi was an ordinary common man with extraordinary convictions, who sold his wife's jewellery to study law in London, returned a barrister but because of his moral uprightness and poor articulation could not become successful in his profession and like thousands of poverty stricken illiterate and unemployed labourers signed a girmit, colloquial of agreement, to practice law for a year in South Africa in the first instance and sailed for a new country in 1893.

This was the beginning of a saga of a common man, who, by his ability to stand up for truth and champion the cause of justice, was transformed from an ordinary person into a great person and ultimately a Mahatma, an appellation used for the most respectable persons in India. Though this transformation from Mohandas to Mahatma was full of uncertainties, sacrifices, renunciations, sufferings and humiliations yet his dauntless courage and spiritual aspirations showed him the path to success.

Gandhi's struggle for bringing honour and dignity to the lives of thousands and thousands of Indians in a foreign country with his newly discovered weapon, *satyagraha,* the philosophy of non-violence or passive resistance, turned into an edict as how to live life and reach self-realization. *Satyagraha* is a relentless search for truth and a determination to teach truth through nonviolent means which was to become the most powerful force in India's struggle for freedom.

General Smuts, (his biggest adversary in South Africa), later referred to the memories of those eventful years on Gandhi's seventieth birthday, "...In jail he had prepared for me a pair of sandals which he presented to me when he was set free. I have worn those sandals for many a summer since then, even though I may feel that I am not worthy to stand in the shoes of so great a man."

Gilburt Murrey wrote about Gandhi in Hibbert Journel of 1914 :

> Persons in power should be very careful how they deal with a man who cares nothing for sensual pleasure, nothing for riches, nothing for comfort or praise or promotion, but is simply determined to do what he believes to be right. He is a dangerous and uncomfortable enemy, because his body which you can always conquer gives you so little purchase upon his soul.

Mahatma Gandhi, a great saint though at the same time an astute politician and Gurudev, an appellation given to Tagore used for a great preceptor, was at the same time a poet are examples and lessons for scholars who work on the great debates of the 20th century between different writers, scholars, philosophers and national leaders. Naravane calls them two banks of the same river, separated yet united and Romain Rolland, the French Noble laureate, as two great minds, both moved by mutual admiration and esteem but as fatally separated in their feeling as a philosopher can be from an apostle.

They met together for the first time in Shantiniketan in February 1915. But it was not until 1919 that their correspondence would take the vital and critical form that made such a major contribution to the future growth of India, world views and their life missions – freedom of India for Gandhi and unity of mankind for Tagore.

Their tributes to each other were unreserved : their differences on major political issues were fundamental. Tagore did not approve of the edges of Gandhi's thought that could be read as not progressive, though in hindsight, we are forced to wonder whether the lack of progressivism lay in Gandhi's ideas or in the perception of his contemporaries. Let us not forget that Tagore or Nehru was part of urban middle-class culture and the majority of Indians are probably not affected by that culture. Gandhi was the only one to connect with the rural India directly, though he himself was a product of the city. Therefore there was in Gandhi a lament for the loss of culture, a savage critique of Western civilization, much more savage than in the case of Tagore.

However he was very candid to say, "Preservation of one's own culture does not mean contempt for that of others, but require assimilation of the best that there may be in all the other cultures." Similarly instead of going for a synthesis between the East and the West Tagore's theory was that there is no other way open to us in the East, but to go along with Europeanization and to go through it. This is a movement of moving beyond your narrow self. It is by stepping outside of ourselves that we can be 'saved' from ourselves and can realize the harmonious nature of the whole or unity of mankind. Going through does not mean acceptance but understanding everything in a larger perspective.

One can see an unfortunate tendency among the modern historians to reduce the Gandhi-Tagore debate, which according to Jawaharlal Nehru was the great debates of the 20th century, into a very simplistic version of a debate between superstitions versus rational thinking or the darkness of tradition versus the enlightenment of modernity or East versus West or a poet versus an ascetic. One cannot draw too neat a contrast between these two great minds because the difference was largely of a degree. The western approach is primarily binary and not holistic as a result even a person like Amartya Sen, the Nobel Prize winner Indian, makes a mistake but this kind of a mistake is inevitable. We go for this kind of comparison even if it sounds extremely odious.

Even Lord Bhiku Parekh, an internationally known political scientist and multiculturalist and having a deep thinking mind, misinterpreted this kind of a glib understanding of the differences between Tagore and Gandhi and said that Gandhi used it as a 'rhetorical strategy' by calling Tagore a poet and himself a 'humble' man of action and thereby i) distinguished him fairly sharply from Tagore and at the same time ii) reduced the impact of Tagore's criticism by warning his readers that Tagore's judgments on matters political were not to be taken too seriously. I cannot imagine that Gandhi, who after Tagore's death had said in his condolence message that there was hardly any public activity on which he had left no impress of his powerful personality and that he was an 'an ardent nationalist', would use this kind of an artifice or duplicity to lower Tagore's position in the public eyes as an ivory tower poet without any understanding of the world of action.

They were not 'close friends' but 'had great respect for each other'. One of the best examples of this friendship was the incident of Bihar Earthquake in 1934. In reply to Gandhi's statement about the earthquake that it was God's chastisement for the sin of untouchability Tagore said on 16 Feb. 1934 that how could Mahatma emphasize the elements of unreason when he inducted in us freedom from fear and feebleness? I am quoting Mahatma's reply which appeared in the same issue of the paper and for once Gandhi seemed to be more poetical than Tagore. It has the power like that of a Hebrew Psalm :

"With me the connection between cosmic phenomenon and human behaviour is a living faith that draws me nearer to my God, humbles me and makes me readier for facing Him. Such a belief would be degrading superstition, if out of the depth of my ignorance I used it for castigating my opponents."

The severe criticism against Gandhi's statement when started pouring in from different quarters Tagore could not stand it and issued a statement :

"To one really great, the real adulation as well as the cheap sneers of the mob means very little and I know Mahatmaji carries that greatness with him."

But what I feel as Ashis Nandi also thinks that Gandhi by his statement was hinting at the collective responsibility and that was not an exclusive conception. President Clinton publically apologized for the sin of slavery of his country for which he was not and nor the white community of his time was responsible even then Clinton apologized being the inheritor of a culture under which, once upon a time, slavery was practiced. Ramchandra Gandhi, the grandson of Gandhi and a distinguished philosopher, with the help of the theory of action within the notion of collectivization of thought of Simone Weil gives a positive explanation of the statement of Mahatma Gandhi on Bihar Earthquake.

In their differences also a level of decorum and gravity was maintained. In this regard one can refer to Tagore-Gandhi controversial debate of 1921 on Charkha, hand operated spinning wheel, passive resistance and non-cooperation movement or burning of foreign clothes.Tagore was apprehensive that passive resistance would turn violent; spinning of the wheel would not generate ideas and that our poverty was not due to our lack of sufficient thread but due to our lack of vitality, our lack of unity; and burning of clothes would hurt our economy. Gandhi called Tagore in an article in 'Young India of 27 April 1921, 'The Great Sentinel' but defended non-cooperation movement and charkha, as a means of livelihood to many poor people and said in the end, "I found it impossible to soothe suffering patients with a song from Kabir. The hungry millions ask for one poem invigorating food."

In reply to this Tagore in his speech on "Call of Truth" at the University Institute in Calcutta spoke against it. He said, "When the early bird awakens, its awakening is not merely for the purpose of looking for food. Its two untiring wings accept the call of the sky. The joy of seeing the light makes him burst out into song. The consciousness of the universal man of today calls out to our consciousness." Tagore made at least one thing clear that if romanticism was a movement for national freedom, which it turned to be, then it also accepted the universalism of the enlightenment.

Mahatma Gandhi in his reply in "Young India" chose to point only to that bird which flies in the sky early in the morning and said," But I have had the pain of watching birds who for want of strength could not be coaxed into a flutter of their wings." In Indian romanticism, around 1920-21 and thereafter as well, the hungry bird also found its place.

Both wore their differences rather lightly and showed their love and admiration more deeply. Once Gandhi requested Tagore to spin the charkha, Tagore immediately responded, "you write a poem, I shall spin the wheel".

In spite of their great love and regard for each other they had fundamental differences on some major political issues and this paradox is difficult to figure out. Even Tagore was frequently driven to his wits' end trying to understand why Gandhi did what he did, in the first place, and moreover, why the Indian public always seemed to follow him no matter how irrational he appeared to be to his colleagues in politics and to the non-political people like Tagore but this, in no way, affected their close friendship and understanding of each other.

The best example of this is that just after one year of his most powerful and comprehensive statement against non-violent, non-cooperation movement,which came out in October 1921 in the Bengali Journal "Prabashi," Tagore wrote his play, "Muktadhara" in 1922. Though a critic of the non violent, non cooperation movement, Tagore surprisingly gave a profound expression to his faith in the Gandhian ideal of a non-violent popular movement. The words on non-violence by the protagonist of the play, Dhananjaya could easily be put in the mouth of Gandhi when one of his followers says that he knows how to give a good beating to his adversary, Dhanjaya exhorts his followers to realize the greater power of non-beating :

> Can't you show him what non-beating is?
> That needs too much strength I suppose?
> asks the follower
> Beating the waves won't stop the storm.
> But hold your rudder steady and you win.
> What do you tell us to do then?
> Exclaims the follower
> Strike at the root of violence itself.
> How can that be done master?
> As soon as you hold up your head and say that it
> does not hurt, the roots of violence will be out

Insinuation of Raja Rammohan Roy by Gandhi created quite a stir during that era. Raja Rammohan Roy came to England in 1831 as the ambassador of the Mughal Emperor Akbar Shah II died in 1833 in Bristol and was initially buried in the grounds of Beech House, but ten years later his friend Dwarakanath Tagore, grandfather of Tagore, had him reinterred at Arno's Vale. A chattri (funerary monument or shrine) was designed by William Prinsep and built with sponsorship from Dwarakanath Tagore was placed over the tomb. In 1997 a full size statue of Raja Ram Mohan Roy was also built at Bristol. The insinuation by Gandhi by calling Raja as a pygmy for thinking and writing in English disturbed Tagore quite a bit not so much for Gandhi's opposition to English as for calling Raja Rammohan Roy, a champion of English education, a pygmy though Gandhi retracted from his original statement available in the collected works of Mahatma Gandhi,Vol.xix, pp.476-78 and published a revised version in Young India now collected in Vol. xx, pp. 42-43 by deleting the derogatory word 'Pygmy' but without shifting from his original stand against English education.

Tagore in a letter to C.F. Andrews from Zurich on May 10, 1921 said, The Mahatma believed Rammohan Roy was limited by his excessive familiarity with English but on the contrary he "had the comprehensiveness of mind to be able to realise the fundamental unity of spirit in the Hindu, Muhammadan and Christian cultures.

Therefore he represented India in the fullness of truth, and this truth is based, not upon rejection, but on perfect comprehension. Rammohan Roy could be perfectly natural in his acceptance of the West, not only because his education had been perfectly Eastern — he had the full inheritance of the Indian wisdom. He was never a school boy of the West, and therefore he had the dignity to be the friend of the West."

Stung by the criticism Gandhi immediately published his reply in "Young India" and made that famous oft quoted statement, "I hope I am as great a believer in free air as the great Poet. I do not want my house to be walled in on all sides and my windows to be stuffed. I want the cultures of all the lands to be blown about my house as freely as possible. But I refuse to be blown off my feet by any."

These lines are engraved in school and college buildings across the land and have recently acquired a fresh lease of life outside India. Thus, as said by Ramachandra Guha, Gandhi's words have been cited in the debates on curriculum reform in the divided campuses of the elite American universities. They are, now indeed, an argument-clinching *mantra* for our multicultural times.

For Tagore India was not territorial (*mrinmaya*) but ideational (*chinmaya*). He said that I love India but my India is an idea and not a geographical expression.

He further said that the word nation is not in our language. India has never had a real sense of western nationalism. Society is in the core of India's civilization and politics is in the core of western civilization and hence the importance which Europe gave to freedom we gave to liberation of the soul.

Tagore replaces the ideology of nation with that of *swadeshi samaj*. When in 1904 on the suggestion by the British that Bengal should be partitioned, an upset Tagore took to delivering a lecture — entitled "Swadeshi Samaj" ('The Union of our Homeland' or 'Social relations') — and instead proposed an alternative solution : a self-help based comprehensive reorganization of rural Bengal. In addition, he viewed British control of India as a "political symptom of our social disease" and that social relations are not mechanical and impersonal but based on love and cooperation as explains

Kalyan Sengupta. He always thought that society and state in India in the past moved on parallel lines without affecting each other. An independent social *swaraj* prevailed in Indian villages which had nothing to do with state or ruling dynasties, and it was only the British- governed Indian state that tried to interfere and politicize the society affecting our civilizational values.

The nation, Tagore views, strengthens the state at the expense of society and undermines the latter's fluidity and rich and vibrant associative life and gears itself to the realization of a single collective purpose, domination, maximization of collective wealth, racial purity or some other.

If one understands Tagore's view that India's unity is a social fact, not a political agenda, it becomes easy to understand that for Tagore universal nationalism is an inclusive plural concept of a nation which goes beyond the idea of exclusive nationalism and where the whole earth is a family. Tagore was for 'non-parochial inclusive nationalism' relevant to humanity. It is very difficult to understand it as people did not understand how a man like Gandhi could bring freedom to a country with the help of salt and charkha as the medieval devotional poets brought a socio-religious revolution with the help of metaphors like *chadar,* bedsheet, *chunri*, scarf or seeds and earth.

Nation state for Tagore has a (i) self destructive tendency, (ii)) which turns violent, (iii) snatches one's freedom, (iv) spreads a homogenized universalism and (v) makes one selfish and exclusive.

At the back of his participation in the Hindu mela for promoting indigenous goods and ideas and Hindu-Muslim unity from the age of 14 to his renouncing the knighthood at the age of 58 after the Jalianwala Bagh massacre where 379 unarmed people were killed and 1,137 injured at the behsest of General Dyer and even after that his anti-imperialist viewpoints forcefully displayed in his last stirring lecture 'The Crisis in Civilization' at the age of 80 in which he mentioned the impertinent challenge by the imperial ruler to our conscience there was no politics.

His anti-imperial disposition was a universal struggle for political justice and cultural dignity and a protest against violence which according to him, was rooted in the notion of nation state. Indeed, it would be logical to infer that much of the cause for the human grief, pain and humiliation in the 20th Century, can be attributed to the conflicting claims of nation states. Far from acting as an instrument for realizing collective or communitarian aspirations and welfare, exclusive nationalism has tragically led to collective despair. Along with nationalism patriotism is also based on the nation state which demands uncritical loyalty by the state even for its criminal activities as it happened in Nazi Germany. For Tagore love of one's country is not to be focused on the state but on the well-being of one's fellow members consistent with due regard for that of the wider humanity.

Hence for Tagore the nonexclusive and active love of the members of one's community could and should give new orientation to our understanding of nationalism and patriotism.

Gandhi broadly shared Tagore views. For him too, the stronger the society, the less it needed to rely on the state to maintain its unity and stability For both, a country is the creation of its citizens and becomes theirs when and to the extent that they identified with and cared for each other. The modern civilization undermined this unity and fragmented and dehumanized the individual and forced him to rely heavily on the coercive institution of the state.

However, Gandhi was definitely more practical then Tagore and wanted people to concentrate on one's attention and energy on one's country and thereafter humankind at large. Gandhi's road map was from nationalism to internationalism and for Tagore both were to be accepted as a single unit.

We can only hope of a world without boundaries as envisaged by Tagore and live with our head high. But it looks a distant dream. The difference between them was their different attitudes to life. Tagore by referring to the first mantra/couplet of 'Isopanishad' would always say, 'rejoice and renounce'. W.B.Yeats, therefore, made a comment about Tagore that he was the only saint who did not refuse to live. This is also diametrically opposite to what Gandhi said to an English journalist when asked to give in five words, the meaning of life, Gandhi said, 'Why five I will give you in three words', 'renounce and rejoice'. For Gandhi morality formed the substance of the good life and beauty was to be defined and judged in moral terms; Tagore took the opposite view and saw morality as a form of beauty. His words were, 'Beauty meant harmony, peace, *ananda* i.e. bliss and morality was about finding blissfulness in living at peace and in harmony with one's fellow men.'

Both were highly concerned for each other in spite of their differences on fundamental issues. In Poone, in Yerveda jail in 1933 when Gandhi went on fast unto death against British Prime Minister Ramsey Mcdonald's communal award Tagore was extremely disturbed hearing about Gandhi's falling health so much so that he could not stay back and came all the way to Poone from Shantiniketan after sending his protest telegrams to the Viceroy and also to the British Prime Minister. When he reached the jail the news came about the Government's withdrawal of the award. As Tagore reached the prison room he found kasturba, Gandhi's wife and many others present in the room. It was the day of silence for Gandhi. He wrote in a piece of paper to Tagore to sing a song of his own while he was offered a glass of orange juice. Tagore sang his famous song – *'jivana jakhono sukaey jai'*, when the life dries up, come like the flow of compassion to fill our lives.

But perhaps we are yet to realize that both were two great lonely men, as said by R.K. Dasgupta, in spite of their tremendous popularity and that they clashed on some principles because they placed truth above everything else and in this they were always in close agreement. Both had the courage and spirit of speaking alone and walking alone. It is not astonishing that because of this Gandhi loved particularly one of the songs of Tagore :

> If they answer not to thy call walk alone.
> If they are afraid and cover mutely facing the wall,
> O thou of evil luck,
> Open thy mind and speak alone.

Chapter Four

Myth, Orality and Folklore in World Literature with Special Reference to Tagore

"The thing truly worth seeing in world literature is the way human beings express their joy in literature and the abiding form in which the human soul wishes to reveal itself through the diversity of this expression." Tagore in his essay on "World Literature"

Myth, orality, folklore, world literature and Tagore the range of the theme of this international conference is all-encompassing and extremely wide. Any critical analysis of a theme or a book for Tagore is an act of worship. In his essay on the Ramayana Tagore writes, "True criticism is an act of worship, *puja*. The true critic is a worshipping priest, who merely gives expression to his own mingled wonder and adoration or that of public at large." Is not the Greek criticism of Homar or the Roman criticism of Virgil a *puja*? T. S. Eliot declared that the greatness of literature cannot be determined solely by literary standards. The concept of *puja* is not an extraneous issue in criticism, but very much a part of history.[1] This keynote is an act of worship, *puja* of the theme of the conference.

Tagore in his essay "The Religion of the Forest" says that Râmachandra, the great hero of our epic, had his initiation to the spiritual life from Vashishtha, the life of inner peace and perfection. But he had his initiation to war from Vishvâmitra, who called him to kill the demons and gave him weapons that were irresistible. Tagore says that reconciliation between these two forces is possible through creation.[2] Creation is the harmony of contrary forces--the forces of attraction and repulsion. When they join hands, all the fire and fight are changed into the smile of flowers and the songs of birds.

While explaining myth Levi-Strauss says that mythical thought progresses from the awareness of oppositions toward their resolution and the element which brings resolution according to Tagore is creation. The Sanskrit term for Creation is '*Srishti*', meaning a manifestation or formation of something that remained occult. Time and space both lay latent in the timeless eternity. The phenomenal creation was only a projection of this transcendent eternity into time and space.

Some of the modern critics of myth have stressed that the myth is essentially related to creation. Says Mircea Eliade, "myth tells how , through the deeds of Supernatural Beings, a reality came into existence, be it the whole of reality, the cosmos, or only a fragment of reality – an island, a species of plant, a particular kind of human behaviour, an institution. Myth then is always an account of a 'creation'.[3] C. G. Jung similarly says that "myth is formed around a figure that may be a god a man or a process that repeats itself throughout man's history whenever creative phantasy is freely manifested."

The miracle of creation is to bring conflicting forces into the harmony of the one. The power which accomplishes that is known as the archetype or eternal cosmic principal or what Levi Strauss says 'universal law of human thought.'[4] It is not a shift from myth as a narrative story to myth as a way of thinking. Both are very closely interrelated. It is first an idea or archetype (*satyadharma*) which becomes the basis of a story to be woven around the idea or thought and hence any mythical story (*devatakhyan*) rests on an idea or an archetype. It is explained by Jung as "the collective unconscious" and he strongly fells that when a man loses his mythical heritage he has really lost his soul.[5] Myth as said by Frank Karmode, "short-circuits the intellect and liberates the imagination"[6] which helps in deriving its universal significance by reconstituting an original event or explaining some fact about human nature and its worldly or cosmic context.

The question of reference or history of myth is still unresolved. In ancient Greece two main theories were put forward to explain myths and they are followed even today by some scholars. One is known as Euhmerist theory, called after its originator Euhmeros (300 B.C.) who saw in myths apotheosis (transformation into deity) of historical events related to human beings and thus Zeus was taken as an actual king of Crete, a human hero, who had overthrown the regime of Kronos and who was deified later by men and turned into a myth. Regarding the origin of Vedic god Indra, R. N. Dandekar has taken a Euhmeristic view, for according to him Indra was originally an war hero of the Vedic Aryans[7]. The other Greek theory upheld by the poets Epicharmus (6th C.B.C.) and Theagenus of Rhegium (5th C.B.C.) and condemned by Plato in his Phaedrus saw in myths, personification of various natural phenomena and thus Zeus was the sky, Poseidon stood for water and like that. Much before that it was Yaska, (7th C.B.C.) in a passage connected with the identification of Vrtra in his book of Vedic etymology, Nirukta, showed that from the very beginning there had been two main schools of interpreting Vedic mythology, the historical school i.e. of the *aithihasikas*, and the naturalistic schools, i.e. of the *nairuktas*. The former believed that Vrtra was a demon, a son of Tvashtr, the later, on the other hand, held that Vrtra is cloud personified or Indra is light personified (*Megha iti naituktah. Tvashtro asuraiti iti aiitihasika,* Nirukta, 2.5.17).

But let me say in passing, as said by Sri Aurobindo about Vedic gods that they are no mythic barbarian gods of clouds, sun and shower, no confused allegories of wonderstruck savages, but the objects of worship to men far more inwardly civilized and profound in self–knowledge than ourselves... They had read the riddle of death and found the secret of immortality; they had sought for and discovered the One and known and worshipped Him, in their glories of his light and purity and wisdom and power.[8]

No doubt the ancient society, not primitive society, was the myth's proper milieu but it will be wrong to follow the Anthropo-ethnological school of scholars like A. Lang, E.B. Taylor, E.Durkheim, Levy Bruhal and call it pre-logical and nothing but 'savage thought'. In fact, it is not savage thought but collective unconscious as Jung explains. For instance, the shaman calling out like birds and animals was not in a state of "possession" but signified at- one-ness or return to a prelapsarian (biblical time before the fall from grace) state of unified consciousness. For Kerenyi, "The going back to the origin and primal time is basic feature of every mythology." This is what Mircea Eliade calls sacral time. It is from this point or place beyond time, that society receives all its functions and sanctions and matters is not when they taught but what they taught and hence "mythological events cannot be judged historically"[9] because the power of the myth resides in a "more-than-historical reality."[10]

The word for myth in Indian context is *purana* and they are episodical. Here history changes into *purana*, so one cannot find a unity which one derives out of a cause and effect relationship. The *purana* keeps up its subterranean historical origin, but goes on adding, multiplying and expanding its body, aiming to bring home the archetypal meaning of the enduring totality. So Mahabharata is *itihasa* as well as *purana*. While explaining the term history as given in Nirukta , Yaska explains that the war between Indra and Vritra is not a historical happening but a symbolic event (*upamaarthena yudha varnabhavanti tatro upamarthena*, 2.16.2), however historical stories like Harishchandra, Nachiketa etc are also to be found. In other words itihasa in the India tradition is both history as is understood in the West and at the same time it is mythical history. Amarkosha defines *itihasa* simply as *puravritta*,i.e. events of the past (1.6.4) but the Indian tradition of Dharmashastra has given a specific connotation to the term *'itihasa'* which stands for a particular class of literature. The Mahabharata defines it as '*Dharmartha kama mokshanam upadesha samanvitam, puravritta samayuktamitihasam prachakshate*' i.e. *itihasa* is the narrative of the past but, at the same time, it contains teaching on *dharma* (religious and moral duties), *artha* (necessities of life. i.e., means of material prosperity), *kama* (fulfilment of desire) and *moksha* (emancipation). Since *itihasa* does not assert 'so it was' but it also reminds us that 'so it has been' hence *itihasa* literally ('thus verily it has been') is a narrative of past events, the recitation of which is a part of the process of self-renewal and regeneration. In the Indian view the 'so it was' aspect remains neither relevant nor real : the most it can achieve is to stimulate one point in a continuum whereas the 'so it has been' view remains continuously relevant and real.

In *itihasa* the emphasis is not on the happenings, however true they may be, but on some teaching, on some ideal. Hence in Indian tradition *itihasa* is coupled with *purana*, 'that which is old and is still new' or 'that which renews the old' and hence timeless and eternal.

From the ancient time in India *Purana* stands for that which is new at the same time ancient, eternal and primordial. Shri Krishna is known as *Purana Purusha*, The Bhagvad Gita says, '*Ajo nitya shashvatoym puranah'*(unborn, eternal, ever existent and primeval is He). In the Rgveda the same epithet is used for Usha – '*Punah punarjayamana purani'*(being born again and again she is primeval).[11] Malinowski calls it 'a living reality'.

Tagore uses the pauranic myths of Ahalya and Uravasi, in his two poems, to give an eternal archetypal meaning by juxtaposing the old with the new consciousness of the modern period. Ahalya recovers from a millennium of sleep, "full youth bathed in a new childhood", "blossoming on a single stock; rising like the dawn/from the blue waters of oblivion" is a myth of renovation of desolateness into life nourishment—an imaginative identification with the vast germinations that fertilise the earth or the human mind. On the contrary the myth of Uravashi as described by Tagore in his poem Uravashi, as an incarnate Eros, is "neither mother, daughter nor wife." She is the eternal beauty which is now lost in the modern world of falsehood and deceit. The pathos evoked by her unavailability in the world as it is – '*phiribe na phiribe na*, she will not come back, not come back' – is not to be found in the epics or the ancient texts. In two other poems Tagore imagines the beauty of the universe as divided into two separate forces – one represents by Urvashi and the other by Lakshmi, the two fair women who rose in the beginning of time from the churning of God's dream. Urvashi stands for that aspect of beauty which is seen in the flowering frenzy of nature and which, in the shape of a woman haunts startles and waylays man. Lakshmi, on the other hand, is the spirit of plenty in nature and of motherliness in humanity, leading men not to the bower of passionate tryst but to the temple of the divine love, wealth and prosperity. The archetypal meaning is clear that life consists of these two opposites and true creativity knows how to unite them into one entity to make life a thing of true joy and happiness and contentment.

As myths are symbolic, it has multiple meaningfulness; it is not unilinear but multilinear; it is not a fact but an experience of the self (the microcosm), his culture (mesocosm) and the universe (macrocosm). It is not a thought-out word but an experienced one, the being of the things themselves.[12] This experience gives a perspective which is not limited by the personal or historical subjectivity but is fostered by centering and unfolding of the individual in integrity and hence the Indian mythical discourse has a holistic world view. It maintains that human affairs do not become intelligible until they are seen as a whole.

There are instances to highlight the point that Indian mythology seen in totality leads us to the conclusion that no part can truly be appreciated unless the whole is understood, and everything can be appreciated only in the light of human destiny. Just to cite one example about the significance of a myth in India is that the story of the myth entertains as well as instructs. Ego sustains man's separation from the Divine and with this separation being primarily responsible for the human fascination for wrong values, disenchantment with such fascination is an inevitable part of the process of progress. Dhruva in his previous life was a young aspirant, yet the luxurious life of a prince fascinated him for a while. He was born as a prince only to be disillusioned and to return to the sunlit path of quest with greater determination.[13]

The myth or the *purana* has a self-renewing, eternalising aspect which appeals to the Indian mind. The story within a story or the 'chain-tale' is a uniquely Indian form of narration used in the Mahabharata which makes the story timeless prototype of human existence. There are stories within stories and the thread of the main story is taken up after many narrations. Sometimes the main story seems almost forgotten or lost, but then it is taken up again which makes the narration move on the level of flux and timelessness. So the stories are primordial and eternal, indefinitely old as well as infinitely new.

In the Indian context it is the myth-making function of history that underlies its dynamic force in moulding the social life, morality and culture of a people. Accordingly, the mutable man is called *Nara*. The man who develops an urge for some creative action becomes

Narottma, the superior man—the inhabitant not of one country and age but of all countries and ages, the maker of enduring myths and traditions and the bearer of the ultimate values ever projected towards which the whole creation moves. Then there is man, the deity—the goal towards which the whole creation moves. He is the eternal man, *Narayana*. So Kalhana, the famous Indian historian following the tradition of historiography says that the historian, resembling *Prajapati* (creator) must possess the divine perception of the past.[14] Tagore by referring to Ramayana and Mahabharata, in his essay on 'The Ramayana' says that they are also history but not the history of actual events, for such a history is limited to a particular period of time, but the history of timeless life of India. Other histories change at time passes; this history has known no change. Within these two vast poetic edifices is enthroned the history of that India strove for, worshipped and purposed.

One cannot deny that the operative sensibility of most of the writers of the world has retained the mythic origin of their historic sense, and as a result the critical idioms developed in literature probe the mythicality of human existence. It has become now all the more necessary because the status of words like 'truth' and 'reality' has turned out to be problematic. Myth has now been accepted as a meaningful unit of the literary text. Tagore's example is very apt in this respect. He says in his essay 'Silent poet, untaught poet'; that it is nonetheless true that on a quite night, moonlight does seem to be asleep. Let them discover every minute scientific fact about the moonlight, let them even demonstrate that it is not a substance at all; people will still say that the moonlight sleeps. Which master scientist will dare call that a lie?'

The next logical question is how this mythic knowledge is communicated? All the important Indian texts whether Vedas, Ramayana, Mahabharata and others were initially narrated in the oral tradition and still orally narrated by the story tellers and *dastagoi* of India in the folk form. Mahabharata was narrated first by Vaishampayana, then Ugrashrava Lomaharshini, then Sanjaya but the original teller was Vyasa. Ramacharit Manas has three pairs of questioners and responders : Parvati, Garuda and Bharadwaja are the questioners and responders are Shiva, Kaka Bhushandi and

Yajnavalkya. These answers are sacred truths as they are '*santan ke vachan*'(words from saints) spoken orally at the four banks of the river. The fourth narrator is Tuilsi Das himself who cleverly transposes all the queries of his readers to the story through these three questioners and becomes a part of the oral narrative structure. He uses the authorial voices of Shiva, kaka Bhushandi and yajnavalkya for engendering in the listener an ever-deepening understanding of life, death and destiny. These voices elevate the story which is a narration of events of at least one eye-witness, and thus turn history into *purana*.

The Indian narrator of the oral culture describes events for the exteriorization of the worldly process, and therefore selects a vantage point in the time past or the time present or the time future which enables him to frequently change his axis in time as well as space. This mobility gives him a holistic vision; time turns circular for him, and he talks with his total existence which may be described as orchestration of all the senses. On the contrary written culture is based on a cause and effect phenomenon, has a linear development, and deals primarily with visual symbols. The axis of the Western narratology is in the written text, and fixity is its main characteristic. Vedas are unique in this respect. Initially it was all oral but at the same time fixity became its main characteristic. In fact, because of auxiliary literature like shiksa, nirukta, vyakarana, kalpa etc , the Vedas offer an example of the written culture into the oral culture, and because of this infixion it becomes the literature of the power class. Oral is for masses and does not believe in fixity.

Malleability is the characteristic of oral culture. The Indian oral culture takes the help of *itihasa* or *purana* or narratology to explain the Vedic truth. So the Mahabharata is the *panchama* Veda. Here you have many different versions, many discrepancies, stories within stories, innumerable legends and episodes, inconsistencies, irregularities but nothing affects the core which remains intact. The core or the nucleus serves as a string holding together numberless legends, episodes, discussions and dialectic portions. Here history changes into *purana*, so one cannot find a unity which one derives out of a cause and effect relationship. The *purana* keeps up its subterranean historical origin, but goes on adding, multiplying and expanding its body, aiming to bring home the archetypal meaning of the enduring totality.[15] So the Mahabharata is *itihasa* as well as *purana.*

Now the question is what the relationship between the oral and the written is. Are they binary opposites? Is there tension between them? Is the written privileged or placed in status in a hierarchical order? The moment we address these seemingly simple questions, a complex field opens up.

Both oral and written become the basis to serve as instruments of communication and dialogue between different levels of society and across regions but it would be fallacious , however, as explained by A.K.Ramanujan, to assume a notion of linear development between the written and the oral or classical and folk. It is more profitable to imagine a history of texts that is made up of written and oral forms contained within cycles of transmission that move up and down through time resulting in manifold possible recompositions within a 'simultaneous order' of texts.[16]

Aditya Malik reiterates the 'simultaneous order' of oral and written tradition and says that oral tradition in Indian context is not restricted to folk tradition and folk lore. While folklore and folk narratives are indeed recited, spoken, sung and performed — orality itself is not confined to folk traditions. In fact in classical and Sanskrit traditions one finds a prevalence of the oral word, in spoken and sung form, both in an epistemological sense — sound as vibration (*nada*) carries knowledge and metaphysical meaning as well as ritual efficacy (*mantra*) — and in a per formative sense. Many Sanskrit texts, for example, Puranas and Mahatmyas, use narrative framing devices that involve a speaker and an audience in dialogue with one another. Even more so, several important Hindu religious texts, such as the Rgveda and the two great epics, the Mahabharata and Ramayana, are not only orally recited and transmitted for millennia, but once written, as is the case with the latter two texts, continued to show signs of having originated out of a possibly oral 'core' that coalesced into their current written form...[17] Kapila Vatsyayan by referring to Amartya Sen and also taking the cue from a sloka of the Mundakopanishad speaks of the two birds on the same branch as the 'experiencer' (*bhokta*) and the 'seer' (*drasta*) – and one cannot live without the other.[18] and then rounds up the issue by stating that the oral and the written are like two birds on the same branch : if the oral is sacred, so also is the written word. Let me quote what did she actually say, "May I draw attention to Nobel Laureate Amartya Sen's book 'Argumentative Indian'? He has delved into the primary sources and other dialogical traditions. However, most humbly, may I say, these dialogues were also oral! This is quite nearly a case of considering *shruti* the word heard as primary and the *smriti* the word written as secondary. The oral and the written are two birds on the same branch : if the oral is sacred, so also is the written word."[19]

It is not easy to draw a line between myths on the one hand and legends, folklore and facts of a remote past on the other. The primordial roots still visible in the oral tradition and folklores have been vital in the growth of the corpus of Indian myth and ritual.

Folk in the Indian context is *loka* and the *loka* and *shastra* (folk and elite) contrast is contrary to the western contrast between great and little Tradition. India does not believe that non-literate cultures are 'Knowledge blanks' which need to be filled in with the modern knowledge of different discipline and dominant cultures. A. K. Coomaraswamy, who many decades ago had written a seminal article "The Bugbear of Literacy", speaks not against literacy but instead that elementary or functional literacy cannot be considered sole criteria for evaluating the total human potentials.[20] The argument holds good even today.

Cultures are never 'blanks'. In some matters, e.g., in the ecological management practices used by tribals are far superior to anything we could teach them. The tragedy is that modernism has imposed a single perspective in dealing with human culture and today this kind of fixed perspective is challenged by the indeterminacy of experience. The search for the one truth in the many is at odds with the relativist experience of anthropology.[21]

In reality traditional Indian mind thinks that *loka* or *desi* and *sastra* or *margi* contrast represents two different expressions of the same tradition and not of different tradition.

These folk literary approaches are not liquidated or co-opted by core literary tradition but assimilated as alternative models of human expressions or as parts of the whole.[22]

In this way, classical Sanskrit literature describes, on one side, the core regions, Dakshina-patha, Kuru-Panchala, Madhyadesa, Gandhara and on the other peripheries like Naga, Shabara, Dasa and Kirata to share the making of Indian literature.

The main narrative view point of Indian literature consists of a classical core trinity. But there is no denial of the fact that the periphery in Indian literature is very vital and hence in Banabhatta's Kadambari or Bharavi's Kiratarjuniam, the periphery always comes and speaks in classical texts. For example, in classical literature, Shiva appears as *Shabara* in Kiratarjuniam. Bana has a Chandala girl as an important character woven in his story. Similarly the modern writers use folk extensively in explaining the modern predicaments.[23]

The focus of classical regional trinity was to create something vital with the help of the periphery, and in the process, both the geographical region and the social sense were brought into focus, but by keeping it outside the framework of the caste system in society. These two literary expressions of core and periphery are always taken together in Indian literary context but of course not as a monolithic unity but as diverse structures complementing each other. Tagore by quoting a *baul* song explains that the distinction and unity are complementary to each other. A school of Vedanta philosophy which admits the truth of what is known as the principle of *bhedabheda* to indicate a belief that *bheda* or 'distinction; and *abheda* or 'unity' can co-exist and be in intimate relation with each other.[24] Substance and attribute, universal and particular, whole and parts, joys and sorrows may seem to be different from, or even opposed to, each other, but really there is no incompatibility between them, for they can be reconciled in a unity which pervades the difference and is its very being. 'Our joys and sorrows are contradictory', as says Tagore in 'An Indian Folk Religion' when self separates them in opposition. But for the heart in which self merges in God's love, they lose their absoluteness. He explains this by quoting a baul song :

> I am the boat; you are the sea, and also the boatman,
> Though you never make the shore, though you let
> me sink, why should I be foolish and afraid?
> Is the reaching the shore a greater prize than

loosing myself with you?
If you are only the heaven, as they say, then what is the sea?
I lie in you, whatever and however you appear.
Save me or kill me as you wish, only never leave me in other's hands.[25]

Orality or folk is never marginalized in India it is always an alternative tradition and alternative is not to be understood as "the opposite". If you want to draw a white line, you need a black or grey or any dark colour background, so it is a mistake to say white is the opposite of black or grey or blue. We have to make use of black or grey or any dark colour to bring out white in all its distinction.

Here in India the glory of "main stream" literature rests not by marginalizing but by accepting oral or folk as complementary. In the folk stories of the marriage of Shiva and Parvati, the words of praise for Shiva are shastra oriented but the words of praise for Paravati who is the mother of the universe, are folk in content.

Similarly the notion of Shakti puja belonging to Anga, Banga, Kalinga and Kamboja regions gets absorbed into the Puritanical Brahminical orthodoxy of the classical core regions which felt psychologically assured to relate itself with Tantric Hinduism. These are examples of many such contacts between the classical creative mind and the culture of excluded peoples and classes.

To give another example of such contacts is the loom of a weaver or the wheel of a potter which are used to explain many intricate literary and philosophical theories. This process of socio-cultural interaction is a dominating factor in India's literary scene that swept all the regions, and with the passage of time, created different important literary movements including the *bhakti* movement, which fostered a sense of identity in the use of languages and cultural specificities, and the historical functioning in the context of the community. But, at the same time, the pan-Indianans of the of the content structure of *bhakti* once again established the fact that the unitary vision of art and literature consisted of profound speculations contained in the systems of Sankhya, Vedanta, and Yoga philosophy and transformed into the living harvest of the people's literature. In this way *loka* and *shastra* were merged together to reveal the essence of Indian philosophical discourse.

In Indian context oral, tribal or folk lore are neither the residue of the past, nor the behaviour of the uncivilized but it is the continuity of a rich culture and also a process of making the present more life worthy and along with *shastra* it gives a complete picture of Indian culture and thought.

Abanindranath Tagore came also to regard the folk arts and village crafts as the finest repositories of Indian tradition.

It was a conscious attempt to appropriate the popular in a sanitized, idealized form within the scope of the reconstructed tradition—to create for Indian art both the legacy of a classical past and the pride of an uncorrupted living tradition.

Notes and References

1. Selected writings on Literature and Languages; Rabindranath Tagore, (Ed) Sukanta Chaudhuri, Introduction, p.10
2. 'The Religion of the Forest',Creative Unity, Rabindranath Tagore, The English Writings of Rabindranath Tagore, Vol II, pp 518-19
3. Mircea Eliade, Myth and Reality, pp.5-6
4. The statement by Jung is referred to by Sisir Kumar Ghose, Lost Dimension, p. 18
5. Levi Strauss, The Raw and the Cooked, p. 10
6. Frank Kermode, referred to by Eric Gould, Mystical Intentions in Modern Literature, introduction, p. 4
7. See, Motifs in Indian Mythology, Their Greek and other parallels, U.P.Arora, preface
8. Sri Aurobindo, On the Veda, p. 284
9. Baynes, Mythology of the Soul, p.790
10. John Crowe Ransom, God Without Thunder, p.65
11. Indra Nath Choudhuri,'IndianNarratology',Comparative Indian Literature;Some Perspectives, p.112
12. Sisir Kumar Ghose, 'Myth : Old and New', lost Dimensions, p. 19
13. Manoj Das, Myths, Legends, Concepts and Literary Antiquities of India, Preface
14. Indra Nath Choudhuri, 'Indian Narratology' Comparative Indian Literature : Some Perspectives,p.113
15. Ibid, pp.110-111

16. Ramanujan, A.K., 'Where Mirrors are Windows' : Towards an Anthology of Reflections, pp. 187-216
17. Aditya Malik, Oral Traditions and Folklore. Koninklijke Brill NY, Leiden, 2010.
18. "Two friendly birds are sitting together on the same tree. One (who is the bhokta or experiencer) is tasting the fruit and the other (who is only a drasta, seer) only beholds without eating." Mundakopanisad, 3.1.1
19. Kapila Vatsyayan, paper on'Pluralism and Diversity in South Asia, presented in the SACEPS World Confwerence on ' South Asia : Democracy,Sustainable Development and Peace, New Delhi, 24-26 February 2011
20. Coomaraswamy, A.K., *The Bugbear of Literacy*, Middlesex, Permanent Books, 1979.
21. Indra Nath Choudhuri, 'Traditions of Folk in Literature, Folklore and the Alternative Modernities, (ed) Nandini Sahu, p. 196
22. Ibid, p. 196-7
23. Indtra Nath Choudhuri, 'The Concept of Regionality in the Indian Literary Context', The genesis of Imagination,p. 83
24. M. Hiriyanna, Indian Philosophical Studies, 1,PP.95-96.
25. Rabindranath Tagore, 'The Religion of the Forest',Creative Unity, The English Writings of Tagore, Vol 2, p.528

Chapter Five

Tagore, Bose and Mahalanobis : The Confluence of Minds

Confluence

In Indian spiritual heritage wherever confluence of rivers takes place that place turns into a pilgrimage – a seat of sacredness. Whenever there is a confluence of minds new ideas spring up generating a social or philosophical movement or a spiritual regeneration of the society as it happened in India during the Vedic times, just to give one example : the Vedic ritualistic world view was replaced by a new ontological configuration brought about by the sharp insightful minds of the Upanishadic seers in their collective wisdom ushering in a renaissance of thought and change of minds in society.

That was the Upanishadic view of oneness between *Brahman*, the unchanging reality or the sacred and the changing world of external appearances or the secular.

When all distinctions between the internal and external vanish, the distinction between the Self and the non-Self vanishes and one experiences Pure Being as Pure consciousness and everything becomes sacred. This was a new religiousness of the Upanishads which could be understood by realizing the intertwining of the sacred with the secular and as a result the creation of a new humanity in which both consciousness and sensuous live together becomes a reality. Any split between these two brings split in the self. We are both together, we are neither just spirituality nor just consciousness – nor are we just matter. We are a tremendous harmony between matter and consciousness.[1]

Similarly in the fag end of 19th century and the first four decades of the 20th century the confluence of these three great minds of India created a new culture of science and related it to literature and spirituality so much so that Ilya Prigogine, a 1984 Chemistry Nobel Laureate went so far to say in 1984 that curiously enough, the present evolution of science is running in the direction stated by the great Indian poet.

To both Tagore and Bose nature appeared to be not merely a physical phenomenon, but a living entity, a transcendental spirit which could lead man to realize the presence of an essential sense of unity in the world of apparent chaos and diversity.

Interrelatedness of living and non –living worlds and Underlying Unity

In this context we may remember the findings of J. C. Bose, who told us that plants had life and they responded to electromagnetic currents. This was in a way no surprise to the Indian psyche because in the Indian world-view the inanimate and animate were inter-dependent and there was as much life in the stone as in the earthworm, the man or the tree i.e. a physical phenomenon. Acharya Bose dealt a blow to the distinction made by the European mind between the animate (organic) and the inanimate (inorganic) or biological realm of plants with the help of sensitive instruments and scientific rigor. Tagore, right from his childhood days, because of the company and training of his father Maharshi Debendranath Thakur, was made familiar with the Upanishads which, in its ancient intuition, proclaims that whatever there is in this world vibrates with life, the life that is one in the infinite."[2]

Having their beliefs firmly rooted to the preachings of the ancient Hindu Upanishads and the Vedas, Tagore and Bose conceived Nature not merely as a physical phenomenon, but a living spirit, which could help man to realize the essential Truth of Life.

Here the microcosm and the macrocosm are seen as interrelated (*yatha pinde thatha bramhande*) and profound synchronization is achieved between the subjective and the objective realms.[3] In the course of his academic career roughly between 1899 and 1902, Bose ventured to go beyond orthodox physics and the traditional methods of science laid by the West, to draw some interesting correlations between the living and the non-living world.[4] It is through this interdisciplinary approach to science that Bose sought to introduce an Eastern spirituality within a materialist Western science and thereby sought to establish a new scientific paradigm to create "a new East for the West to appreciate."[5] While working with his electric wave receiver, Bose became preoccupied with the question of responses to electric touch upon various objects and went on to compare metallic fatigue and excitation with that of excitation in living tissue.[6] Thus he pursued in a research to draw a link between the animate and the inanimate in their responses to electric stimulus, and wrote his seminal book, 'Responses in the Living and Non-living'.[7]

This project of Bose or this idea of interrelatedness and the underlying unity he elaborated in his presidential address at the Bengal Literary Conference in 1911 :

"You are aware that, in the West, the prevailing tendency at the moment is, after a period of synthesis, to return upon the excessive sub-division of learning... Such a caste-system in scholarship, undoubtedly helps at first, in the gathering and classification of new material. But if followed too exclusively, it ends by limiting the comprehensiveness of truth. The search is endless. Realization evades us. The Eastern aim has been rather the opposite, namely that, in the multiplicity of phenomena, we should never miss their underlying unity. After generations of this quest, the idea of unity comes to us almost spontaneously, and we apprehend no insuperable obstacle in grasping it."[8]

The poet and the scientist had become affiliated with each other in pursuit of the same objective. Tagore expressed this alliance in his dedication of his "Katha O Kahini" to Bose :

"You gave the jewels of Truth, I give you in return its words and vision."

This idea of Tagore and Bose of relatedness and unity of matter and consciousness, of animate and inanimate which was based on ancient Indian spiritual thought of oneness, created a big controversy in the West and also in India about Bose as a scientists and Tagore as a thinker and a poet.

Controversies over Tagore and Bose

When Tagore's 'Gitanjali' came out in English translation and he was awarded the Nobel Prize in the West because of their overactive life it developed a thirst for the infinite peace and feeling of the Eternal. Contemporary notices of "Gitanjali" during that time confirm this, one said, "They are offerings from finite to infinite".

Another said, Mr. Tagore "uses things as if they were thoughts; something which had the imprint of the gods." This peace and feeling of the eternal is possible if one tries to understand the unity of mankind – an idea which was so much needed for people to realise during that time in the war ravage Europe.

Sturge Moore, after hearing Tagore's reading of his poems at Rothenstein's had remarked to Yeats that the poems were 'preposterously optimistic'. To this Yeats replied : "Ah, you see, he is absorbed in God".

That was true. Tagore's poetry appeared at that time as an antithesis to pride of life and disquiet about absolute evil, and as a release into another world. England and Europe, during that time were under the spell of an existential dilemma and angst and were searching for an answer as how to transcend this angst and get rid of the fabric of pessimism and realized that in Tagore's poetry, one can find a message and that is that one can possibly transcend pain and sorrow and celebrate life. It was during that time due to a psychological situation in England and Europe in which people were ready to listen even to a mere message because his poetry in its original though true and great poetry yet in translation did not have that much a form and style but the message of the poems which, however, because of a genuine, European, emotional demand did impinge.

In the initial exuberance shown at the time of his receiving the Nobel prize Tagore was accepted by the West as a spiritual guru, the great mystic from the East, a gentle Christ with a putative message for the West a messenger of peace and unity of mankind and transcendentalism who found god in nature and man, a man from the orient belonging to a culture of the other, a voice from Asia.

From the very beginning of his western career this stereotypical figure of Tagore as latter-day Wise Man from the East, the prophet did lingering harm to him. Nirod C Chaudhuri in his book 'Thy Hand, Great Anarch' said that very soon the literary alternative to Tagore came from the post war poets and novelists and above all from the Bloomsbury group and then with the loss of psychological topicality of his message the initial exuberance faded away very soon and the Western man's disillusion dawned in and criticism started.

Graham Green said about Tagore, the bright pabbly eyes of the theosophists. The fact that the West oscillated so widely from one extreme of exaggerated praise and admiration to another extreme of contempt and rejection only proves that they were fanatasized images of Tagore which had very little to do with reality.

Same thing happened with Jagadish Chandra Bose. After 1900, Bose extended his study to the effects of radiation on plant and animal tissues, his highly sensitive apparatus revealing striking but at the same time controversial similarities in the responses to electrical stimulus of living and non-living substances. He thus became more physiologist than physicist, though his work on plant physiology, with its mystical overtones, was never accepted in the way his work in physics was, either during Bose's lifetime or subsequently. According to C.V. Raman, India's first Nobel laureate in science, Bose "did some very clever physics before he started on all his mumbo-jumbo."[9] But surprisingly he was speaking almost the same language. Amongst Raman's many remarkable insights was the emphasis on identifying geometry in nature, both of organic world as also inorganic.

West chose to see Bose as the embodiment of a unique yet typically mystic Eastern mind endowed with the capacity and the imagination to grasp the absolute and simple truths of the earth and the universe and in due course he was accepted as a scientist offering the alternative orientations to science and understanding of scientific creativity outside the normal habitat of science. As a physicist his admirers such as Albert Einstein, Bernard Shaw, Henri Bergson, Aldous Huxley, and Romain Rolland found in him the personification of a historical civilization which had a more humane concept of science and a more integrated view of the organic and inorganic worlds than the West would offer. Even when he had fallen from grace he was accepted as a scientist of alternative sciences, in whom one can see a symbol of Indian science, where a book of surgery is written in verse and God is invoked before a scientist embarked in any kind of scientific activity. Bose was accepted as a pioneer who had Indianized modern science to make it compatible with the culture of an ancient society. London Spectator emphasized his 'easterness' and called him having a "sanyasi mind".[10]

Geddes described him as an Indian *rishi (hermit)* free from greed.[11]

Modern and Alternative Sciences

This raised the modern versus alternative sciences debate by drawing an instinctive relationship between science (technology) and "western" people and exemplifying a prevalent discourse within which non-western people are relegated to a particular ontological position in relation to "modern science" (and technology) that can be characterised as "waiting room" of scientific sociability. It constituted modern science as a universal knowledge and relegated scientific research in the non west to "waiting rooms" of history and development.[12]

In this debate the Eurocentric modernists by borrowing a term 'bricoleur' from Levi Strauss argue that the engineer (the engineer according to Levi Strauss creates specialized tools for specialized purposes. The bricoleur is a "jack-of-all-trades", who uses few, non-specialized tools for a wide variety of purposes. There is a loose connection between, on the one hand, the bricoleur and "primitive" societies, and, on the other, the engineer and modern societies) is always trying to make his way out of and go beyond the constraints imposed by a particular state of civilisation while the "bricoleur" by inclination or necessity always remains within them.[13]

Modernity and Tagore

But, however, the colonial west felt extremely surprised when both Tagore and Gandhi warned us in the beginning of the 20th century about the danger of developing a colonial mentality or mental colonisation.

Tagore said in those days that true modernism is freedom of mind and not slavery of taste. He observed, "You must apply your eastern mind, your spiritual strength, your love of simplicity, your recognition of social obligations in order to cut out a new path for this great unworldly car of progress shrieking out its loud discards as it runs"[14] and thereby debunked the whole notion of exclusivity of Western modernism and the development project and hence, while defining modernity, he had no hesitation to declare in Beijing in 1924 that 'The impertinence of material things is extremely old. The revelation of spirit in man is modern. I am in its side, I am modern.'[15]

Both Tagore and Bose had the courage to speak of other modernity or what Bhikhù Parekh says, 'critical traditionalism'[16] to infuse the Eastern spiritual resources and Vedantic beliefs leaving a distinctly Indian imprint in the corpus of modern science and widen its worldview.

Revelation of Spirit in man is the core philosophy of Tagore. Tagore's was not the lone voice during those days. Jose Ortega Y Gasset, considered to be the greatest Spanish philosopher of the modern time, developed a philosophical system known as 'ratiovitalism' had said clearly that modernity brought two common elements Disorientation and Dehumanization in poetry and as a result it led to violence and vivisection.

Science, Eastern Spirituality and Nationalism

Proponents of alternative sciences have been deeply concerned with violence perpetuated through "modern western science". They have criticised modern science for its qualities of "extreme use of reason directed towards the extreme use of violence"[17] and vivisection as explained by Ashis Nandi[18] and Shiv Viswanathan[19] and according to them, qualities of violence and vivisection are intrinsic to modern science and not simply are a result of, for example, its misguided application. The effort of the advocates of alternative sciences has been to look for epistemological alternatives to modern science in order to search for non-Eurocentric, non-violent, and non vivisectionist ontological possibilities.

The main purpose of Bose was to raise the question about the issue of modernity intertwined with science and Enlightment and challenge the Western vision of a fully autonomous science and reveal the tendency of the Western mind to forget that every culture produces its own science as surely as each scientific achievement produces new cultural realities.

By leaving a distinctly Indian imprint in the corpus of modern science; and secondly, by widening the worldview of modern science Bose brought a refreshing spirit to the excesses of Western scientific methodology by infusing the Eastern spiritual resources and Vedantic beliefs which proclaim the ideal of the Unity of Life. Bose made a valiant attempt to give a different orientation to the study of science, which, however, was not acceptable by his critics both in the West and India and which became a part of alternative sciences.

Bose sought to introduce an "eastern" spirituality within a "materialist" Western science, much like Mahendra Lal Sircar[20] and Reverend Father E. Lafont[21] but with a definite conscious assertion of 'Indian' spirituality.[22] It is emphatically said that for purposes of discipline–intellectual, moral, religious–the most efficient study is–Science… concerns all mankind for all times.[23] In this respect I may recall the words of D. S. Kothari, a very distinguished humanitarian physicist who said, "science provides an understanding of and control over nature, but it is the moral and spiritual insights which give meaning and purpose to life, individually and collectively".[24]

The perception of Bose and Tagore was to protest and resist the colonial political agenda by propagating the study of science and disproving that India is a "nation of dreamers" and they are incapable of grasping the depth of disciplines like science, notwithstanding the fact that the ancient India produced scientists like Aryabhata, Varamihira, Bhaskara, Brahmagupta and many others and discovered zero. Science became a symbol of nationalism and culture. After Bose's triumphant return from his visit of Europe Rabindranath called on Jagadish Chandra to offer him his congratulations on his successful mission abroad.

But not finding the scientist at home he left a bunch of champak flowers on his table[25] and after some months wrote a poem addressed to Bose which was later on published in his volume of poetry, "Kalpana" :

Vigyan lakhir priya paschim mandire
Door sindhuteere
Hey bandhu, giyecho tumi; jayamalyakhani
Seethe hote aani
....
Se vani pashibe sudhu tomari antare
Kheen matree sware

The nationalist message is clear and in due course Tagore urged Bose to take up larger responsibilities in the Indian struggle for national pride. Bose wrote to Tagore, how he was feeling uneasy before a lecture of 10th May 1901 at the Royal Society, when he envisioned a woman (was it mother India?) in rags who muttered, "I have come to greet you" and all his uneasiness instantly disappeared.[26]

Science in the discourse of both Tagore and Bose acquired a nationalist and spiritual configuration. In 1900 Bose, in a letter to Tagore from London wrote :

> "I heard the call of mother in your words of enthusiasm."

In the same year Bose, as a delegate of the Govt of India, took part in the International Congress of Physicists at Paris and while presenting his paper he, for the first time drew a parallelism between the living and the non-living. The paper was regarded as one of the most important received by the Congress and it was published in its volume. The audience in the conference was awestruck. Among them was Swami Vivekananda, who saw in Bose the embodiment of a new India and wrote in a letter :

"Here in Paris have assembled the great of every land, each to proclaim the glory of his country.... Among these peerless men gathered from all parts of the world, where is thy representative, O thou the country of my birth? Out of this vast assembly, a young man stood for thee, one of thy heroic sons, whose words have electrified the audience, and will thrill all his countrymen."[27]

Bose created a new paradigm of nationalism with the help of scientific essence. He is now hailed as a symbol of Indian nationalist culture, its national pride. Tagore hoped that through scientific researches India would regain its old glory and in a letter to Bose wrote a poem about it :

> Alone at the deep centre of all things;
> Where dwells the One alone in Sun, Moon and flowers,
> In leaves and beasts and birds and dust and stones,
> Where still one sleepless Life on its own lap
> Rocks all things with a wordless melody,
> All things that move or seem motionless.
> Call thou thy scholar-band come forth
> Out on the face of nature, this broad earth.
> Let them all gather. So may our India,
> O once again return to steadfast work,
> To duty and devotion, to her trance
> Of earliest meditation.

One can realize how exciting were the days when great minds like Tagore, Bose and others, in search for a nationalistic construction, made use of scientific essence , Vedic monism of "the unity of life" and the ethos of the traditional India to give expression to their nationalistic zeal. It was a unique confluence of ideas to infuse the people of India with the spirit of nationalism. This could be possible because they had a deep understanding of India- both of its past heritage and its present and created a new archetype of modernity where past does not pass off but past and present together create the future In that archetypal construction emerged their vision of India. On one side they salvaged the scientific essence and the modern scientific research by Indians and that became a means of pilgrimage to that essence, of realizing the Indian scientific spirit so as to create a national pride among Indians and on the other side both of them with the help and scientific experiments and philosophical speculations searched for the unity of life based on Vedic monism. In his letter to Tagore, dated 29th November, 1901, Bose acknowledged his responsibilities as a scientist to revive the national pride of his country :

"I am alive with the life force of the mother Earth, I have prospered with the help of the love of my countrymen. For ages the sacrificial fire of India's enlightenment has been kept burning, millions of Indians are protecting it with their lives, a small spark of which has reached this country ."

In his another letter to Tagore, dated 30th August, 1901, Bose gave expression to Vedic monism to raise the feelings of nationalism :

"There is a great gap between the living and the non-living, and I was experimenting on the responses on plants to make a connection between the two. Just now I got the amazing results; Same, Same, all are the Same!"[28] Poetically he wrote, "These trees have a life like ours. They eat and grow, face poverty, sorrows and suffering.

This poverty may induce them to steal and rob, they also help each other develop friendships, sacrifice their lives for their children."

This depiction of Nature, as a means to realize the essential unity in all existence, had been also evoked by Tagore in many of his writings. In his essay, "The Relation of the Individual to the Universe" in *Sadhana* the poet said :

"In ancient India we find that the circumstances of forest life did not overcome man's mind, and did not enfeeble the current of his energies, but only gave to it a particular direction.

He felt that truth is all-comprehensive, that there is no such thing as absolute isolation in existence, and the only way of attaining truth is through the interpenetration of our being into all objects.[29]

These are the fullest articulation of Vedic monism for creating a nationalistic feeling of the unity of people irrespective of their caste, creed, religion or social status. They did not stop there only and by using the folk wisdom and ancient Indian religious beliefs went back to their roots. Immediately after his marriage, he began, with his young wife, Abala Bose, to devote the two annual vacations to seeing and knowing India and to realizing what India stood for. He tried to understand the mythologies and folklores of India and some of the stories out of the great Indian epics *Ramayana* and *Mahabharata* which almost all Indian children used to grow up with and attempted to create a nationalistic spirit for India, its heritage, ethos and all that India stood for. Bose translated the myth of the origin of the river Ganga and used the anti-rational view prevalent in our racial unconscious : "Ganga, where do you come from?" I used to ask the river. “From the matted hair of Mahadeva”, she would reply. And where do you end? She would reply, “At the feet of Mahadeva”, “I could clearly hear this answer in the murmur of the river.”[30] Tagore now found in his work the true meaning of the universe which Indian saints discovered long ago.[31]

The New Way of Science

Fortunately today the Enlightment’s concept of science, from which the dominant culture of science draws sustenance, is changing. In the West many developments took place in the 18th and 19th centuries, culminating in the assertion of pure objectivity and definitiveness of science. Science became abstract and mathematical to a point of discomfort. Voices of dissension could be heard. The vision of India or Tagore or J.C. Bose of the spiritual unity of all existence is taken up seriously now in the Western frontiers.

This is corroborated by Peter Tomkins of “The Secret Life of Plants” :

“While we in England were still steeped in the rude empiricism of barbaric life, the subtle Easterners had swept the universe into a synthesis and had seen the one in all its changing manifestations”.

Fritz of Capra (1939-) in his book, The Tao of Physics’ endorses this view and says that the basic element of the Eastern world view are also those of the world view emerging from modern physics and further says that his book aims at improving the image of science by showing that there is an essential harmony between the spirit of Eastern wisdom and Western science. (1983, p.25) At another place Capra refers to the basic unity of the universe as upheld in Eastern mysticism and modern physics :

“The most important characteristics of the Eastern world view is the awareness of the unity and mutual interrelation of all things and events... The Eastern traditions constantly refer to this ultimately the indivisible reality, which manifests in all things and of which all things are parts.”

The famous German physicist and philosopher, Werner Karl Heisenberg, Nobel Laureate in Physics in 1932 for his ‘Uncertainty

Principle' met Tagore in Calcutta at his Jorasanko house in 1928 and had long conversations with him about Science and Indian Philosophy. He is reported to have said in 1972 that Rabindranath's philosophical ideas had been of help to him as a physicist. Heisenberg, aged 27 then had several conversations with the mature poet of 67 years old about relativity, incommensurability, inter-connectedness and impermanence as fundamental aspects of physical reality. After the conversations he said : "Some of the ideas that had seemed so crazy, suddenly made much sense. That was of great help for me."[32] His enduring fascination with the relationship between Man and Nature, notably in his Hibbert Lectures "The Religion of Man" at Manchester College, Oxford University on May 19, 21 and 26, 1930, brought him close to Albert Einstein. In the same year on July 14, Tagore and Einstein had a seminal discussion on the issue of scientific truth and one about the physical world. One dialogue from their discussion is worth quoting :

> Einstein – That the universe exists is a matter of faith for me.
>
> Tagore – The universe can exists only if I know that I am Human.

Einstein is emphatic in his belief that the world as a reality is independent of human consciousness. Tagore, on his part, affirms that his conception of truth is also impersonal, and that it is not therefore dependent on the perception or consciousness of any particular person of any particular time and place. "Truth" according to him, " is one with the Universal Being, must essentially be human, otherwise whatever we, the individuals, realize as true can never be called truth... In science we go through the discipline of eliminating the personal limitations of our individual minds and thus reach that comprehension of truth which is in the mind of the Universal Man."[33] According to Tagore's Vedic-Upanishadic vision, the individual in the universal (simar maje ashim tumi bajao apan sur) i.e. the later is articulated in and through the former. The valid vision of truth is integral – both individual and universal, both real (experientially real) and ideal (transcendentally ideal).[34]

Brain Josephon, physics Nobel Laureate has commented,

'Tagore is, I think, saying that truth is a subtler concept than Einstein realised.'[35]

Understood in this light, in Indian knowledge system, there is no conflict between modern science and spirituality, physical sciences and literature, between empirical knowledge and metaphysical, between reason and imagination and between scientific and aesthetic values. Capra endorses the view that imagination is what helps critical reason to develop into creative intuition and says, "The rational part of research would, in fact, be useless if it were not complemented by the intuition that gives scientists new insights and makes them creative."

This creativity is in no way different from the literary creativity.

Tagore and Bose : Creative Use of Science

Both Tagore and Bose made use of literature and Science respectively not only creatively but in their writings one can see science or literary creativity intermingling with each other. Tagore's only expressly scientific poem was on 'The Sensitive Plant' which appeared as preface to his collection of poems called *kheya* (*The Ferry*). In beautiful poetic terms it summarizes J.C.Bose's findings on the sensitive plant. However, scientific thought permeated even his early poems. In *Prabhat Sangeet* – one of his earliest poetic publications - there are two complementary poems *Anananta Jivan* (Endless Life') and *Anananta Maran* (Endless Death). These two are full of scientific illustrations. There is a third poem *Sristi Sthiti Pralaya* (Creation, Conservation and Destruction) which is a marvelous synthesis of pictures of the world's beginning depicted in modern science and in Hindu mythology. Edward Thompson in his book on 'Rabindranath Tagore : His life and work' said about the poem :

"Thought is lit up by imagination, and we have an unforgetful picture of the vast wastes and of primal Energies at work... Space is filled with whirling fire fountains, and burning nebulae, shaping themselves to become world."

The theme of creation is an extremely favourite one with Tagore. He reverts to this theme again and again and describes with scientific precision the story of earth's beginnings. In the poem *sandhya*, (twilight) in his collection of poems called *chitra,* he says :

Aake aake andhokare hoteche bahire
Aakate aakte dipta tara, sudur pallir
praddeeper moto| Dheere jeno uthe bhese
mlan chobi dharanir nayononemeshe
kato jug- juganter atit abhash,
kato jeev heebaner jirna itihas|
Jeno mone pare sai balya niharika;
Tar pare projwalanto joubaner sikha;
Jeeva dhatri jananer kaj bokhe loye
Lokkho koti jeev – kato , kato klesh,
Kato judho, kato mritu, nahi tar shesh

There is large number of Scientist- writers, who gave copious examples from Tagore's writings to establish the fact that in a good number of his creative writings - poetry and prose - one can find allusions after allusions of his scientific knowledge and expression of unmistakable scientific imagery.[36] He also wrote articles and books on pure science but in Bengali so that the people of Bengal can understand its nationalistic value and use it for their progress and development but both Tagore and Bose were for the humanization of Science and explained to the West that when the European peoples would be able to realize deeply that their scientific heritage is rooted in their culture, history and humanity, the science will be self-conscious and well founded and the crisis of civilization, which was Tagore's stirring lecture at the age of 80, would be gradually over. In fact, Science and Culture are "the two birds on the same branch". The Katho Upanisad speaks of the two birds on the same branch as the 'experiencer' (*bhokta*) and the 'seer' *(drasta)* – and one cannot live without the other.

Personal Relation of Tagore with Bose

This paper will remain incomplete, if I do not mention the personal relationship between Tagore and Bose and remove some misgivings created by some scholars. In the poet's own words :

"I found in him (Bose), a dreamer, and it seemed to me, what surely was a half truth, that it was more his magical instinct than the probing of his reason which startled out secrets of nature before sudden flashes of his imagination. In this I found our mutual affinity but at the same time our difference, for to my mind he appeared to be poet of the world of facts that waited to be proved by the scientist for their final triumph, whereas my own world of visions had their value, not in their absolute probability but in their significance of delightfulness."[37]

Tagore met Bose in 1891, but their close friendship began after Bose's triumphant return from Europe in 1896. Thereafter on numerous occasions they met together and Bose influenced Tagore to write short stories, poems like *Karna-Kunti Sambad* and many others and listened to his delightful songs and Bose, on his part, told Tagore about science and discoveries. Tagore was Bose's greatest Bengali advocate. Though by his own admission he hardly understood Bose's scientific achievements, he raised money from the Maharaja of Tripura to enable Bose to stay in Europe and carry on his researches. It is said by Dutta and Robinson by quoting Ashis Nandy that this friendship lasted for ten years. Bose was a touchy, somewhat vain man who found friendship and collaborations difficult. The success of Shantiniketan and the award of the Nobel Prize to Tagore seemed to have provoked Bose to jealousy.[38] Bose was now seemed to be looking for an excuse to break away from a man he had once declared was one of his best friends.[39] But it is difficult to accept this allegation of jealousy when one reads the letter to Tagore by Jagadish on Tagore's receiving the Nobel prize :

"All these years, I felt a deep anguish that you had not been bedecked with the world's greatest honour. Today, I do not feel so any more. How may I express my gratitude to Almighty God? Go from strength to strength. Let victory be always yours. Let "Dharma" be your eternal companion."

There was another letter written in 1919 after Tagore relinquished his knighthood after the Jallianwala massacre in Punjab shows how tight was the bond of friendship between them. Bose wrote just a line to Tagore in appreciation :

> Dear Friend, You have divine blessings on you...

It is true that the letters exchanged between the two were much fewer than before. There may have been some misunderstandings but the warmth of their love remained till the end. Both of them were getting busier, having set up two Institutions and finding it hard to sustain them.

Jagadish dedicated his famous book "Nervous Mechanism in Plants" (1926) : To My Life Long Friend Rabindranath Tagore.

Tagore's reply to Bose's letter on his return from the US was :

> When I received your book, I realized, 'here lies our Truth, the Light and Life, the eternal manifestation of India. The fatigue that had come over me dissolved by the warmth of friendship that was conveyed by your letter.

Jagadish's letter to Tagore in 1932 expressing his delight after Tagore's visit to Iran and also his grief on the death of Tagore's grandson (the son of Meera, Tagore's daughter), and the one in 1936, sending some money to help Tagore's Visva-Bharati University were sincere expressions of his feelings. Bose died in 1937 and the memorial address by Tagore after Bose's death bears testimony to the love and respect they had for each other. It is true that the letters exchanged between the two were much fewer than before and their might have been have been some misunderstandings between them but the warmth of their love remained till the end.

One was an *acharya* and the other was *gurudev* but the meanings of these two appellations are different. One is a theoretician, who creates theories (aachenoti arthaan) and asks people to follow the right path for investigation (aacharam grahayati) and the other is a preceptor. A theoretician works mostly in isolation and hence has less visibility, a teacher works in society having more visibility. The search of both was for an alternative idea of India but not for a revival of ancient India. Bose was searching for a creative philosophy of science and looked for inputs in India's ancient heritage and Tagore also went to the ancient heritage in search for living and reasoning in freedom for the unity of mankind. As we have come to a new millennium, we may arrive to a position to affirm in the coming decades that Europe did not say the last words about science and other issues. Time may still vindicate the vision of the two dissenters.

Mahalanobis in this Scenario

Where does Prasanta Kumar Mahalanobis fit in in this scenario?

Despite a 30-year difference between the two, Prasanta Chandra Mahalanobis "was one of Tagore's rare friends who did not place him simply on a high pedestal full of only aura and fame, but treated him as a lively intellectual and affectionate companion." Rabindranath Tagore also took a liking to young Mahalanobis, being particularly impressed by the combination in him of a love of literature with a flair for logical analysis.

"Just as Tagore sought to bring humanity closer through Visva-Bharati or his one-nest-world university at Santiniketan, Prasanta Chandra strove to use the ideal of humanism through statistics," "Statistics for human welfare" was a stated goal in the Memorandum of Association of the institute.

While Tagore coined the Bengali word for statistics *rashi vigyan* or *rashi vidya* and wrote a poem in the inaugural issue of the journal of the Indian Statistical Institute, Mahalanobis served as the first joint secretary of Visva-Bharati for 10 years and framed the constitution of Visva-Bharati in 1921. Tagore would often call upon Prasanta for advice on 'political' matters. He also travelled with Tagore several times on his foreign tours. Prasanta acted as Tagore's secretary in Europe in 1926 and in one of his letters to E. J. Thompson he wrote, 'we have been going from place to place like gypsies. Poet had a nervous breakdown in Prague... there are two different sets in Prague, Czechs and Germans, and everything had to be repeated twice.'[40]

Mahalanobis's analytical turn of mind manifested itself at a very early age and he was given to arguing things out with his friends and even with his superiors.

Though undoubtedly a clever man but this trait was not liked by many including Leonard k Elmhirst, the English man brought by Tagore from Cornel University, where he did a course in agriculture, to take charge of Sriniketan. In 'Poet and Plowman' Elmhirst writes that Prasanta Mahalanobis, the newly appointed secretary to the new Visva-Bharati University wanted Elmhirst to write out a prospectus so that the news would go around and the whole country come to know about the work at Sriniketan and also to write a column every month in 'The Modern Review' and then there would be no dearth of financial help from different parts of the country. Elmherst had to decline his ideas as he thought it would be too early to go into print till they were much further in their feet and concluded that Prasanta's 'torrent of suggestion without penetration flowed on'[41] but he did not think, it was worthwhile.

Prasanta was attracted towards Tagore because of his demeanour, poetic grandeur, interest in science and love for the country. Another reason for his fascination was Tagore's analytical force which brought into focus some very original issues like nationalism, traditionalism, educational commitment, freedom of mind and interpretational epistemology which created a tremendous awareness all over India and the world; each area provided insights into his scientific and Upanishadic faith of the unity of universe. Prasanta joined hands with Tagore in repudiating the violent nationalism and wrote in a letter to Edward J. Thompson in 1921 that Tagore never "supported nationalism, not in any form or guise. Even at the height of the *swadeshi* movement he was protesting against some particular aspects".[42]

Mahalanobis copiously read the writings of Tagore and wrote to him often. The renowned statistician was also a most meticulous chronicler of Tagore's life and put together a year-by-year calendar of Tagore's activities. But here the conflict between litterateur Tagore, and historian Mohalanobis came on the surface. Tagore wanted to give recognition only to his later day mature writings and hence dismissed the rationale of Mahalanobis of chronologically chronicling of his writings and humourously referred to a poem that he wrote to Prashanta in 1935 : '*Aami chele gale phele rekhe jabo pichu*'[43] and politly asked him not to do so. But the history of Tagore study has proved that a synthesis between the literary and historical ideals of Tagore and Mahalanobis can truly take us to our covetous destination.

Let me here refer to an unpublished letter of Mahalanobis to E.J. Thompson which on one side shows Rani and Prasanta's great love and regard for Tagore that continued unabatedly till Tagore's last days as well as, Tagore's exceptional optimism of hope of a good time in a situation of great crisis :

"As you know the Poet was very seriously ill in September (1937). Just before this he was staying with us in Calcutta. I left for Shimla for a committee meeting; two days letter, after a great deal of hesitation, he went back to Shantiniketan, and the same night he became un conscious. As the telegraph office was then closed, the railway people sent a telephonic message to our house at one o'clock at night asking that doctors should be sent to Shantiniketan immediately without waiting for the morning train as otherwise it might be too late. Rani (Mrs Mahalanobis telephoned to my uncle Sir Nil Ratan Sarkar (a famous Physician); (they) left for Shantiniketan at two o'clock by car and reached there early in the morning. Poet was then completely unconscious and the local doctors thought it was a case of apoplectic stroke. He however recognized Rani, smiled and said 'So you have come'; and again became unconscious. When doctors arrived from Calcutta they found that it was a very bad attack of erysipelas complicated by kidney trouble. For sixty-two hours he was completely unconscious and all hopes were given up. Rani was near him all the time almost continuously as nobody else could administer medicine or food. He apparently retained a subconscious touch with her and it was only she who could manage to do anything. Once he regained consciousness recovery was very rapid. As soon as he could speak he said that he wanted to write a poem or to paint a picture. As writing a poem would be more strenuous, he asked for his pigments and brushes. Within a few hours he painted quite a large picture. The whole of the foreground is a dark and ill defined veil of primitive forest, a warm flood of golden light breaks through in the centre showing the distance view on the other side."[44]

At the End

This warm flood of golden light breaking through the centre in the painting of Tagore, and showing the distance view on the other side, is extremely significant. It reveals the other side which definitely brings a message of an alternative world, a world within us – a world which can give meaning to our life and solace even to a soldier going to war. Let me quote here a letter which one Susan Owen, the mother of a First World War soldier Wilfred Owen wrote to Tagore in 1920, describing his last conversation with her son before he left for the war which would take his life at the age of 25 only. She writes, 'Wilfred said goodbye with those wonderful words of yours – beginning at "When I go from hence, let this be my parting word."

When Wilfred's notebook was returned to me, I found "these words written in his dear writing – with your name beneath".[45]

Thank you for your exceptional attention and patience to listen to my address.

Notes and References

1. Indra Nath Choudhuri, Seminar paper on 'The Sacred and the Secular : Conflictual or Complementary" presented in an extended and closed seminar organized by the Centre for study of Culture and Philosophy, Washington in 2009.
2. Rabindranath Tagore, ed. Sisir Kumar Das. New Delhi : Sahitya Akademi, 1966, Vol. III : p. 827, henceforth referred to as EWRT.
3. Usha Choudhuri, Vedic Mythopoeia : An Approach to religion, Myth and Poetry, Delhi, 1983, p.2
4. J. Lourdusamy, Science and National Consciousness in Bengal 1870-1930. New Delhi : Orient Longman Private Limited, 2004, p. 102.
5. Pratik Chakrabarti, *Western Science in Modern India.* Delhi :, 2004, p.
6. Patrick Geddes, *The Life and Works of* Sir Jagadish Chandra Bose. London : Longman, Green and Co., 1920, pp. 88-89. Cited in Chakrabarti, p. 193.
7. J. C. Bose, *Responses in the Living and Non-Living.* London : Longman, Green and Co., 1902
8. Jagadish Chandra Bose, Sir Jagadish Chandra Bose : His Life, Discoveries and Writings.Madras, 1921, pp. 60-61.
9. Quoted in Dutta and Robinson, Rabindranath Tagore, 1995, p.403
10. Quoted in Pratik Chakrabarti, Western Science in Modern India : Metropolitian Methods, Colonial practices, ranikhet, p.185
11. 1. P. Geddes, The Life and Work of Sir Jagadis Chandra Bose (Longman, Green and Co., 1920).
12. Dipesh Chakrabarty (Chakrabarty, Dipesh, *Provincialising Europe : Postcolonial Thought and Historical Difference,* 2000) argues that as a result of Eurocentric historicism the non-west is relegated to waiting room of history, a stage that is perpetually characterised as "not yet". Veena Das throws light on this issue in her analysis of Louis Dumont's(a French anthropologist) criticism of A K Saran (an Indian anthropologist),that the latter's theoretical

position stemmed from his being a Hindu/Indian. Das argues that while Saran is shown as "doubly entrenched,"as a social scientist and an Indian/Hindu, similar double entrenchment is not seen by Dumont for himself , Das Veena, Critical Events : An Anthropological Perspective of Contemporary India,1984

13. Levi Strauss, The Savage Mind,1966, pp.19-20.
14. Rabindranath Tagore, The English Writings of Tagore, Vol.III, 1996 (edited by Sisir Kumar Das, p. 368 & p.365
15. Ibid, Vol. II, 1996, p. 585
16. The critical traditionalists wanted to mobilize their indigenous resources, borrowing from Europe where necessary, Bhikhu Parekh, Colonialism, Tradition and Reform, New Delhi, 1989, p.35
17. Sardar Z, The Revenge of Athena : Science Exploitation and the Third World, 1998, P.1
18. Ashis, Alternative Sciences : Creativity and Authenticity in Two Indian Scientist, 1995, p.68
19. Viswanathan,Shiv, Carnival for Sciences : Essays on Science, Technolgy Development, 1997
20. Mahendra Lal Sircar established the Indian Association for the Cultivation of Science (IACS) in 1876 and articulated his goals in his first article to set up a nationalist agenda and to create a culture of science in India trough its practice and popularization (M.L. Sircar, 'On the Desirability of the National Institution for the Cultivationof the Science in India', in Indian Association for the Cultivation of Science, Calcutta, 1877, p.8).
21. Father E. Lafont, a man with keen interest in science who was engaged in building a spectra-telescope observatory at St Xavier's College. He always thought that study of science is compatible with unearthing the spirituality of Christianity and the practice of science has moral significance. See Andrew Cunningham, 'How the Principia Got Its Name Or, Talking Natural Philosophy Seriously', History of Science, vol. xxix, no.83,part 4, 1991, pp. 377-92
22. Pratik Chakravarti, Western Science in Modern India : Metropolitian Methods, Colnial practices, 1910, p.181
23. Annual Report of the IACS, 1899, p.18
24. Kapila Vatsyayan, Culture and Science, Lecture delivered at the Indian National Science Academy Platinum Jubilee celebration in New Delhi on 10. 1. 2009

25. Manoranjan Gupta, Jagadish Chandra Bose : A Biography, 1964, p.68
26. J. C. Bose, *Patraboli (Letters of J. C. Bose)*, ed. D. Sen (Basu Vigyan Mandir,1994).
27. The Complete Works of Swami Vivekananda, Mayavati Memorial Edition, 1962, Vol. Vii, pp. 379-80
28. Dibakar Sen (ed.), *Patrabali Acharya Jagadish Chandra Bose* (Bengali). op. cit., p. 82.Cited in Chakrabarti, 210.
29. Rabindranath Tagore, *Sadhana* (*The Realization ofLife*).op.cit. p. 4.
30. Jagadish Chandra Bose, Abyakta, pp. 73-74
31. Ashis Nandi, Alternative Sciences : Creativity and Authenticity in two Indian scientists, p. 65
32. Capra Fritzof, The Book of Tao, 1972,
33. Rabindranath Tagore, The Religion of Man, London, 1931, p.19
34. D.P. Chattopadhyaya, 'Tagore on Humanization of Science', Interdisciplinary Studies In Science, Society, Value and Civilizational Dialogue, (ed. D.P. Chattopadhyaya), Shimla, 2004, pp. 161-180
35. This meeting of Tagore and Einstein was reported in the New York Times by the journalist Dmitri Marianoff (Einstein's step-son-in-law) : "It was interesting to see them together; Tagore–the poet—with the head of a thinker, and Einstein–the thinker–with the head of a poet'. It seemed to an observer as though two planets were engaged in a chat".

    Tagore again met Einstein in mid-December, 1930, in New York for the fourth and last time. They shared a deep mutual respect. Einstein alluded to Tagore affectionately as "Rabbi" (affectionately called him so) and Tagore felt so much concerned for Einstein that he turned down the offer of an Honorary Doctorate from Berlin University as a protest against the Nazi treatment of Einstein.
36. Scientist and Writers like Partha Ghosh, B.M. Chaudhuri, D.P. Chattopadhyaya, Sisir K Majumdar, D. M. Sengupta, Biswanath Banerjee and others
37. J. C. Bose, Patraboli (Letters of J. C. Bose), ed. D. Sen, Kolkata, 1994).
38. Krishna Dutt and Andrew Robinson, Selected Letters of Rabindranath Tagore, 1997, p.57
39. Ashis Nandi, Alternative Sciences : Creativity and Authenticity in Two Indian Scientists, 1995, p.56
40. Quoted in Selected Letters of Tagore (ed) Dutta and Robinson, 1997, p. 359

41. Leonard K. Elmhirst, Poet and Plowman, Visva-Bharati, 2008, p.137
42. Prasanta Mahalanobis to E. J. Thompson, December, 1921 : E. P. Thompson, "Introduction" : Rabindranath Tagore, *Nationalism* , London, 1991, p. 12.
43. Letter no 130 of Tagore quoted in Kalyaneyeshu Prashanta, (ed) Prashantakumar Pal, 1904
44. Qouted in Selected Letters of Rabindranath Tagore, (ed) Dutta and Robinson, 1997, pp. 484-485
45. Robert B. Silvers and Barbara Epstein, India : A Mosaic, New York, The New York Review of Books, 2000, p. 6

    The complete poem is from Gitanjali, no. 96, The English Writings of Rabindranath Tagore, Vol. I, (ed) Sisir Kumar Das, New Delhi, 1994, p.76

    "When I Go from hence let this be my parting word, that what I have seen is unsurpassable.

    I have tasted of the hidden honey of this lotus that expands on the ocean of light, and thus am I blessed —let this be my parting word.

    In this playhouse of infinite forms I have had my playand here have I caught sight of him that is formless.

    My whole body and my limbs have thrilled with his touch who is beyond touch; and if the end comes here, let it come —let this be my parting word."

    (It will be worthwhile to bring from memory a parallel idea given by Rumi : If I die, don't say that he died.

    Say he was dead, became alive, and was taken by the Beloved).

Chapter Six

Rabindranath Tagore : Children's Writing and Juan Ramon Jimenez

It was not a coincidence that after Rabindranath Tagore shot into fame particularly in 1913 when it came to be known that the poet from India, with an unpronounceable name had got the Nobel prize in literature, a young blonde Spanish girl, Zenobia Camprubi, with her eyes as blue as the Mediterranean where she was born, with a very feminine and gentle appearance, and a very distinct speech although a little hurried, who passed long periods in the United States came across an English book of poems for children written and translated by Tagore himself, 'The Crescent Moon.' in 1913 Which included translations of a collection of poems in Bengali called 'shishu' (The Child), which appeared in 1903 just after the death of his wife Mrinalini in 1902, and also some other poems. Zenobia was so much impressed by the poems that she began translating them in prose, in Spanish and in one of her visits to Madrid in 1915 approached Juan Ramon Jimenez, then a well known celebrated poet and author of several volumes of poems, who was to get Nobel prize in 1956, to help her by going through her manuscript containing a literal translation of the "Crescent Moon", the help was available to her immediately. One can imagine that Juan Ramon's eagerness to polish the translation was more because of his love at first sight, which turned into passionate love for Zenobia though as he went through the translations his admiration grew for Tagore. Jimenez not only polished the translation but wrote a poem as an introduction to the volume which was the first evidence of his admiration for Tagore. His six lines four paragraph introduction dedicated to the Indian child of "La Luna Nueva" written in a prose that approximates poetry, began thus.

"You are here, yes; we feel that you are amongst us, but where are you? Are you playing in your village among the sun-bathed lilies, and we here you speaking to yourself, when the breeze unfolds the layers of sand on the beach, the breeze that guides your tiny paper boats; or are you already in the sky, boatman of the moon, pouring a blue ray into the vigil of your mother?"

An infinite freshness and endless tenderness tell us you exist. But I do not know how or why. But where, where are you? I think, I know you, but do you know us? We see you without your seeing us... or do you see us, without our knowing it, across the border of a dark cloud of a summer night?"

In this introductory poem, which is of four units, the warmth and profundity of Juan Ramon's response to the world of Tagore is clearly manifested. He realizes that the poems of "The Crescent Moon" are not only poems for or about children but they are celebration of childhood. He feels the existence of the child of Tagore in his essence though he fails to visualize him exactly in concrete details. He feels his presence and accepts him as a part of the known reality and yet his feelings stretch into the frontiers of the unknown. The 'nino indio' slowly transcends his national limitation and finds himself merged into the child eternal.

The relation between Juan Ramon and Tagore that began with the translation of "The crescent Moon", deepened with the passage of time, but it certainly played a significant role during the years between 1914 and 1916. All lovers of Juan Ramon have noticed that a great change in his writings came around 1916. The change coincided with a great change in his life; he had fallen in love with Zenobia as the translation brought them closer and finally united the lovers. In this game of love Tagore played a role – the role of cupid – without knowing it. Let me say here in passing that Zenobia who lived as life partner of Ramon all her life helping him even in owning property by paying from her royalties from Tagore translations died of cancer just three days after the Swedish Academy voted to award Jimenez the Nobel Prize in Literature.

The Spanish readers found a world of innocence and beauty in the poems of "The Crescent Moon" and also a striking similarity between Juan Ramon and the Indian poet. The Spanish translation acquired a felicity of expression, as it incorporated qualities that have been called by an English critic as "catchy as a hit song" and "music of words.". The result was that these poems and passages could be recited and remembered by a large number of people enhancing its immense popularity.

The first review of the translation that appeared in Gil Blas (12th Oct 1915) said "this book of the Indian poet whose name is difficult to pronounce... appears like a comet in the sky of our language... Juan Ramon is so much a kindred spirit of Tagore, a brother of Tagore (hermano de Tagore) that one can find his own spirit in these pages..."

It is indeed the similarity between these two poets that made the translation so welcome to the Spanish reader despite the foreign ness of the original. The reviewer found the child of the crescent Moon more delightful than his European counterpart. "This child is more a child, noble and pure, more naked and clean, more angelic and remote, more humane and graceful" and "Tagore has presented the child with such vividness and depth that the alieness of the landscape does not prevent one in visualizing him in his fullness."

Jose Ostega Gasset Spain's greatest thinker of the last century, writing a three-part serial on the Indian poet in Madrid's newspaper, El sol, in 1918 paid a rich tribute to Zenobia Camprubi for bringing the genius of Tagore within the reach of the Spanish public. The philosopher Gasset, who is remembered for his famous sentence, "I am what I am and what my circumstances are", praised Tagore for his universal quality,

"Rabindranath, on the other hand, does not need anything historical or sumptuary, anything particular of a time or a people, with a little of sun, sky and cloud, of springs and thrust, of tempest and river-bank, with the hinge of a door, or the frame of a window from which to peep out, above all, with a little of loving fire and fever towards God, he weaves his songs. This lyric is, thus, composed of universal things, which is there everywhere and which has been there everywhere and which suddenly make it a bird which sings out from every branch."

Further Ortega Y Gasset refers to "this Indian who has the profile of the Aryan Christ" who is a great poet because he can "tell us something which no one has told us before, but which is not new for us".

Tagore's range of poems and prose writings on children is extremely wide and full of variety which includes whimsy, nonsense and fantasy, but also moral pieces, social narratives and historical tales. Tagore took the issue of writing for children extremely seriously. In his works written for children a strong emphasis on bringing the heritage of India to the knowledge of the children can be visible. In these writings he valourizes qualities of honesty, chivalry and bravery embodied in heroes of legend and history and also describes idyllic scenes from rural Bengal with the sole purpose to stimulate the imagination of the children.

Tagore wrote several poems for children confirming their `hidden longing to act like adults. In one of poems, the boy says that when he grows up like his father, in the evening he will pick up his walking stick and go to the local club. And at that time, if the tutor comes and asks for his books and homework, then he will say, 'Don't you see I am grown up now like my father and there is nothing to study?' The tutor will then reply, ok, babusahab, and then I go.'

It is not that a child wants to grow up like an adult but a proper childhood is important in the formation of the adult and hence Wordsworth's phrase, "The child is Father of man" is interpreted so wildly to bring home this point. Sukanta Chaudhuri in his Preface and Introduction to the Oxford Selected writings for Children says that Tagore credited children with power of absorption that adults may well lack, and laid before them the entire range of human experience : the comic, the fantastic and the reassuring, but also the tragic, the philosophic, even at times the grim and horrific. The poems of 'The Crescent Moon' are very funny, or exciting and amusing at the least, particularly to comfort and amuse the younger children : they had just lost their mother. But others in the collection are sad and thoughtful pieces, obviously written for grown-ups to read and therefore it is said that a child may extend his mind in many directions after reading Tagore's literature for children but this may be even truer of an adult and it means that the line between grown-up stories and children's fairy tales and realistic ones, is sometimes hard to draw.

The story, "Wishes Come True", is a story which is to be found in the anthology of stories for the adults as well as for children. This is a strong reason that a great poet of Jimenez' standing, after working on the translation of "The Crescent Moon", could write to his friend Maria Martos in 1915 that Tagore is an extraordinary and true poet. Graciela Palau De Nemes, a famous Spanish critic with a an analogical and perceptive mind, could notice the parallelism between Tagore's "The Crescent Moon" and Jimenez, best known work, first published in 1914 long before the translation "Platero and I". She says.

In Jimenez' landscape in Southern Andalusia there is no banana plants, no areca palms, no cocoa nut trees, but Jimenez could as well have written, for example, the opening lines in Tagore's "The Flower School" :

> When storm-clouds rumble in the sky and June showers Come down,
> The moist east wind comes marching over the heath to blow its bagpipes among the bamboos.
> The crowds of flowers come out of a sudden, from nobody know where, and dance upon the grass in wild glee.

There was no shaggy-headed banyan tree standing on the bank of the pond to attract the little child Jimenez, but there was a tree in the yard which, while he lived in that house, was the first source of his poetry, as Tagore's banyan tree had been to the child.

The children in both poets have golden dawns and silver moons; both fear lightning and thunder : "scratching the sky with its nail," said Tagore; "like an enormous cargo of rocks falling from the zenith on the town," said Jimenez.

Both the Indian and the Spanish child dream their dreams behind the locked gate : "I can see through the gate of that house the gardener digging the ground...I wish I were a Gardener," wrote Tagore and Jimenez :

> I would place my face against the bars and look...
> there is a wide, low road that I have never travelled.

Tagore remembers the girl who went away "when the trees were in bud and the spring was young" and Jimenez "the little girl in her crib (who) sailed down-river toward death...Oh melancholy summer!" Nemes quotes the lines of Tagore.

"The burning log bursts in flames and cries, this is my flower, my death" and then says that as we read it, we know we are also reading Juan Ramon Jimenez. Only the Spanish poet could have written Tagore's lines with the perfection with which they are rendered into Spanish. Those of us who know his works could have easily been deceived into affirming that Jimenez was the author of 'Stray Birds".

Tagore says in 'Stray Birds' :

> Do not say, 'it is morning,' and dismiss it with a name of yesterday. See it for the first time as a new-born child that has no name.
> And Jimenez in Indice : 'Yesterday's illusion shall be left, without greed, as a flower or a germ, to yesterday's corpse.

One can easily realise that Nemes was trying to disprove those critics who were loud about the possible influence of Tagore on Juan Ramon and establish the fact that there are striking resemblances and close affinity rather than any influence of Tagore on Jimenez. I think she is correct. There is no doubt that Jimenez had spent a considerable part of his creative life in translating Tagore with the active help of his wife, and translations of Tagore form more than one-third of his total writings.

Rarely indeed has any creative writer of his status and power devoted so much of his time and energy in translating a foreign writer and rarely a creative writer does translate one author so consistently and enthusiastically over such a long period of time without an inner compulsion. There was an inner compulsion, Ramon discovered in Tagore a kindred spirit, a spiritual companion and also "a flame of love soaring towards God." As his wife Zenobia wrote to Tagore in

1919, "I think you will understand how constantly you have been our spiritual companion since we began to know you five years ago. It has been a wonderful companionship to have and you seem to pervade everything for us."

All the prefatory verses to Tagore's work by Juan Ramon as well as the verses directly addressed to Tagore which we have already referred to indicate that Juan Ramon penetrated deep into the world of Tagore and he made it a part of his own poetic world. Any study of parallelism will be too crude and too inadequate to explain the mysterious ways of the poetic process. Whether his understanding of Tagore was right or wrong is irrelevant. What is relevant is that he understood and appreciated Tagore in his own way, and that Tagore he understood became a part of his poetic personality– This is to emphasize only our anxiety to know how did Jemenez receive Tagore and what way did he reveal his response. Let us have a look at his "Song to Dead Amal" which introduces "El Cartero del rey" (The Post office) :

> Be in sleep. Sudha remembers you; the king comes to you tonight, Amal. Sleep quietly, be in sleep; and when you get up your eyes will behold in your hands Sudha's flowers, and in front of you the King's countenance. Be in sleep.
>
> Sleep well. Be in measured, untroubled sleep... be in your sleep for ever, child; in this night you shall see the polar-star above his grand black palace.
>
> Be in sleep, let all the doors of your room be unlatched and opened for your soul's wanderings. Amal; the stars that know you well fetch you during the king's arrival. Be in sleep... from the bowers of eternal garden. I know you shall return, Amal because the flowers that are in your hand, the flowers of Sudha, await your awaking... sleep, be in sleep.

This is in perfect consonance with the Tagorean spirit evoking the most poignant moments in the play. Let me say in passing that on that night when Hitler's Nazi army attacked Paris in the beginning of the 2nd World war, the Radio Paris was that time broadcasting the

French translation of "The Post Office" and in Hitler's concentration camp in Poland this same play was staged by prisoners knowing well that very soon their life would end in gas chambers. Such was the appeal of the play and its insightful depth.

But in Tagore's "Malini", which is a play of sharp conflict of ideologies between two friends, appears to Juan Ramon as a play where all contradictions are resolved, where duality is an illusion. The prefatory poem Malini has obvious connections with the play, but Sisir Kumar Das while explaining Ramon's disagreement with Tagore in his book" "Indian Ode to the West Wind" says that as the complex imagery of sky and earth develops Tagore slides in the background and Juan Ramon appears in full glory :

> Everything is the earth; the sky is everything; one and the only eternal landscape! The universe, like the senses, like the cadence, like an enormous rose of flesh speaks only one word, a word unnecessary to pronounce; Love!

This is how, says Sisir Kumar Das, Tagore had been working within the mind of Juan Ramon. He did not borrow from Tagore, nor did he imitate him. He entered into the world of Tagore only to return to his own replenished with new intuitions and ideas.

When Tagore died in 1941 at the age of eighty, Juan Ramon was sixty years old and considered to be one of the greatest poets in the Spanish language. Eight years after Tagore's death in 1949 Ramon wrote a poem addressing it to Tagore which can't be called a belated obituary but an acknowledgement of a very deep relationship that Juan Ramon had with the poet of a distant land whom he had never met, nor with whom he ever corresponded. The piece of prose-verse of Juan Ramon Jimenez was first published in 1955 in the complete works of Rabindranath Tagore in Spanish under the title "Cenizas de Rabindranath Tagore : obra escojida :"

> I stood on a familiar beach that day, I picked with my hands the foam of a wave which looked like fresh ashes from the mother-of pearl, remaining frothing in my palms.
>
> I do not know why an idea within turned into a

> word, exact and natural; and I explained 'The Ashes of Tagore!'
>
> Why did I say that? That was what you heard me say; you witnessed in the palms of my hand the remnants of ashes unglued and sparkling anew.
>
> The Ganga bore the precious life of Tagore, now in ashes; towards the complete sea and the poet in ashes now become one with the waves of the great ocean. Why would they not enter my hands, hands that moulded the rhythm of his soul's immensity into our Spanish frame?

But long before Tagore became a part of the "complete sea," he became a part of Juan Ramon's life and consequently of his poetry.

❑❑

Chapter Seven

Tagore as a Transnational Writer

When Ananya Vajpeyi in her book "Righteous Republic" says that :

> "how monumental an error of judgment occurred in designating Tagore as India or Bengal's national poet can be judged from the fact that both India in 1947 and Bangladesh in 1971 adopted two of his songs as their respective national anthems. These gestures consolidated the misreading of Tagore as a poet of nationhood when he was in fact anything but that ".

It sounds apparently true but it is also misleading at the same time. He was a transnational poet, no doubt but he was a nationalist with a difference at the same time and always, as says William Radice, near to his people.

He himself, no doubt, once said, "I am a poet of the world, 'I try to capture its melody, wherever it rises" (aikatan, harmony) but this melody emanated from the soil and spread in far distant horizon.

Transnational means that one who is beyond one's nation and not affiliated with particularity of only one's tradition, culture, society or ethos and ready to be a part of the world at large and having a universal vision of life.

Tagore was no doubt a strong critic of nationalism and the concept of nation -state. It is his complete apathy towards violence that he was so much against nationalism based on the concept of a nation-state which does not hesitate to kill in the name of sovereignty of a nation and rather went for universal humanism and cosmopolitanism but not as an enlightenment project or homogenized universalism.

Universal humanism, trans national, cosmopolitanism or glovalism are expressions apparently look like having only shades of difference in meaning and that they are all used for Tagore and even sometimes interchangeably by scholars like Martha Nussbaum.

But in reality there is quite a difference at least between transnational and cosmopolitan and universal humanism.

When we look at Tagore as a transnational we actually find him turning it into a notion of transnationalization of nation state. It is Tagore's universal nationalism which is an inclusive plural concept of a nation which goes beyond the idea of exclusive nationalism and where the whole earth is a family. Tagore was for 'non-parochial inclusive nationalism' relevant to humanity.

To speak of cosmopolitanism with reference to Tagore is to refer to a transformation in self-understanding as a result of the engagement with others over issues of global morality and ethics. But for Tagore this self-transformation allows him to realize the other as self- same.

While discussing the issue of the self and other, Levinas says, "The foundation of ethics consists in the obligation to respond to the other." "In being for the other only the sense of responsibility (goodness, mercy, charity) calls forth." For Jacque Derrida "the foundation of ethics is hospitality, the readiness and inclination to welcome the other into one's home." Levinas and Derrida's theories of ethics – responsibility and hospitality – no doubt reveal a new consciousness emerging in the West about crossing the boundaries and looking beyond one's nation but it is still a broad view of particularism. It holds out the possibility of acceptance of the other as different but of equal standing. This is no where nearer to the Upanishadic idea of oneness, as referred to by Tagore in his acceptance speech of the Nobel Prize delivered on 26th June, 1921 at Stockholm :

> One who perceives all the beings in his own self and own self in all the beings does not hate any one anymore.
> (Yastu Sarvani bhutaniatmanyevanupashyati, Sarvabhuteshu chatmanam tatonavijugupsate.)

Universal humanism is almost the same as cosmopolitanism except that it does not talk only of identity of the self with the other but at the same time it is meant for Tagore a little more and also different from others because of his notion of the unity of inspiration of the self with the Infinite as he said :

> The Infinite wants the finite's intimate comradeship,
> And the finite wishes to lose itself in the Infinite.

The word cosmopolitanism as we perceive relates to the discursive level of knowledge and communication. Universalism as Tagore explains it transcends this discursive level and includes the spiritual aspect of being as well and hence he says in his essay on "Nationalism in the West" :

> Neither the colourless vagueness of cosmopolitanism, nor the fierce self-idolatry of nation-worship is the goal of human history. And India has been trying to accomplish her task through social regulation of differences, on the one hand, and the spiritual recognition of unity, on the other.

I argue that though the meanings of these above terms are unequivocal but at the same time the innumerable interpretive ambiguities of these terms undergird Tagore's life and vision and that form the foundation of his open –ended all embracing philosophy of universal humanism.

His optimism of some spiritual emancipative power coming to save the humanity is also vividly spelt out at the end of his last lecture, "The Crisis in Civilization" delivered at the age of 80 :

> "Today I live in the hope that the saviour is coming that he will be born in our midst in this poverty shamed hovel which is India. I shall wait to hear the divine message of civilization which he will bring with

> him, the supreme word of promise that he will speak unto man from this very eastern horizon to give faith and strength to all who hear." (Crisis in Civilization)

Another man before his death in 1940, a German, Walter Benjamin, said also almost the same thing :

> "For every second of time was the straight gate through which the Messiah might enter." (Theses on the Philosophy of History)

Both of them are not talking about their countries but of the whole world, of the whole humanity. Both Tagore and Benjamin were not talking about the superiority of the spiritual domain over the material domain but were trying to find a way out for the redemption of the total humanity and developing a discourse of universal humanism. This should not be equated in any way with the German Sonderweg discourse. It is the normal path and not any unique German or age-old spiritual Indian path where spiritual exceptionalism does not exclude universalism but cohabits with that. Both the exceptionalist and universalist discourses are the head and tail of the same coin and it is, indeed, to Tagore's everlasting credit that his great cosmopolitan vision never sacrificed the richest possible sense of tradition.

The cosmopolitan attitude here is not derived from a conception of reason that universality always tends toward abstractions; rather, it is dependent upon reason's articulation of the universal through an engagement with the local.

"When we understand this truth in a disinterested spirit, it teaches us to respect all the differences in man that are real, yet remain conscious of our oneness (Tagore, Creative Unity).

It is this solution—unity through acknowledgement of differences—that India has to offer to the world" (Tagore, Nationalism). This conception is the principal element of Tagore's idea of cosmopolitan universality or universal humanism.

For Tagore it was easy to hint at the transnationality of the nationalist imagination, accept cosmopolitanism and to making tradition as a part of it as he says :

> "I have come to feel that the mind, which has been matured in the atmosphere of a profound knowledge of its own country and of the perfect thoughts that have been produced in that land, is ready to accept and assimilate the cultures that come from other countries" ("The Way to Unity").

Otherwise also in the assertion of Marc Bloch that "all history is comparative history" hints at the transnationality of the nationalist imagination, for comparative history throws lights on the peculiarities of a given national history and, thus helps to understand 'the national' within the broad frame work of international discourse. National history itself is a product of worldwide cultural interactions and transnational discourses. It would thus be more appropriate to keep in mind the configuration of national and transnational history; it is in this transnational space that one can figure out the strategic location of the historiographical exceptionalism or in Tagore words tradition or local.

Tagore has called himself a wayfarer; he loved to visit distant lands and his correspondence reveals his contacts through his travels around the world and his deep engagement with the global course of history.

His faith in humanity encouraged him to speak against injustice, violence and narrow view of nationalist exceptionalism and crime against humanity. He wrote against the fascist regime of Mussolini in *Manchester Guardian* which ruthlessly suppressed the freedom of expression; against the cannibalistic political culture of Nazism that shook his 'faith in modern civilization' particularly when his friend Albert Einstein was removed from his academic position in Berlin in 1932 and ultimately had to leave Germany. He renounced knighthood at the age of 58 after the Jalianwala Bagh massacre where 379 unarmed people were killed and 1,137 injured at the behest of British General Dyer. He also expressed his sentiments against the war mongering Japan whose military authorities were bent upon devastating China. But the most pathetic incident for him was the appeasement of Nazi Germany at Munich treaty in September 20, 1938 by the British Prime Minister Neiville Chamberlain, who was one of the signatories of the treaty along with Edouard Daladier, the then Prime Minister of France and sent a message to President EdvardBeneš of Czechoslovakia expressing his deepest sympathy on behalf of India. A week later he wrote his famous poem :

> Those crushed and trodden lives of the meek and the weak /which are sacrificed as food offerings for the mighties...
> We will not fear, overcoming the distress, victory for us at the end(Prayaschita).

When he sent a message to American President Franklin D Roosevelt on 15th June, 1940 stating that 'all our individual problems of politics today have merged into one supreme world politics', it was Tagore's all time realization that 'the ideal of universalism' is inseparable from the domain of global politics where it needs to be worked out in real time'.

This global voyage into the foreign which also nurtured his ideals of universalism encouraged Tagore to talk in 1906 of 'Vishva Sahitya' world literature as a synonymic term for comparative literature. The term was first coined by Goethe in 1827 though Goethe hinted in his journal *Propoylen* about the use of the term by Christophe Martin Wieland some 13 years ago and presented his thesis that " There is no such thing as patriotic art or patriotic science... Both belong to world literature".

There is no doubt that in the age of transnationalism and globalization Goethe's concept cannot be ignored but it was against national literature and was based on insulating identities—one region, one religion, one race, one language and one literature. He said, "I am more and more convinced that poetry is the universal possession of mankind, revealing itself everywhere and at all times in hundreds and hundreds of men... I therefore like to look about me in foreign nations, and advise everyone to do the same. National literature is now a rather unmeaning term; the epoch of world literature is at hand, and everyone must strive to hasten its approach. (Eckermann : Johann Peter *Gespräche mit Goethe in den letzten Jahren seines Lebens,* trans. John Oxenford as J. W. von Goethe, *Conversations with Eckermann,* repr. North Point Press, p.132, 1994).

But where is this one, one world? It is already divided by the West into three – 1st, 2nd, and 3rd world and hence Franko Moretti, and Pascale Casanova, stressed the inequalities of the global literary field, which Moretti described as 'one, but unequal.'

In Tagore's term Vishva Sahitya, the adjective vishva is not world, but the total universe. In this case, *vishva* is something that is spread all over; something is extended first and then it spreads. It does not have geographical or regional territories, and is not limited by the boundaries of countries and continents or even by the earth. It is not a binary term as opposed to nation but holistic as a concept broader, dynamic, and more catholic and inclusive.

Vishva Sahitya is based primarily on his concept of *Vishwamanava,* the universal man. To him universal humanity expressed itself in literature. Let me summarize what Tagore says :

In his Address, he discussed the concept of world literature in terms of universal man. Tagore envisaged *Vishwa Sahitya a*s a *mandir* (temple) which is a construct but not an ordinary one. The temples have their master plan but it has no visible master plan. It should, however, not be construed that it does not have its master-builders. In this temple each writer is an artisan and a worker contributing according to one's natural capacities to the whole. Whatever does not stand the test of time falls off on its own. The workers are no ordinary mortals, they are the universal men and they are not paid in terms of wages but become recipients of prestige accorded to an *ustad* (master).

'To judge literature by this model is to draw on the support of humankind's collective wisdom.'

In Tagore's concept the most important factor is recognition of inter-relatedness of all human beings, their faculties and their relations with all elements in the universe and everything that is there. All faculties of human inner being exist to forge a relationship with all.

The bond of joy is 'in knowing others as our own'. (Tagore 139) Moreover, he saw inter-relatedness, as he began with the metaphor from the world of dance, in which birth and death, deliverance and bondage, beauty and ugliness, pain and joy are conjoined and all dance together in ecstasy. In the complimentariness of the opposite Tagore finds the meaning and joy of life. The dance relates to *natraj* as the highest point of reference who with his one step destroys and with another step creates.

Tagore refers to Lord Krishna, Mathurapati or the king of Mathura, dancing with the milkmaids of Vrindavan. This bond of joy 'erases all distances' (Tagore 139) because there is no self-conceit, or concealment or calculation. Rather there is surrender of ourselves to the small and weak.

In Bangla storytelling formula, says Nabaneeta Dev Sen, a tale begins, *Ek je chhilo raja,* ("There was a king"). In one of his last pieces written in 1941, just before his death, he begins his tale with this formulaic expression *Ek je achhemanush* ("There is a man"). He makes two enormously important changes in the formula, he changes its tense from the past to the present, and changes its subject from a king to a common man. Instead of *"there was"* he writes *there is,* and instead of *a king* he writes *a man,* meaning a *human being.*

These were the alternatives he offered to mankind, to grapple with the crisis our civilization had created for itself, and the world was passing through in 1941. The focus was to shift from the past to the present, not the present moment but the continuous presence, *bartaman*, indicating the eternal presence of mankind upon this planet and ascertain a shift from the royalty to the common man, from the source of political power to the source of moral strength, and from colonialism to democracy and from exclusive nationalism to transnationalism – a recognition of inter-relatedness of all human beings and with all elements in the universe and everything that is there.

❏❏

Chapter Eight

The Conflict between the Other Asia and the New Asia : Rabindranath Tagore, Liang Qichao and Kakuzo (Tenshin) Okakura and the Politics of Friendship and a Love Story

This is the story of three men and their activities in the first three decades of the twentieth century. Rabindranath Tagore (1861-1941), Kakuzo Okakura (1862-1913) and Liang Qichao (1873- 1929) of India, Japan and China respectively. These men occupied the East Asian stage as three protagonists with very different visions of Asia. This paper will unveil the complex friendship between the three within - and against - the background of a unified Asia that concealed considerable political differences.

Okakura, Japanese writer, founder of a radical art school (Nihon Bijutsuin) and well known art curator, was an ultranationalist, who followed Fukuzawa Yukichi's (1834-1901), philosophy of *Datsu-a Ron,*[1] meaning 'saying goodbye to Asia' while casting Japan's lot in with the civilized nations of the West. His prime intention was to adopt a militaristic nationalism to compete with the West, thus bringing about a new Asia.

But there is quite a lot of ambivalence in his notion of Asia, which can be perceived in his envisaging an image of pan-Asian unity – a unity apparently based on the oneness of oriental art but covertly establishing the supremacy of Japanese art. Hence in his book "The Awakening of the East" (written by Okakura during his stay in Calcutta and, for unknown reasons, not published during his life-time) he wanted us to believe that we are one...Asia is one[2] but his Japanese identity disrupted his own idea of the unity in 'we' and created an Asia as a part of two mighty civilizations, the Chinese with its communism of Confucius (according to Rustam Barucha what he meant was communitarian ethics)[3] and the Indian with its individualism of the Vedas; these, like two sides of a triangle, with Japan as the apex of the triangle, and thus made unabashed display of his ultra-nationalism.

In his ultra-nationalist wisdom, denigration of India and China was crucial to establish the supremacy of Japan and hence he spoke of India as the "orphaned child of Asia"[4] and of China as the victim of the "White disaster in the Opium War"[5], thereby implicitly suggesting that we are not one Asia.

One should not, however, find in this any post-colonial strain of destabilizing a monolithic perspective of unitary culture at Asia's level; but it was Okakura's own futuristic thinking along ultra-nationalistic and imperialistic lines which was soon revealed in Japan's war with Russia (1904-05), and with Korea, turning it to a protectorate in 1905 and then in 1910 – forcing it to surrender its sovereignty following wars with China in 1894-95 and 1937-1941.

Among the other pan-Asianists, Okawa Shumei, who had converted himself into a pan-Asianist in 1913 after reading a book about India's dire state under the British, forgot, in due course, all his idealism and accepted Pan-Asianism with Japan as the future imperial conqueror.[6]

Indeed, the "Unified Asia" of which Tagore and Okakura appeared to dream together was imagined on significantly different grounds. For Okakura it was a triumphant call for a new Asia in the guise of Japanese imperialism and for Tagore it was the perennial Asia reworded as the "continental mind of Asia" i.e. an Asia of "one mind." A votary of Asian cultural unity and not an advocate of a political federation of Asia, Tagore invoked this notion of -a single -continental mind of Asia in his third visit to Japan in 1929, while paying his highest tribute to Okakura, who died in Boston in 1913, while serving there as the curator of the Museum of Fine Arts.

Let me pause a little in this narration to look back to the time when Okakura came for the first time to India for a period of 9 months on 6 January, 1902 and met the Tagores in their Jorashanko residence. There is no record of what kind of discussion took place between Rabindranath and Okakura but one thing is sure - the mutual affection and respect which each had for the other was very much visible in their behavior. However, they never exchanged letters and their friendship remained mostly speculative but what cannot be denied is the intensity with which it was celebrated.[7]

After 1902 Tagore met Okakura for the second and last time in his life in February 1913 in Boston. It is possible that Okakura had a premonition of his own imminent death as it was recorded by him in a letter to Priyambada Devi Banerji. She was a widowed *bhadramahila* (educated Bengali lady) and a poet, distantly related to Tagore, with whom Okakura fell in love at first sight on his last visit to Calcutta in 1912. This meeting led to a long distance love affair conducted by passionate letters written to each other. Following Tagore's visit, Okakura wrote to Priyambada on 3rd March 1913, "It is snowing here still and I long for the sunshine and flowers of the orient. Your uncle (Tagore) has left for Chicago and I feel a sudden loneliness."[8]

Liang Qichao, an ardent Orientalist and President of Beijing Lecture Association, had a radical mindset in his younger days and hero-worshipped Mao Zedong in his youth but later turned away from radicalism and also from Europe's Universalist ideals of the Enlightenment – which he saw as a moral cover for unjust racial hierarchies- to seek strength and dignity in a revamped Confucianism.[9]

On his invitation, Tagore visited China in 1924 but this gave rise to a virulent campaign against Tagore, so much so that in Hankou he had to hear such slogans as : "Go back, slave from a lost country!" But let us not forget what Lu Xun (1881-1936), a celebrated Marxist poet and story writer of world fame pointed out in 1927 : "All the ancient civilization of the world, Chinese and Egyptian included, had lost their voices. Nor was there any voice in Annam and Korea.

There was only one voice still living and that was the voice of Tagore in India."[10]

No doubt the hostility against Tagore in China was partly because of his hosts Liang Qichao and Zhang Junmai. Both were targets of severe criticism by the leftist radicals who disliked their so called "reactionary politics". In spite of a statement by Liang[11] that Mr Tagore and he had no connection with each other, and… Tagore did not come to China to assist him, the resentment against Tagore continued. No doubt Liang's questioning of China's tradition, and his skepticism about China's old Confucius tradition's ability to adapt to the harsh world of competition, were the basis of both radical new despair and also hopefulness for the New Culture which ushered in the May 4 Movement in 1919.

But Liang could not get the credit for this as his disastrous strategy of aligning himself, during the post-Qing state, with the violent and corrupt warlords, compromised his position and ultimately led to his becoming politically irrelevant and, tragically, a target of criticism involving Tagore.

Resentment against Tagore notwithstanding, it is difficult for me to accept terms like 'reactionary' or 'revisionist' or even 'obscurantist' for Liang Qichao, which were used by the left radicals to demean Liang as well as his mentor Kang Youwei (1858-1927). Liang was known as China's first iconic modern intellectual, who stressed the urgency of political reform as more important than technological reforms and was nothing less than radical in his demand for political innovation and public participation in government; he tried to reformulate Confucianism by adding to it some of the virtues of the West, particularly 'Mr Democracy and Mr Science' as mentioned by Chen Duziu and his friends associated with the journal, Xin Quignian (New Youth).[12] I shall come back to this point later.

The resentment was also because of Tagore's criticism of the Western model of development and the notion of Western modernity[13] and also because of the upsurge of Chinese nationalism after the May 4 movement. Though Tagore wrote three important articles on China; The Death trade in China (*Chine Maraner Byabasay*), Social differences (*Samajbhed*) and letters of a Chinaman (*Chinemaner Chithi*) and also profusely referred to Chinese civilization and contemporary Chinese life and political turmoil in his writings , yet he did not realize the intensity of the repugnance for Confucianism and aversion from a moribund feudal culture in China among the younger generation and that failure made it very likely that he would be misunderstood amid the clamour of that seething internal strife.

But at the same time there were many scholars, writers and intellectuals who expressed enthusiasm forTagore's visit in abundant measures. These included Zheng Zhentuo, the editor of 'The Fiction Monthly', (Xiaoshuo Yuebao), Xu Zhimo (1895-1931) and Zhang Wentian (1900-1976), a close associate of Mao Zedong and Guo Moruo, the distinguished writer who was critical of Tagore but at the same time wrote of his experience of reading Tagore's writings : "I felt I found my 'life of life', my 'fountain of Life.'"[14] Though in 1924 Guo Moruo had drifted far from Tagore,[15] yet one should not overlook the ambivalence in his use of terms like *baoda* which means to repay one's indebtedness. Though he criticized Tagore but at the same time repaid his indebtedness by establishing, at the same time, his spiritual communion with Tagore.[16]

No doubt Tagore was deeply hurt by the scathing criticism meted out to him by the leftist radicals. However, he did not change his views about the danger of adopting the Western materialistic model of development and ignoring the country's heritage of the past. At the same time did not hesitate to say, "We have a great thing to accept from the people of the West – their treasure of intellect, which is immense and whose superiority we must admit."[17] Lu Xun in his "remembering Tagore's visit, 1933", aptly summed up the reasons for all criticism and hostility against Tagore : 'Perhaps if our poets and others had not made him a living fairy he would not have been so confused and the Chinese youths would not have been so alienated. What bad luck now.'[18]

In spite of all kinds of controversy and virulent attack Tagore's love for China did not weaken. When Tagore was leaving Beijing somebody asked him : "I hope you have not left anything." Tagore shook his head gently and said in a sad voice, "Nothing except a portion of my heart."[19] But he could not say this for Japan as after Japan's brutal aggression against China Tagore acknowledged, "I can no longer point out with pride the example of a great Japan."

Tagore formulated a non-nationalist ideal of Asian cosmopolitanism early in his life, and never departed from it. This is his perennial Asia which has now become 'other' within its own boundaries and the tussle between the new and the other, and the slogan of one Asia in different connotations, and how it led to the politics of friendship has become the main issue in this narration.

It was not Okakura but Yone Naguchi (1875-1947), who was among the best-known Japanese writers in the first two or three decades of the 20th Century and an associate of W.B. Yeats and Ezra Pound, and who met Tagore in Calcutta in 1902, when he came to deliver a course of lectures in Calcutta and other universities. Naguchi became a very popular figure among Indians and was greatly respected by Tagore.

Naguchi's poetry was most romantic and devoid of materialistic spirit but Tagore was stunned to receive a letter from him in mid 1938 – after a gap of 36 years – arguing vociferously for Japan's spiritual and moral role in sending an army to China and wanting to use their friendship politically, but Tagore's ideology was much more important to him than friendship and his firmness towards that proposal was exemplary. Tagore had only one ground on which to counter the machinations of realpolitik of friendship : humanity.

It was very difficult, though, in case of Naguchi, who became a close friend on Tagore's first visit to Japan in 1916 and supported his views on nationalism or to be precise against nationalism. It is surely ironic that their break-up was directly related to Naguchi's significantly altered views and his reversion to Nationalism in 1938. In 1916 Tagore said in a lecture :

> I sincerely hope that Japanese people will not forget the old Japan. The new Japan was only an imitation of the West. This will ruin Japan.[20]

In fact Tagore was differentiating between the New Asia and the perennial Asia, which by then had become the other Asia of philosophy, idealism, humanity and love for all, or universal humanism, but the new Asians were bent upon discarding it and during Tagore's visit to China in 1924 the radicals circulated leaflets denouncing Tagore by stating :

"We have had enough of the ancient civilization."

Definitely, for the Chinese and the Japanese it was important to build their nations on western lines - and they were surprised to find Tagore not worried at all about his country's political subjugation and to hear him speaking instead of spiritual liberation.

They had no idea of the real nature of Tagore's thinking. For Tagore, India's unity was a social reality. It was not a political agenda. His ideas of *samaj*, social upliftment and then *atmasshakti*, self reliance and thereafter *swaraj,* self rule, form a sequential progression to true national freedom wherein there is no scope for violence.

Underlying his participation in the Hindu *mela* from the age of 14, his renouncing the knighthood after the Jalianwala Bagh massacre at the age of 58, and even after that his anti-imperialist viewpoints forcefully displayed in his last stirring lecture 'The Crisis in Civilization' at the age of 80 - in which he mentioned the impertinent challenge by the imperial ruler to our conscience - was a completely non-political attitude. His anti-imperial stance was in fact an aspect of a universal struggle for political justice and cultural dignity, and a protest against violence. Years after Tagore left China Lu Xun had to acknowledge, "I did not see this clearly before, now I know that he is also an anti-imperialist."[21]

In his classic autobiography, *Errata : An Examined Life* (1997), George Steiner, one of the foremost philosophers of the 20th century, wrote :

> "It is possible to suppose that the period since August 1914 has been, notably in Europe and Russia, from Madrid to Moscow, from Sicily to the Arctic Circle, the most bestial in recorded history."[22]

Steiner's epitaph to the essential tragedy of the 20th century may well serve as a postscript to Rabindranath's critique of nationalism. Indeed, it would be logical to infer that much of the cause for human grief, pain and humiliation in the 20th Century, can be attributed to the conflicting claims of Nation States. Far from acting as an instrument for realizing collective or communitarian aspirations and welfare, nationalism has tragically led to collective despair.

Friendship

It is almost impossible to imagine laws determining friendship. Friendships are "voluntary, unspecialized, informal and private" says Allan Silver[23], and this definition would fit the friendship of Tagore and Okakura very well.

Naguchi definitely introduced politics into his friendship to placate Tagore so that he withdrew his statement about the Japanese invasion of China as "slaughtering madness".[24] Naguchi explained in his letter to Tagore that the Japanese invasion of China was the means for establishing a new great world in the Asiatic continent', a war of "Asia for Asia" – one Asia. But for Tagore 'one' is a very suspect term because there is no unity in one.

He said, in his essay, *Shikshar Milan* (The Unity of Education), 'a man who is alone or one is meaningless because there is no unity in one. The one with many is truly one because in that one, one can see the unity and this unity gives the message of truth.'[25] Tagore condemned Naguchi's so- called idea of one Asia , which destroyed others so as to establish one's own one new Asia. Tagore in that long exchange of letters ultimately said, "Wishing your people whom I love, not success, but remorse."[26]

Liang Qichao's friendship was different and so was of Okakura's. It is generally surmised, though wrongly, that under attack by the Chinese radicals Tagore's host Liang Qichao and his interpreter, the poet, Zhang Junmai, used Tagore's talent to instill in young China their conservative and reactionary tendencies[27] and used his great name in pursuing their ulterior motive.

Could this be true of a man of Liang's stature who – as I have said before – believed, like Tagore in "broad nationalism", as opposed to what he called "narrow nationalism",[28] and also believed in Confucian *ren, yi, xiao* i.e. benevolence, propriety, filial piety, and the correct modes of behavior. He was politically more pragmatic than his mentor, Kang Youwei, and also, by invoking Patrik Henry's famous words, "Give me Liberty or give me death", spoke about freedom as an absolute necessity for China. Could a man of such vision ever use Tagore's name for his so called ulterior interest? It was just not possible.

Tagore before leaving China also said, 'I have done what was possible – I have made friends' Tagore celebrated the day in 1941 when he was given the new name "Zhu Zhendan" in a poem concludsing with the sentence : 'Where ever we find friends there begins a new life'.[29]

Tagore's friendship with Okakura was definitely different. In Okakura's mind the place of Japan was supreme as was India in the mind of Tagore. But if Okakura showed his desire to create a new Japan in Asia, he was equally enthusiastic to assure Tagore that "China is great."[29] 'This big-hearted Japanese thinker' had always displayed his idea of the welfare of total Asia but when looking at it politically, he would give Japan the supreme place in it. Otherwise, as mentioned by Sister Nivedita in the 'Introduction' of his book "The Ideals of the East" (1903), when Okakura looked at Asia culturally he would see it not as "the congeries of geographical fragments", but rather as a "united living organism, each part dependent on all the others, the whole breathing a single complex life"[30]

In Tagore's concept of one Asia there is no political motivation. His was a non- political ideal of Asian cosmopolitanism with all the Asian Nations living in harmony but not in uniformity or, in other words, acknowledging the real differences between them yet seeking some basis of unity.[31]

Okakura's transformation from his earlier nationalist avatar was already evident from 1908 onwards in the mellowing of his nationalism through cosmopolitanism, which he developed by moving into the World of Oriental Art as a curator and thus realizing a fundamental unity across different cultures of the Orient. In the last year of his life, in 1913, primarily through his correspondence with Priyambada, we find more conclusive evidence of his emergent cosmopolitan humanitarianism.

Written to Priyambada from Akakura Springs, Echigo, Niigata prefecture, the letter says, "yet, I am in perfect peace with the universe and grateful, oh, so grateful for all it has granted me of late. I am perfectly content and even boisterously happy. I laugh at the clouds that sweep and swirl round my pillow."[32].

Tagore in his lecture, almost an obituary lecture, given in 1929 in Japan said that Okakura had a feeling of reverence for his neighbouring country, China, and had developed a true "continental mind of Asia".[33] Tagore is talking for the first time with reference to Okakura about Asia as an idea in a world facing severe economic depression, hatred and suspicion fanned by exclusive nationalism and hearing with dreadful fear the clamouring of the drums of war. In that situation it was Tagore's message, a message of Asia, the Other Asia, to the people, urging them not to think of the world as territorial but as an idea (ideational) in order to save it from total annihilation.

What happened to Priyambada? It is a long story not meant for today except to say that at Okakura's request Priyambada sent her most favourite Tagore song, *Tobu mone rekho Jodi dure jai chole* in English translation to Okakura. Okakura liked it immensely and remembered it by repeating those lines again and again, one can assume, till the last days of his life :

> Even so, remember me
> If I should move far away, even so
> If the old love should be lost in the mazes of a new passion
> Even so, remember me
> And if although I am near
> My presence, like shadow, is shrouded with doubt
> Your eyes might cloud with tears.
> And if one lovely night this game should end
> Even so, remember me...

Notes and References :

1. Refer to David J. Lu's Japan : A Documentary History (London : M.E. Sharpe, 1997), pp. 351-3
2. From Okakur's book'The Awakening of the East' (written by Okakura during his stay in Calcutta and not published in his lifetime; it is a mystery and later retrieved by members of the Okakura family and published in 1938 in original Japanese language and English translation in 1940)
3. A fascinating book on Tagore and Okakura by Rustom Bharucha 'Another Asia; Rabindranath Tagore and Okakura Tenshin, Oxford, (2006) p. 17

4. Okakura Kakuzo, The Awakening of the East; Collected English Writings, vol. 1. 1984, p. 141
5. Ibid, p. 138
6. From the Ruins of Empire, Pankaj Mishra, (2012) p.155
7. Rustam Bharucha, Another Asia : Rabindranath Tagore & Okakura Tenshin, (2006) p. 174
8. Okakura Kakuzo's letter to Priyambada Devi Banerjee, 3 March 1913, Okakuro Kakuzo, Collected English Writings, vol. 3, p. 182
9. For a useful study of Liang see, Josheph R. Leavenson, Liang Chi-ch'ao (Berkley, 1970).
10. 'Wushengde Zhongguo' (The Voiceless China). Lu Xun Quanji, Vol.IV, p. 15
11 Published in Chen-Pao, 31 May 1924, quoted by Stephen Hay, 'Asian Ideas of East and West (1970)p. 214
12. Please see, From the Ruins of Empire, Pankaj Mishra, (2012) p.182
13. It was difficult for the 'Moderns' to understand the definition of Modernity by Tagore which was an extension of the notion of continuity in the Indian ethos : The revelation of material things is extremely old. The revelation in spirit in man is truly modern; I am on its side, for I am modern. 'Autobiographical', Talks in China, The English Writings of Rabindranath Tagore (Now henceforth EWRT) (ed) Sisir Kumar Das, Vol. II reprint 2012, p. 585
14. "I still remember when I got those books in the autumn of 1916 at the Kang Shan Library I felt I found my 'life of life', my 'fountain of life'" quoted by Sisir Kumar Das, Tagore in China, Visva-Bharati, (1999), p. 160
15. 'The literature of yesterday is an unconscious sacred recreation for the aristocrats who hold supremacy in life. Like the poems of Tagore and the novels of Tolstoy, I feel they are offerings alms to the hungry ghosts'. Guo Moruo's letter to Cheng Fangwa in Zhonguo Xin Wenxue daxi, Essay, Vol. I, p, 219
16. Sisir Kumar Das, Tagore in China, Visva-Bharati, (1999)
17. First Public speech at Beijing near Zhonghai, the Middle Lake, referred to by Sisir Kumar Das in his article 'Tagore in China' included in Talk in China : Rabindranath Tagore, (ed), 1999) p.167
18. Quoted in From the Ruins of Empire :The Revolt Against the West and the Remaking of Asia, Pankaj Mishra 2012, p.218
19. Lun Taoge'er. Op.cit., pp.180-81
20. On June 13, 1916 in front of some 250 dignitaries, who came to Kaneiji Buddhist Temple to honour Tagore at a formal reception where the Prime Minister, the Mayor, the President of Tokyo

Imperial University, the Minister of Education "all the famous people of the day" present. The meeting was opened by Dr Takakusu Junjiro, Japan's most eminent scholar, after which Heki Mokusen (who like Takausu had visited India) senior priest of the Soto Sect of Zen Buddhism, read an address of welcome. Tagore replied in Bengali with a succinct restatement of his message to Japan. The Prime Minister thanked him. See Stephen N Hay : Tagore and his Critics in Japan, China and India (1970), p.66

21. Amiya Dev and Tan Chung (eds), Tagore and China, p.37
22. George Steiner, Errata : An Examined Life, (1997), p.103
23. Silver, Allan, Friendship and Trust as Moral Ideals : An Historical Approach, Archives curopeenes de sociologie 30, (1989), p.274
24. The term 'slaughtering madness' was used by Naguchi as a synonymic expression to present Tagore's extreme criticism against Japan's invasion against China, see the letter by Naguchi to Tagore on July 23, 1938, EWRT, Vol. III. p. 834
25. In 1922 in Pune in the Kirlosker Theatre he gave a lecture on Indian Renaissance, elaborating this idea, the Bengali version of that is titled : '*shikkhar milan*' See Rabindra Rachanvali, (Tagore-s Collected Works), Vol. XI, p.671,WB Govt Publication in 15 Volumes, 1961
26. Tagore's letter to Naguchi, October 27, 1938, EWRT, Vol. III, p. 845
27. Pankaj Mishra, From the Ruins of Empire : The Revolt Against the West and the Remaking of Asia, p. 236
28. Ibid, p. 177
29. It is mentioned in Naguchi's letter to Tagore on October 2, 1938. EWRT, Vol. III, p. 839
30. Sister Nivedita, 'Introduction', Okakura, 'The Ideals of the East', (1903), p.11
31. Tagore, 'Indian Nationalism', EWRT, Vol. III, p.453
32. Okakura Kakuzo, Collected English Writings, Vol. 3, p.217
33. 'On Oriental Culture and Japan's Mission'. EWRT, Vol. III. p. 606.

Chapter Nine

The Formation of Tagore's Spirituality and the Evidence of it in his Artistic Endeavour

The old concept is that spirituality is something against materialism. To renounce the pleasures of matter, of body, of mind is defined as spirituality. The Sanskrit word for spirituality is *adhyatma* i.e. that knowledge which is related to atman or spirit, soul or self or it is life in depth, in ultimate depth.

In other words it is a communion with the inner self or the higher body. Spirituality says that what is important is a seeker's inner attitude. Through practicing spirituality we seek to develop an inner shrine in our own heart. But a non-religious man can never be spiritual.

Immediately the question comes in our mind what is religion and what is the connection between religion and spirituality particularly when in India, China and Japan people are still repeating the old, hackneyed statement that Western civilization is materialistic, while the East Asian civilization is spiritual. It is completely erroneous to think like that though, as Hazime Nakamura had said that it was generally felt that East Asian peoples, menaced by the invaders labeled the West "materialistic; on the other hand, the West characterized the less advanced East Asian peoples in science and technology itself as "soulful" or "spiritual."[1] This is no more applicable today.

West, no doubt, is religious and through following their religion, great saints have attained the fruits and realizations of a mystical approach to God. This includes Christian mystics such as St. Teresa of Avila, St Francis of Assisi, and Sufi saints like Rabaya, Rumi, Hafiz and Attar or Hindu spiritual saints like Sri Ramakrishna Paramahansa, Sri Aurobindo, Swami Vivekananda, Maharshi Raman and many others.

Each religion has produced spiritual seekers of the highest order. Religion is a path to God. Spirituality is also a path to God. However they have differences in approach. Religion places more emphasis on outer forms and outer rituals. Spirituality is less concerned with outer rituals. The term 'spiritual' as distinct from 'religious' is first encountered in the 19th century in the writings of Ralph Waldo Emerson. Spirituality places little importance on religious dogma or belief system, but is concerned with growing into and experiencing the Divine consciousness.

Spirituality or *adhyatma* does not reject the material world but only advises us as how to make a journey to move beyond the material world for the realization of the self, or atman or divine consciousness.

Tagore explains this by bringing a girl and her doll and says that when a girl's life outgrows her doll, when she realizes that in every respect she is more than her doll is, then she throws it away. By the very act of possession we know that we are greater than the things possess. It is not rejecting the doll but going beyond the doll. [2] Thus man truly realizes his soul by outgrowing his possession, by moving beyond the material world.

Renunciation here has a special meaning i.e. self expansion and to be one with nature and this vast universe which is pervaded by the Supreme Self and immerse oneself in *ananda* or joy or bliss.

Krishna Dutt and Andrew Robinson, while comparing Tagore with Mahatma Gandhi, say that both of them spoke and wrote constantly of joy and the spirit of renunciation but by following different connotations of the notion of renunciation and gave opposite emphases to these two notions of joy and renunciation. Tagore, referring to the first mantra/couplet of "Isopanishad", would always say, "rejoice and renounce". W.B.Yeats, therefore, made a comment about Tagore that he was the only saint who did not refuse to live. This is diametrically opposite to what Gandhi said to an English journalist when asked to give, in five words, the meaning of life, Gandhi said, "Why five? I will give it to you in three words, 'renounce and rejoice". [3]

Here 'renounce' means negation of the self or the world. Thus Tagore speaks of renunciation as self expansion as well as self negation and in this way displays a deep ambivalence of his mind.

The issue becomes further complicated when in a letter to Charles Andrews from New York on 17 December 1920, he quotes from Brihadaranyaka Upanishad, the episode of Maitreyi, and her husband, Yajnavalkya, who offered his property equally to his two wives Maitrayi and Katyayini before taking the path of *sanyasa*, the ascetic path of renunciation. But Maitreyi refused to accept the wealth as she realized that it would not make her immortal which was her life-objective.

Let us not forget that Tagore is quoting Maitreyi and that too just seven days before Christmas in New York where he must have seen during that time the display of unrestrained wealth, affluence, worldly prosperity and plenitude and wrote in reaction :

> I should not let my dignity be soiled by the sordid touch of her dollars; mere lack of means should not be allowed to mock the majesty of my soul...the spirit of India comes to me in the midst of my spurious activities and whispers the immortal *mantram* of Maitreyi to my inner spirit :
>
> *Yenaham namritasyama kimaham tena kuryama?*

What shall I do with that which will not make me immortal.'

Let us not bring a psycho-analyst to explain it as Tagore's inferiority complex in the language of psychology rather place the explanation which Amartya Sen gave of this statement of Maitreyi.

If one reads the statement of Maitreyi carefully, as says Amartya Sen, "it will be revealed then that Maitreyi is not discarding material life. Maitreyi's worldly worries might well have some transcendental relevance (as Indian religious commentators have discussed over many centuries) but they have certainly worldly interest as well.

While there is a connection between opulence and our ability to achieve what we value, the linkage may or may not be very close." But at the same time if we are concerned with the freedom to live long and live well for doing action for 100 years and seeking true knowledge as says Ishopanishad and that what quotes Tagore,[4] it is to be self less action and then only spiritual knowledge becomes a reality. Maitreyi also knows that without worldly fulfillment of needs which only wealth can provide, one cannot make a journey from attachment to non attachment.

Amartya Sen is justified to say that as with the freedom to live long and live well, our focus has to be directly on life and death or I would add on the transcendental relevance of our self , and not just on wealth and economic opulence. Let us not forget that there is a connection between the two, however distinct it may be. [5]

In Tagore's notion of renunciation the harmonious blending of worldliness with renunciation is the inbuilt unity principle in it and is not to be forgotten. I shall take it up as the last point of my paper.

Tagore also spoke against Gandhi's movement of temple entry by the untouchables and wrote to Gandhi that he did not at all relish the idea of divinity being enclosed in a brick and mortar temple and strongly believed that it is possible for simple hearted people to realize the presence of God in the open air, in a surrounding free from all artificial obstruction. [6]

In the same letter Tagore spoke of illiterate Bauls, the dancing mendicants of Bengal, who reject the Brahminical tradition of worship and enjoy a perfect freedom of worship profoundly universal in character.

The pride of the Baul beggar, writes Tagore is not in his worldly distinction, but the distinction that God himself has given to him. [7] When asked by Tagore these Baul ascetics explain that that they have first of all to know their own soul under the guidance of their spiritual teacher, and when they have done that they find him, who is the supreme soul, within us. This realization, Tagore says in "Religion of Man" gives us a clue of the divinity of man and also that their religion is never about a God of cosmic force but rather about the God of human personality, the *maner manush*, God as the man of my heart.[8]

Being a Poet Tagore has more of poetic thinking rather than analytical, argumentational, calculative thought and Heideggar found absolutely this trait of Tagore in the German poet, Holderlin and called him a poet of world-disclosure and remarked that there is a great need – specially in a modern age in which we have forgotten, how to think poetically – for disclosive or originative, poetic mode of thinking. [9]

Metaphysical argument is not the only possible approach to truth. "Reality in all manifestations", writes Tagore, 'reveals itself in the emotional and imaginative background of our mind, we know it not because we can think of it, but because we directly feel it.[10] We must give credit to Tagore, because of this kind of ideas, which was in accordance with the Upanishads, converted the most famous Cartesian notion, "I think therefore I am" to "I am, therefore I think". Man therefore seeks to discover what he is.

Tagore further says, 'all that I feel is from vision and not from knowledge.'[11] Let us not forget that in Sanskrit the word for philosophy is *darshana* i.e. vision.

Now the issues are :

(i) Whether Tagore's quest was a cognitive quest for an understanding of ultimate reality with Truth, consciousness and joy as its main fundamental constituents as one finds in the Upanishads or was it a spiritual quest where Infinite is defined with reference to humanity with truth, love and joy as its predominant essence.

(ii) In this spiritual quest did Tagore avoid worldly materialistic life or did he create a synthesis between finite and infinite to become complete in our selves.

Like the medieval Indian devotional poets Tagore is also known as a mystic and religious poet but he never believed in the existence of iconic gods or in idol worship but in a supreme power which pervades everything, even the leftovers or those which are thrown away by us. Tagore would always quote a Vedic mantra *'yajne hutasishtasya odanasya...'* etc to establish an extraordinary idea that in the leftovers resides Brahman, the original source of the universe. [12]

In other words, Brahman is boundless in its superfluity which inevitably finds its expression in the eternal world process. By referring to a Baul women Tagore mentions this in a letter from New York to Charles Andrews on 17 December 1920 [13] and also speaks about it in his essay "An Indian Folk Religion" published in 1922 :

> One day in a small village in Bengal, an ascetic Baul women came to see me. She fixed her star-like eyes upon my face and startled me with the question, 'When are you coming to meet me underneath the trees?
>
> Evidently she pitied me who lived (according to her) prisoned behind walls, banished away from the great meeting-place of the All, where she had her dwelling.
>
> Just at that moment my gardener came with his basket, and when the woman understood that the flowers in the vase on my table were going to be thrown away to make place for the fresh ones, she looked pained and said to me :
>
> 'You are always engaged reading and writing; you do not see.'
>
> Then she took the discarded flowers in her palms, kissed them and touched them with her forehead, and reverently murmured to herself :
>
> 'Beloved of my heart.'

Tagore says that he felt that this woman, in her direct vision of the infinite personality in the heart of all things, truly represented the spirit of India.[14]

Tagore is a mystic, romantic than religious poet like Dante or medieval religious poets. True mysticism calls for an effort to understand the quest for a hidden truth and an aspiration to realize the "Great Beyond"; it is the expression of the innate tendency of the human spirit towards complete harmony with the transcendental realm.

Tagore is slowly moving towards creating his notion of spirituality – it is self expansion based on the unity principle where world-acceptance as well as world- negation coalesce with each other leading to the realization of God of human personality. He calls it the unity of life.

Tagore's mystic affiliation for the unity of life which is same everywhere as he says in Gitanjali :

> The same stream of life that runs through my veins night and day runs through the world and dances in rhythmic measures.

Again in another song in Gitanjali :

> It is the same life that shouts in joy through the dust of the earth in numberless blades of grass and breaks into tumultuous waves of leaves and flowers.[15]

The vital identity with the rhythm of life goes hand in hand with devotion. But yearning and waiting rather than fulfillment are the characteristics of the poet. Tagore is more a poet of *viraha* (separation) than *milan* (union) as he says :

> He came and sat by my side, but I woke not. Only I feel a faint of perfumes of the presence in the air.[16]

But the Divine in Gitanjali is not complete unto himself as he says, "without me, O Lord of three worlds, your love would have been in vain"; but at the same time Tagore feels separated with a sense of perpetual waiting 'to be with me, how long have you been coming'.

Let us not forget that Tagore's lifelong urge was to bring harmony in this duality of separation, (*viraha*) and union (*milan*). He becomes sad when he does not find harmony around and rapture when harmony takes place and this extends to other dualities – man and nature, India and the West, folk and classical, human and divine.[17]

In the harmony of two contradictory forces everything rests. Tagore wrote in his letter to Andrews on 7 September 1915, Contradictions may seem to hurt each other "like the finger and the string' but this contradiction produces music; when one predominates there is the sterility of silence".[18]

He further writes to Andrews in the same letter that 'whenever our logic tries to simplify things by reducing the troublesome two into one it goes wrong... Truth is beyond logic, it is the everlasting miracle, it is static and dynamic at the same time it is ideal and real, it is finite and infinite.'

One can go with logic as Shankaracharya the greatest 8th century Indian philosopher did but up to a certain point and there comes a moment when it cannot go beyond – but to go beyond it too the intuition starts playing its role.[19] Intuition is not against logic it is beyond logic. From logic to intuition was the journey Shankaracharya made when he turned from non- duality to harmony of duality in his devotional songs.

I am reminded of a conversation between Tagore and Einstein on this similar topic in one afternoon of 14 July 1930 at Einstein's residence in Kaputh :

Einstein said to Tagore : "If there would be no human beings any more, the Apollo of Belvedere would no longer be beautiful?"

Tagore said, "no".

"I agree with regard to this conception of Beauty, but not with regard to Truth", said Einstein

"Why not?" , Tagore said, "Truth is realized through man... It is the perfect comprehension of the Universal Mind."

"I cannot prove scientifically that truth must be conceived as a truth that is valid independent of humanity; but I believe it firmly", said Einstein.

"Truth, which is one with the Universal Being, must essentially be human", asserted Tagore... "According to Indian philosophy there is Brahman, the absolute Truth, which cannot be conceived by isolation of the individual mind or described by words, but can only be realized by completely merging the individual in its infinity."[20]

This longing for the union with the Supreme reality and inversely the longing of the Supreme reality also for the union with the finite can be realized, as says Tagore, by anyone who is in peace and has the feeling of the eternal and if one tries to understand the unity of mankind. Tagore is slowly taking us at the threashold of the exact meaning of spirituality through the path of the unity of mankind.

In the unity of beings one realizes the spirit, *atman.*

Revelation of Spirit in man is the core philosophy of Tagore.

Tagore makes a very important statement which clearly distinguishes spirituality from religion but at the same time mentions about the closeness of the two. He says :

The highest wisdom of the East holds that it is not the function of our soul to gain God, to utilize him for any special material purpose. All that we can ever aspire to is to become more and more one with God... In the spiritual world , which is the region of unity, we grow by losing ourselves, by uniting.[21]

One can be complete when the difference between finitude and infinite vanishes and the person becomes one with the Ultimate Truth. This is so nicely explained by Gorakhnath, a Siddha i.e. enlightened living between (2nd century BC – 2 century AD) by one of his poems :

Die, o Yogi die, die
Sweet is dying
Gorakh says, I teach death
The death I passed through when I became awakened
It was the death of sleep not of me
The ego died, not me, duality died , not me
Duality died and I met the eternal
The small constricted life broke,
And the drop became the ocean.[22]

Yes, when the rain drop falls into the ocean it is certainly dying in one sense, it is dying as a drop and in other sense the drop attains for the first time to the great life – it lives as an ocean and hence dissolve, die –but it is the ego that dies – then the divine manifestation, the union or the realization of oneness or completeness becomes a reality.

This consciousness of oneness beyond all boundaries is the consciousness of the soul. This soul exceeds all boundaries, and yet is bounded by myself.

Let us be very clear here that Tagore believed in unity of the infinite with finite but not in the Vedantic oneness where self, the finite looses itself completely in the Infinite.

Tagore replaces Upanishadic concept of oneness by a more personal and intimate relation between the divine and the human and creates his concept of Jivan Devata (the god of life) which evolves in three stages, i) as the 'beloved lady'; ii) as his inner being (antaraatma); and ultimately iii) Goddess of life who is the Infinite Being and gives his core spiritual message as enumerated in Gitanjali :

> The Infinite wants the finite's intimate comradeship
> And the finite wishes to lose itself in the Infinite.[23]

Tagore thereafter reveals the core content of spirituality and that is joy because the soul which is the unifying principle in me finds its perfection in its unity realizing ourselves outside us :

> We come to know it through the joy of this truth.
> Our delight is in realizing ourselves outside us.[24]

The medieval poet Kabir explains this joy so poetically :

> The inward and the outward has become as one sky,
> The infinite and the finite are united :
>
> I am drunken with the sight of this all[25]

I don't agree with William Radice when he says that in the poems of Gitanjali Tagore is essentially a dualist emphasizing always on relationship between the infinite and the finite, or on an interplay between the poet and the divine but he turns himself to be a non-dualist as a musician in his songs.[26]

On the contrary in songs after songs one may find the union but not the non-dual oneness of the infinite with the finite; however, the essence of Vedantic oneness can also be traced and this takes Tagore very close to the very distinguished 11th Century philosopher, Ramanujacharya and his philosophical concept, *vishishtadvaitavada* or qualified monoism [27] showing unity in diversity where both unity and the diversity are a reality.[28]

Tagore speaks of it again and again in his life. In 1922 in Pune in the Kirlosker Theatre he gave a lecture on 'Indian Renaissance', elaborating the very idea that :

> a man who is alone or one is meaningless because
> there is no unity in one. The one with many is truly
> one because in that one, one can see the unity and
> this unity gives the message of truth.

The distinguished psychologist Sudhir Kakar challenges the claim that Hindus are unique in self-knowledge and self-development. His contention is that Hinduism encourages men and women to be members of groups rather than self determining individuals. The contention of Kakar is erroneous particularly with reference to Tagore, who, however does not talk of Hinduism but the spirit of India. Tagore has said this umpteen times that unity with the infinite is possible by self sacrifice but at the same time it results in self blossoming and that establishes the fact that man's personality is much more important than his becoming one with the supreme or non-duality. [29]

Tagore says that true spirituality is calmly balanced in strength, in the correlation of the within and the without. [30]

In simple terminology it is a balance between worldliness and renunciation.

Then he says freedom i.e. freeing oneself from all kind of worldly entanglement or in other words, the knowledge of truth is not possible without submission to law. Law here is *rita*, the worldly or the cosmic law and this law also controls action of a person who does all to live in this world. The spirit, atman or Brahman is bound by this truth and also free from it in its joy. We are bound by worldliness as well as we are also bound by our desire to renounce this world and have the feel of blissfulness. The state of blissfulness is the ultimate in spirituality.

I have another point of difference with Sudhir Kakar when he states in his latest book on "Young Tagore : The Making of a Genius", that Tagore attributes his creativity to spiritual unconscious, which he calls the "One within me". However he corrects himself by stating that (though) it is analogous to the pleasure principle governing the Freudian dynamic unconscious, it can be said that Tagore's creativity is governed by the 'unity principle'.[31]

In fact it is not unconscious but 'pratyabhijna' or recognition of that supreme self and to be in union with it as mentioned by the 9th century distinguished poetician Abhinava Gupta and one can find a repetition of it in Mirza Ghalib, the great 19th century Urdu poet :

> Aate hain gaib se ye/mazamiin khyal mein/
> Ghalib sareer e khama/navaye farosh hai'

My thoughts come to me/From somewhere beyond/
When Ghalib is attuned/To the music of the stars(pen).[32]

If in his poetry Tagore is spiritual, it can equally be claimed that his creativity displayed in his art, particularly landscapes, is also fundamentally spiritual. In his landscapes – dark trees outlined against a ghostly twilight, or rows of trees and the masses of dark clouds – Tagore can be found gazing into nature with such an empathy of a *sahridya* (a cognoscente) that as he seems to be connecting with the universal self. [33]

Following what the distinguished keeper of Indian Art in the Museum of Fine Arts in Boston, A. Coomaraswamy said about artistic creativity, one can say that it is a two-step yoga, one, a spiritual stance of a meditative monk, and two, mindfulness of a skilled executor . One finds this yoga in Rabindranath of a meditative monk and the mindfulness of an arrow maker. Shankaracharya speaks about the arrow maker, who perceives nothing beyond his work when he is buried in it.[34]

To come to the last point whether in Tagore's scheme of thought on spirituality is there any space for worldliness. Though I have spoken about it yet it needs a little more elaboration.

Tagore says that only by living life fully can you outgrow it.[35] Life is perpetual creation; it has its truth when it outgrows itself in the infinite. Tagore says that the two aspects of human existence worldliness and spirituality go together and this knowledge leads one to achieve the state of blissfulness (*anandam*). Knowledge only of the finite, of worldliness is like lamp without its light, it is accumulation of knowledge without any illumination. But the greater darkness, says Upanishads, is the sole pursuit of the infinite.

The absolute infinite is emptiness. Tagore by endorsing Upanishads says that it will never do the least good to attempt the realization of the Infinite apart from the world of action or the existence of the finite.

Therefore Tagore says that the infinite and the finite are one as song and singing are one.[36]. The lotus grows in the mud of this world, the symbol of worldliness and history but when it opens to light and sun symbolizing the transcendent it blooms and hence both the transcendental spiritual and the worldliness together creates our joy'.

Our delight is in this world and to see infinite in humanity therefore Tagore says :

> Deliverance is not for me in renunciation. I feel the embrace of freedom in thousand bonds of delight.[37]

This strikes the keynote of Tagore's notion of spirituality. Despite his deep Vedantic background, Tagore was against any world-negating asceticism. In many of his poems and songs he made this point clear :

In Gitanjali Tagore says :

> Whom dost thou worship in the lonely dark corner of a temple with doors all shut?[38]
>
> and thereafter makes his point forcefully that

'we can never go beyond man in all that we know and feel.....I feel that I have found my religion at last, in which the infinite became defined in humanity.... reality is the definition of the infinite which relates to the person. [39]. In his acceptance speech of the Nobel Prize, which he delivered at Stockholm after eight years of its declaration in 1921, he speaks of the spirit of unity of all races and, by quoting Upanishad he gives this philosophical message, which he says is the message of the East to the West :

> He who sees all beings in his self, and his self in all the beings does not hate any one, and knows the truth[40]

Once we acknowledge this oneness, we are necessarily inhibited from doing harm to others. What is emphasized above all in the Isopanishad is amity or loving kindness towards other people and the corresponding rejection of apathy, cruelty, violence and everything else that is destructive of cordial, harmonious relations with one another.[41]

This is Tagore's spiritual universalism. It is not the negative kind of universalism which belongs neither to one nor to another. It is not an abstract soul, but it is my own soul which I must realize in others. It gives us delight. When I love, in other words, when I feel I am truer in someone else than myself, then I am glad, for the One in me realizes its truth of unity by uniting with others, and there is its Joy. [42]

One can present the true meaning of Tagore's notion of spiritual universalism with an imagery of a lotus. Lotus is symbolic in the sense that it tells how can one live in this world but remain untouched by it. The lotus grows from mud in the water and it is a worldly reality but it remains untouched. The light and sun which help the lotus to bloom and its fragrance to permeate is also a reality. Lotus is a symbol of transformation. Mud is transformed into the most beautiful and most fragrant flower. By remaining untouched it impregnates our mind with a sense of transcendent spirituality and then one can hear the sublime urge of the soul, "Light, oh where is the light"? The transcendental luminosity leads man to final deliverance and realization that spirituality is nothing but love for humanity.

This is the most enlightening message which Tagore offers to the people of the world.

Notes and References

1. Hazime Nakamura, Ways of Thinking of Eastern Peoples, 1964, p. 15
2. Tagore Rabindranath, The English Writings of Rabindranath Tagore (henceforth EWRT), Vol. II, reprint 2012. pp.339-40
3. Notes on letter no 266, Selected letters of Rabindranath Tagore, (eds) Krishna Dutt and Andrew Robinson, 1997, p.425
4. Rabindranath Tagore, EWRT, Vol.II, p. 327
5. Sen Amartya, The Argumentative Indian : Writings on Indian History, Culture and Identity, 2005, pp. 8-9
6. Selected letters of Rabindranath Tagore, (eds) Krishna Dutt and Andrew Robinson, 1997, P. 425, letter no 264, p.421
7. Tagore Rabindranath, Creative Unity, EWRT, Vol. II, p.527
8. Tagore Rabindranath, 'Man's Universe', The Religion of Man, EWRT, Vol. III, reprint 2012, p. 89
9. J.G. Gray, 'Poets and thinkers – Their kindred roles in the Philosophy of Heidegger', in Edward N. Lee and Maurice Mandelbaum(eds), Phenomenology and Existentialism, Baltimore : The john Hopkins University Press, 1967, p.97
10. Tagore Rabindranath, 'The Artist', The Religion of Man, EWRT, Vol. III, p.138

11. Tagore Rabindranath, 'The Vision', The Religion of Man, EWRT, Vol. III, p. 127
12. The Religion of an Artist, Contemporary Indian Philosophy, (ed) S. Radhakrishnan, Muirhead Library of Philosophy, 3rd reprint, 1958, p. 34
13. Selected letters of Rabindranath Tagore, (eds) Krishna Dutt and Andrew Robinson, (1997), p.245
14. Tagore Rabindranath, 'An Indian Folk Religion', Creative Unity, EWRT, Vol. II, p.523
15. Tagore Rabindranath, Gitanjali, song 69, EWRT, Vol. I, pp.66-67
16. Ibid, song 26, p. 50
17. Kakar Sudhir by quoting Jung that 'every creative person is a duality or a synthesis of contradictory aptitudes' says that if there is one creative genius who bears witness to Jung's observation it is Rabindranath, Young Tagore : The Makings of a Genius, 2013, p. 62
18. Letter of Tagore to C.F. Andrews. 7 September. 2015, cited in Sudhir Kakar, Young Tagore : The Makings of a Genius, 2013, p.63
19. Osho, India my Love : Fragments of a Golden Past, 1994, p. 91
20. David L. Gosling, Science and the Indian Tradition : When Einstein met Tagore, 2007, p.162
21. 'The Realization of the Infinite', Sadhana, EWRT, Vol. II, p. 341
22. Osho, India my Love : Fragments of a Golden Past, 1994, p. 29
23. Rabindra Rachanabali, Vol. 2 ,Gitanjali (original),1961, Song 120, p. 292
24. The exact wordings of Tagore are : 'Through the help of logic we never could have arrived at the truth that the soul which is the unifying principle in me finds its perfection in its unity in others. We have known it through the joy of this truth, Our delight is in realizing ourselves outside us', 'The World of Personality', Personality, EWRT, Vol. II, p. 373
25. Ibid, p. 375
26. Radice William, Gitanjali : A new Translation by William Radice, 2011, Introduction, p. xii
27. Ramanuja's concept of unity is not unity but union; for from a logical point of view it is only union and not unity that can be thought of as being constituted of ultimately distinct and separate parts...Ramanuja's Absolute, unlike Shankara's, is not unqualified identity but identity-in-difference.

28. Ramakrishna Puligandla, Fundamentals of Indian Philosophy, 1975, p. 259 and M. Hiriyana, Outlines of Indian Philosophy, 1932,, p.398
29. Abu Syeed Ayyub in his book 'Adhunikata O Rabindranath, 1983 writes under the sub title 'The Gitanjali Period' that ' the mind of a devotee (imbued with bhakti-rasa is singularly preoccupied with god, not absorbed in own self........But the poet of Gitanjali is not at all oblivious of himself; in the world of Gitanjali, the giving is as generous as the demand for reciprocation is unashamed; self-sacrifice and self-blossming are held together in a single container. The second element is not heard in purely devotional poetry as in Kabir's dohas, for example...the tune is of love... not bhakti; the lover always expects something in return, otherwise his love is unrequited, his giving himself futile...(Excerpts from the translation by Amitaava Ray)
30. Tagore Rabindranath, 'Realization in action', Sadhana, EWRT, Vol II. p. 329
31. Kakar Sudhir, Young Tagore : The Making of a Genius, p. 204
32. Cited in kakar Sudhir, Young Tagore : The making of a genius, p. 205
33. Coomaraswamy, A , The Transformation of Nature into Art, 2010 (reprint) pp.7-8
34. Cited in Coomaraswamy, Transformation of nature into Art, p.8)
35. Tagore Rabindranath, 'The World of Personality', Personality, EWRT, Vol. II, p. 372
36. Ibid, p.369
37. Tagore Rabindranath, Gitanjali, poem 73, P.68, EWRT, Vol. I
38. Ibid, poem 11 p. 46
39. Tagore Rabindranath, 'The Vision', Religion of Man, EWRT, Vol. III, p. 122
40. Tagore Rabindranath, 'The Nobel Prize acceptance Speech', EWRT, Vol. III, dated, 26 May 1921, p. 966
41. Kalyan Sen Gupta, The Philosophy of Rabindranath Tagore, 2005, p. 10
42. Tagore Rabindranath, 'The World of Personality', Personality, EWRT, Vol. II, p. 373.

❑❑

Chapter Ten

Paintings of Tagore and his Notion of Art

In 1915 itself in his introduction to his play Chitra, an English version of his Bengali play Chitrangada, Tagore said that people thought of him as an idealist talking only of the hopes and aspirations of the people and painting a rosy picture of life, This was not true.

He felt concerned about the sufferings of the humanity. That was a continuous concern which made him create a world of the eerie and the bizarre, the distorted and the dark in his paintings as well as in his poetry. The strain is more strongly marked in his latter period.

It all happened after 1924-25 at the time of 63 and 64 years of age, after the formal inauguration of Visva-Bharati. Tagore left for an academic tour of China and Japan and then South America. On his way to South America he fell critically ill. He had to keep himself inside the cabin all the time. The boat crossed over the equatorial line. The crossing was very rough and his mind was distraught with the saddest thoughts of the tragedy of love and death. It was in this mood that he strove to pass the painfully dragging hours in his cabin writing poetry. These were the poems of *Purabi* with their calligraphic erasures about which he wrote :

> When the scratches in my manuscript cried, like sinners
> for salvation and assailed my eyes with the ugliness of

> irrelevance, I often took more time in rescuing them into a merciful finality of rhythm than in carrying on what was my obvious task.[1]

And while explaining the reason why he did so, he wrote :

> The only training which I had from my young days was the training in rhythm, rhythm in thought, and rhythm in sound. I have come to know that rhythm gives reality to that which is desultory.[2]

In fact, while making corrections he scored out some words or erring lines and then he found that scratches looking very ugly. [3] He was also not systematic in his writing. The *Purabi* poems reveal a degree of desultoriness induced probably by the state of his mind and health during the crossing. He gave some kind of a form to these scratches which turned into figures.

His mind was very much disturbed in face of the violent crisis in the world, caused by the unchecked terrors of fascism, and he found himself evoking the primitivist world of crawling snakes, sharp beaked birds, globules of rough faces, square –jawed humans and heavy brooding ghostly forms, bursting flowers.

Shri Sovon Sen while giving a very authentic and matter of fact explanation of the genesis and development of his world of paintings, said that in order to give a cosmetic treatment to the erring lines and corrections that defaced the manuscript 'like a maze of deserted trenches in a self-ravaged battlefield', he took more time in covering them with linear traceries than in writing.

He was more concerned to counter the ugliness then these erasures caused. These cross-outs tracked through the horizontally composed writings, creating a unique flowing design. As Tagore conjoined stray deletions with extended lines, the coverings attained a unity of design as well.

These were neither sought after nor were some pre-planned designs; on the contrary, the tip of his pen found them on its journey to a fulfilment. In his case, it was not the brush that created the design, but it was the same tip of the fountain pen that wrote poetry which found the seeds of the visual form and paved his way to the domain of painting. He contoured the erring lines with thin pen marks adding cartouches (decorative panel) and orgees (a weired trick to remove age spots) as design elements and filled up the deletion with playful hatchings and delicate curves.[4].

There must have been a distinct style and depth in Tagore's paintings which must have induced W.G. Archer, an acknowledged art critic, to remark that he is the first modern painter that India has produced.

From the area of silence thus emerged a world which shows men and women as they really affected the artist in their true reality as demons, humans or angels.

But think of Tagore who after his first visit to Japan in 1916, severely criticising Japan's imperialist policy towards China in his two lectures, 'The Nation' and 'The spirit of Japan' which roused considerable resentment, wrote to his two artist nephews from Japan :

To Aban :

> The more I travel in Japan the more I feel that you should have been here too. How vital it is to get into close contact with the living art of this country in order to infuse life into our own art – this you will never realize squatting there all the time in your South verandah. Our country has no artistic atmosphere, there is no arterial link between our social life and our art – for us art is a superficial thing, neither here nor there; which is why you people can never derive your full nourishment from indigenous sources.[5] If you come here, you would see how the Japanese race lives in the lap of art- every aspect of its life is artistic. Had you come, the scales would have fallen from your eyes, and the goddess of art in your innermost being would have received her proper homage. [6]

But on one hand, he praised the traditional Japanese art and its aesthetic beauty, and on the other when it came to painting he created a primitivist world and what he wrote about his own art could be summarised as follows :

(i) He was an expressionist (a style in art, literature, and music in which the artist emphasizes emotions and reactions to things instead of objects as they really appear), urging to revert to primitive sources of inspiration in order that the imaginative creativity might be renewed and the hateful routine of cut-and-dried realism abandoned.

(ii) His lines often expressed passions that were abstract and evolved characters that drew upon subtle suggestions.

(iii) The perfect representation of an object, say a horse, by an academician can fail to move us, yet one of his weird creatures could be very compelling. He illustrates this with a story : "A child comes to me and commands me to tell her a story. I tell her of a tiger which is disgusted by the black stripes on its body and comes to my frightened servant demanding a piece of soap. The story gives my little audience immense pleasure, the pleasure of a vision."

(iv) Tagore did not have any academic training, but he bypassed known techniques and relied on pure artistic instinct. It is the element of unpredictability in art that fascinated him, and the resultant effect of that that his pictures do not represent a scheme preconceived in his mind. It is often said that he entered into the domain of art almost in a somnambulistic (walking in sleep) way.

(v) Tagore shared a common trait with Paul Valery, Nicholai Gogol, W. M. Thackeray, Vladimir Mayakovsky, William Blake and that was that their painting and writings supplemented each other. They continued their writings in paintings and vice-versa. [7] K G Subramanyan, in a more positive sense attempted at initiating a process of *de-exceptionalising* Tagore's painting from his "author-function"by trying to associate it with the nature of the poet's thoughts and deeds in other domains of his activity. [8]

(vi) Tagore pursued a kind of 'automatic' writing by allowing his painting tools to move about on the surface of canvas in a diagrammatical manner, presumably without any prefixed idea, so that the painting tools would find images of their own.

(vii) Artists in a natural consequence shift from figuration to abstraction, in Tagore case it happened the other way round. After returning from Argentina, Tagore started creating rhythmic forms in black on white paper and thus moved from abstraction to figuration.

(viii) Tagore did not name his paintings. Ramananda Chattopadhyay, the legendary editor of a Bengali monthly journal, wrote a letter to Tagore requesting him to name the paintings selected by him for printing in *Prabasi.* Tagore wrote to him that "it is absolutely impossible to give a name to my pictures, the reason being that I never make a picture of any preconceived subject. Accidently some form, whose genealogy I am totally unaware of, takes shape out of the tip of my moving pen and stand out as an individual. It is like Sita coming out of the furrows made by King Janaka's ploughshare. For him it was easier to give a name to that one accidental factor – the more so when the name had no relation to the actual subject matter. For me it is hopeless to try to register the names of the progeny of my pen who come unhidden and in such numbers. I do realise one does not feel happy as long as *rupa* (form) is not given a *nama* (name). [9] Incidentally Tagore was the first Indian artist who abstained from naming his visual work.

Tagore called his paintings doodles (scribble drawings) and his Argentinean hostess Victoria Ocampo took them seriously and requested him to commence painting pictures for their own sake. She arranged the first exhibition of his paintings of 1924 and then 25, 26, 27 and 28 at Paris in 1930 and thereafter in England, Germany, Denmark, Russia and America.

By 1940 Tagore created 2000 drawings and paintings. Tagore also wrote about the process of his paintings :

(i) First there is the hint of a line;

(ii) Then the line takes a form;

(iii) The more pronounced the form, the clearer the picture of his conception and

(iv) This creation of form is an endless wonder. Tagore has said in a poem

"Fragments of forms stored in the mind
Combines in pictures on the magic touch of art." Yet in another place he has observed :

> A strange face uninvited
> Hovers before my brush
> Making me wonder
> Whence does it appear[10]

His subjects are :

(a) Natural scenery, e.g. flowers, creepers, trees etc.;
(b) Human images;
(c) Animals and queer objects.

Western connoisseurs have discovered affinities of style and theme between the works of Tagore and those of Modigliani (Italian painter and sculptor 1884-1920), Pollaiuolo (Italian painter1429/1433-1498), Edvard Munch (Norwegian painter and print maker 1863-1944), Emil Nolde (German Danish painter and print maker 1867-1956), Paul Klee (German-Swiss painterexpressioninst 1879-1940), Morgenstern (German landscape painter 1805-1867), Alfred Leopold Isidor Kubin (1877 – 1959) was an Austrian printmaker illustrator and occasional writer, representative of Symbolism and expressionism), Franz Marc (German painter and print maker, 188—1916, an expressionist) and a host of moderns. But a statement by Henri Bidou, previewing Tagore's visual work prior to the exhibition in Paris in 1930, very straightforwardly established the fact that Tagore was not at all influenced by the West :

> These forms begin by having an abstract character. Little by little, whether by kind of self-produced evolution, or because the influence which guides them is touched by some memory of the common world, they acquire a certain resemblance to what we call nature... Only those who have never recognised the mysterious currents of thought and feeling, the outcome of the age itself, which penetrate all souls as by osmosis (something done gradually and without any obvious effort), and give direction to a whole epoch, will be surprised that these pure paintings, absolutely

> sincere and wholly uninfluenced by our studio customs, should resemble now and then the most recent researches of the painters of the West. There can be no question of imitation, but the convergence of the spirit is remarkable.[11]

One can conclude that :

(i) In his pictures one finds a staccato (disjointed) rhythm of our puzzled times. They bring out the stress and strain, conflict and confusion of a civilization crumbling into a vast ruin;

(ii) There are also luminous landscapes symbolizing the hope of a dawn arising out of the East;

(iii) He created a new language of purely visual expression, because he felt the spoken language did not convey everything.

As in paintings, so in his poems written in the later stage of his life, Tagore finds himself in a state of utter despair. He describes this feeling in one of his poems :

> I see secretive hatred murdering the
> helpless under cover of night
> And justice weeping silently and
> Furtively at power misused,
> No hope of redress.
> I see young men working themselves
> into a frenzy
> In agony dashing their hands against
> stone to no avail.
> My voice is choked today;
> I have no music in my flute;
> Black moonless night
> Has imprisoned my world, plunged it
> into nightmare
> And this is why with tears in my eyes, I ask :
> Those who have poisoned your air,
> Those who have extinguished your light,
> Can it be that you have forgiven them?
> Can it be that you love them?[12]

These are questions which he goes on asking again and again

and for many of them he fails to find an answer, but this does not deter him from seeking the truth. He describes the inevitability of suffering and death, nevertheless, he talks of the power to endure them – power which presents man in a new glory. In his last stirring lecture, "Crisis in Civilization" at the age of 80, a few months before his death, he spoke in the same vain and I quote, "A day will come when unvanquished Man will retrace his path of conquest, despite all barriers, to win back his lost human heritage."[13]

But the problem starts when persons like Prithwish Neogy, a well known Harvard- educated art historian, who acted as a curator of Rabindra Sadan in Visva-Bharati wrote in Sahitya Akademi Tagore Centenary Volume, though in a difficult style and English that :

> As though impelled by his intimations of the revelatory transposition of perceptive faculties in art, the aging poet's runaway experience of painting had powerfully aided in setting comparatively free the conclusive phase of his literature from lingering aristocratic, formal and traditional compunctions and the inhibition of the last century. Rabindranath Tagore had come to belong fully to the world of his time, the modern world.[14]

When Neogy said, modern world, he meant the Western world where modernity developed because of the impact of Enlightenment. In Western terminology, modernism is a breaking away from established rules, traditions and conventions, and implies fresh ways of looking at man's position and functions in the universe, and inheres in some cases remarkable experiments in form and style. In 1784, Immanual Kant, in a short essay, "Enlightenment", speaking in the same vein, was talking about the way the present was draw out the meaning of enlightenment, or the definition of modernism but Tagore, right from the very beginning, rejected the Western modernism and declared in Beijing in 1924 that the impertinence of material things is extremely old. The revelation of spirit in man is truly modern : I am on its side, for I am modern [15]. He said all this while in the same academic tour of China, Japan, and South America when in a state of ill health he painted while travelling by boat the bizarre, the distorted and the dark, the eerie and the primitivist and continued to do so in the coming years. In fact before that in his visit to Japan in 1916 he had already stated that true modernism is freedom of mind, not slavery of taste. It is independence of thought and action, not tutelage under European school –masters.[16]

When Tagore said that modernity is freedom of mind and not slavery of taste he was actually hinting at a critical openness that allows one to retrieve, rediscover and redefine elements of culture in a creative way, by a return of pride in one's roots, while looking ahead and hence when in the modern times Tagore could still write :

> Thou hast made me endless
> Such is Thy pleasure (*Gitanjali*)

Yeats could not but talk of a particular historical strain in the western modernist movement :

> Things fall apart; the centre cannot hold.

Tagore's poem speaks of the spiritual bond between the self and the universal self and rejects any kind of narrow approach related to humanity.

Yeats' line of the poem reveals that Europe with all its materialist advancement and prosperity seemed to be haunted by a TS Eliot – Wasteland feeling of inner desolation so prominent in her poetry and art - What Heidegger was to call the feeling of homelessness?

Tagore had the courage to speak of other modernism and even create a world of paintings as a creation of a mind which was very disturbed because of the tragic crisis in the world and unchecked terrors of fascism and saddest thoughts of the tragedy of love and death. But for Tagore, who believed in the creative unity, of harmony of life, to talk all of a sudden of disharmony and dissonance in his paintings can encourage any body to find the influence of the West in it and place him in the modern world of his time. Tagore's views on these subjects may look contradictory but at the same time under a school of *bhedabhed* of Indian philosophy contradictions are complementary to each other, which is an age old philosophical concept of India and China known as "complementariness of the opposites" and hence for Tagore it was easy to hint at the harmony and dissonance in his art creation.[17] In fact in a famous song of Tagore he showed how the opposites- death and birth dance together, beauty and ugly complement each other and joy and sorrow together make the life a complete whole.

Indian mind believed in double time order, one, is the level of reality which has a time marker, so it has a linear tension. The other is the level of man's hopes and aspirations – the world of gods having a cyclical rhythm. The double time-order reveals the basic nature of Indian art which knows no anti-thesis between the immediate and the ultimate, the earthly and the heavenly, the sensuous and the transcendental, enjoyment and liberation, harmony and dissonance and accepts them as complementary to each other. Tagore conceived of these orders in unison. Tagore says in his *Atmaparichaya* , I am the messenger of Vichitra, the variegated or the Universal Soul. This Universal Soul manifests itself into *bahu*, multiforms so that he may go on playing his divine game in playful tune, songs, dance, painting, words and other forms. [18] In his poem, *samanjasya*, he reveals that :

> *The Infinite wants the finite's intimate comradeship*
> *And the finite wishes to lose itself in the Infinite.*

The true principle of art, Tagore says, is the principle of unity between the Infinite and the finite.[19] But the Infinite is not impersonal. In all creative activity, Tagore says, reflects directly or indirectly, man's lavish desire for the manifestation of Person. The communication of a person to a person is the creative act but sometimes person's ego hinders the contact with the Universal Self. Egoism is the biggest thief of the world.[20] The egocentric individualism conflicts with the concept of unity. Tagore relates an excellent incident about this :

> Tagore often used to go on his small house boat and live for months on the beautiful river, surrounded by thick forest, in absolute silence and aloneness.

One full-moon night, it happened that he was reading a very significant contribution to the philosophy of aesthetics, by Croce. In the middle of night, tired from Croce's very complicated arguments, he closed the book and blew out the candle. He was going to his bed to sleep, but a miracle happened.

As the small flame of the candle disappeared, from every window and door of the small house boat the moon came dancing in.The moon filled the house with its splendour. Rabindranath Tagore remained silent for a moment. It was such a sacred experience. He went out of the house, and the moon was immensely beautiful in that silent night amongst those silent trees, with a river flowing so slowly that there was no noise.

He wrote in his diary the next morning, the beauty was all around me, but a small candle had been preventing the whole universe from rushing into me. Because of the light of the candle, the light of the moon could not enter and hence the first step towards creative act is to blow out the candle in other words, to replace the egocentric individual with the living growing personality. The ideal of harmony is fully consistent with recognition of the value of personality in aesthetic creativity and then only the whole universe penetrates you from every nook and corner.

Tagore, while explaining the creative act, has said about *riupa-bhedah*, separateness of forms. He says that in sheer oneness, form can have only a potential existence but the varied forms if they remain separate only, there would be fearful loneliness of multitude. Hence the varied forms, in their very separateness, must carry something which would indicate the paradox of their ultimate unity. Otherwise there would be no creation and for that Tagore refers to the term *pramaanaani*, proportion which indicates relationship, the principal of mutual accommodation and the harmony of the fact. But beauty cannot be always proportionate or symmetrical. One may discover symmetry in a lotus or in the structure of the Taj Mahal but the deep, dark forest, the starlit shadowy pathway in the silent night, the many splendoured aspects of human life as depicted in the Mahabharata or the shabbily dressed, pulled down languishing Shakuntala wearing a single plait cannot possibly be branded as 'symmetrical'.[21] More than outer proportion these examples reflect an inner harmony of *bhava* which inspires the artist and evokes the spectator to wonder and enjoy.

Thing which is abundant, left-over, surplus, which overlaps one's absolute need, in that resides the Divine. There is a remarkable verse in the Atharva Veda which attributes all that is great in the human world to superfluity. It says :

Ritam satyam taporashtram sramo dharmascha-karmascha
Bhutam bhavishyat uchisthe viryam lokashmeer balambale

"Righteousness, Truth, great endeavours, empire, religion, enterprise, heroism and prosperity, the past and the future dwell in the surpassing strength of the surplus." The meaning of it is that man expresses himself through his superabundance which largely overlaps his absolute needs. Tagore says, "In superfluity or transcendence, we have the genesis of creation and therefore the origin of art". Here Tagore talks about the artist who goes beyond one's needs, one's desires, one's worldliness and turns into a creative artist without any ego, a no-mind, only then one realises the Divine, the Eternity in this universe with whom the creativity starts. When one abandons ones needs and goes for left over which is symbolical of Brahma, the Creator (*yajnye hutassistasya odanasya sarvajnayatakaranbhuta bramhavedena*), One, in fact makes the shift from outer harmony to inner harmony where the Divine manifest itself in the self or the poet. Then only the poet is transported to the higher plane of transcendence where he becomes one with the Universal Self and the creativity takes place.

These two forms of harmony may sometimes move in parallel or may at times coalesce with each other or at other time disentangle themselves from each other. In any event these forms are responsible in the creative act leading to the expression of beauty.

To conclude, it is not the outer harmony but the inner aesthetic harmony caused by superfluity defines art. In our lives all around us are scattered things of our needs, of our desires and of our material interest but if we can remain untouched by them and pass through the world without carrying impression, any impact, any scratch only then in that state of super abundance the creativity takes place and the inner harmony of art is realised.

Notes and References

1. Quoted by I.N. Choudhuri "Poems and Paintings of Tagore : An integrated Vision", Comparative Indian Literature : Some Perspective, p. 230, Delhi,1992
2. The prefatory note that Tagore wrote for the catalogue of his exhibition of paintings at the city gallery of Birmingham in 1930

3. In a letter to Leonard Elmhirst, Tagore wrote "You have expressed your hope that this pen of yours will help me in my cult of frenzied drawing. You had the opportunity of observing me in the flowering session of my eccentricity which comes from an excess of dream energy. I have hardly enough left of it even for writing poems. Of late I have occasionally been compelled to write prose compositions which tracks across them of scratches–but they remain there undisturbed like a maze of deserted trenches in a self-ravaged battlefield. Pages full of them rebuke me in pathetic silence claiming for some harmony in this anarchy of forms." Letter to Leonard Elmhirst, The Tagore Centre, London 1991a : 98
4. Sovan Sen, Tagore's Paintings : Versification in Line, p.33, 2011
5. These comments recall of W.G. Archer on Abanindranath in his 'India and Modern Art' :

   "As (Abanindranath's style) developed over a period of thirty years, it became identified with certain qualities – hesitant, indecisive line, misty vagueness of form, sombre murkiness of colour, likings for wistful girlish stances, dainty wanness, anaemic sentimentality… due, in part , to the mystical nature of Havell's teaching… In essence, however, they derive from the contemporary (cultural) situation. They are the qualities that go with tepid shrinkage from reality, faltering distrust, a failure in courage." W. G. Archer, India and Modern Art, London, 1959, p.37
6. MS original at Rabindra Bhavan, Shantiniketan; letter published in Visva-Bharati Patrika, Magh- Chaitra 1353 (Jan.- April 1947), pp. 135-6
7. See, Sovan Sen, Tagore's Paintings : Versification in Line, p.19, 2011
8. See, the article by Subramanyan, K.G. "The Amateur and the Professional" from the book *Rabindranth Tagore and the Challenges of Today*, eds. Bhudeb Chaudhuri and K. G. Subramanyan. This reference is taken from the article Tagore's Paintings : a Creation of *Geniusi* Rajdeep Konar Jawaharlal Nehru University, New Delhi, India
9. Letter to Ramananda Chattopadhyaya, December 18,1931, Chitipatra, Vol 12, Visva-Bharati, 1986
10. See, Tagore's paintings : Versification in Line, Sovan Sen, p.33 2011

11. Bidou Henri, Rabindranath Tagore's Drawings, Visva- Bharati Quarterly, May-October,1941
12. A poem 'Question' by Tagore
13. Tagore, 'The Crisis of Civilization', The English Writings of Rabindranath Tagore, Vol iii, (Ed. Sisir Kumar Das), p.726, 1996
14. Prithwish Neogy, ' Drawings and Paintings of Rabindranath Tagore, A Centenary Volume : Rabindranath Tagore 1861-1941, Sahitya Akademi, 1987, 3rd print
15. Rabindranath Tagore, 'Autographical' (Talks in China), The English Writings of Rabindranath Tagore, Volume ii, (Ed. Sisir Kumar Das), 1996, p. 585
16. Rabindranath Tagore, 'The Spirit of Japan',The English Writings of Rabindrnath Tagore, Vol iii, (Ed. Sisir Kumar Das), 1996, p.368
17. M. Hiriyanna, Indian Philosophical Studies (1957), pp.95-96, Mysore.
18. Tagore, Atamaparichaya, Rabindra Rachanabali, X Vol. p.206
19. Tagore, 'What is Art', Sadhana, The English Writings of Tagore, Vol ii, (Ed. Sisir Kumar Das), 1996, pp.348-362
20. Tagore, Atmaparichaya, Rabindranath, Vol X, p.182
21. I.N. Choudhuri, 'Shakuntalam in the context of Western Dramatic Art and Modern Aesthetics', Comparative Indian Literature : Some Perspectives, 1992, p.158.

❑❑

Chapter Eleven

William Butler Yeats The India Connection : Kabir and Tagore

Of all modern Western poets the one to have been most deeply and continuously influenced by India is the greatest of all – William Butler Yeats (1865-1939). As an art- student in Dublin Yeats and his friend the poet and mystic George Russell (AE 1837-1935) were among the founders of the Dublin Hermetic Society in the year 1885, under the auspices of the Theosophical Society in London. Theosophical society did bring the metaphysical thought of India to the west and what Yeats has described as 'the rise of soul against intellect' began to make its first inroads into the entrenched positions of naïve materialism.

While tracing Yeats's journey from Swedenborg (who in the eighteen century recorded his visions of the inner worlds) and Blake to theosophy to Cabbala (a Jewish mystical system of belief based on mystical insight into the nature of God and the soul) to folklore and psychical research to Neo-Platonist to Noh theatre, (where on the stage a spectator can see incarnate and discarnate spirits meeting in dramatic encounter,) Kathleen Raine finds Yeats turning finally and definitively at last to the venerable root of all immaterialist thought, the Vedas.(*Yeats The Initiate*, London, 1986, p.332). With the help of his teacher Shri Purohit Swami translated ten principal Upanishads (1937) and in this way kept his connection with India till he made his full discovery of the tradition of Indian thought related to the unity of the Indian view of life, of body and spirit (*atma*) as indivisibly one.

An Indian barrister Mohini Chatterjee was sent to Dublin as an Indian Theosophists by the London headquarters of the Theosophical society to give a lecture at the contemporary club in Dublin on "The Common Sense of Theosophy" in 1886.Yeats was already a member of the club from 1885 and the influence of Chatterjee's lecture on Yeats was to prove enduring so much so that half a life time later in 1928 Yeats in his poem "Mohini Chaterjee" was to recall the lesson he had learnt from his first teacher about the doctrine of rebirth; a belief he himself retained, claiming besides to find traces of Indian idea of rebirth in Irish folklore. Rebirth, in Indian philosophy, is the result of one's worldly desire and past actions, impelled by the law of karma and the aim is to escape the cycle of birth-death and rebirth and attain moksha, emancipation or a state of transcendental bliss. But surprisingly Yeats in his poem 'Kanva on Himelf' wishes to return to the cycle of birth-death and rebirth and does not advocate suppression of desire and a joyful acceptance of rebirth which ultimately will lead to a state when birth hour and death hour meet and the soul stays beyond birth and death, dancing on deathless feet : Yeats says :

> Then wherefore fear the usury of Time,
> Or Death that cometh with the next-life key?
> Nay, rise and flatter her with golden rhyme,
> For as things were so shall things ever be.

The theme of reincarnation of soul is found in many other poems such as "Death', 'Ephemera', 'Fergus and Druid', 'Broken Dreams' and 'He Mourns for the Change". In 'Ephemera' the lover says :

> Ah, do not mourn... That we are tired
> for other loves await us;
> ...Before us lies eternity...

Tagore in his famous poem in Gitanjali (poem 73) speaks about his love for this world and people around him and boldly remarks that deliverance is not for him in renunciation.

Certainly, the Indian elements of Mohini Chatterjee's discourse had influenced Yeats's mind as it was evident in his early poetry and later recollections. What Yeats found in Brahmin Chatterjee's conversations was a doctrine of withdrawal from worldly matters as he said, "all action and all words that lead to action were vulgar and trivial."

Initially he accepted it but very soon we find him saying, 'Ah, how many years it has taken me to come out of that dream.'

Definitely it is a new approach of living a life of worldly desires which we find in the materialistic philosophy or Lokayata, the philosophy of the people of Charvaka.

Yeats admitted that "when I try to remember Mohini Chatterjee's philosophy as a whole, I cannot part from what I myself have built about it, or have gathered in the great ruined house of the prophetic books of William Blake', and evidently the ideas which clung to his memory were those that had stuck a cord with him in 1886 but more to develop 'his own valid synthesis.' i.e. an ascetic aestheticism".

He records in the "Pathway" which is more akin to the exquisite reclusion of his own protagonist in "Rosa Alchemica" (1897) than to Krishna's advice of disinterested action in the Gita, which appeared in Chatterjee's translation in 1887, the year after his visit to Dublin.

This shows his vacillation of mind between India and the making of his own ideas and love for Ireland as he says in the 1908 volume "*Collected Works in Verse and Prose*" :

"When I first wrote I went here and there for my subjects as my reading led me, and preferred to all other countries Arcadia and the India of romance, but presently I convinced myself.... that I should never go for the scenery of a poem to any country but my own, and I think that I shall hold to that conviction to the end."

However the Indian influence continued throughout Yeats's life with periodic ebb and flow, and reaching its strongest manifestation in his final decade in his friendship and work with Shree Purohit Swami in 1931. In fact, his veneration for Indian thought was so deep that he could never leave it and found solace in equating Ireland with India as an image of the pre-schism Christian existence and an image of early Irish Christianity. His words are, "I said that for the moment I associated early Christian Ireland with India." (Mokashi-Punekar, p. 247).

Marsh, Janet Zimmerman in his paper in Yeats Eliot Review, Winter 2005 on *The Influence of Hinduism in William Butler Yeats's poem "Meru"* says that when he met Purohit Swami in 1931 his interest in the Indian philosophy intensified and lasted to the end of his life. Two years before his death Yeats said he had "fed on the Upanishads" all his life (Joseph Hone 459). The Upanishads, part of Hindu sacred scripture, explain how the individual self (Atman) finds the ultimate reality (Brahman) by an inner spiritual journey. Yeats's interest in the Upanishads is reflected in "Meru" (1934). Thematically, "Meru" is distinctly Indian in its philosophical content and its formal structure parallels the process of man's ascent to Truth according to the teachings of the Upanishads, a structure which augments the meaning of the poem.

Yeats wrote "Meru" after reading Shri Purohit Swami's "The Holy Mountain", a work to which he also wrote an Introduction. Mukashi-Punekar has published in his book *'The later phase in the development of W. B. Yeats'* some 30 letters of Yeats written to Swami, the last was written on December 22, 1938 just one month and six days before his death. No doubt Yeats was indebted to Swami, particularly for resolving his doubt about the term "subjective abstraction" which is not recoil and evasion but having a subjective life, practice and conduct and as a result whatever Yeats wrote remained Yeatsian in form and content.

During 1886 itself, Yeats political consciousness evolved rapidly along with his exploration of the occult and wrote a poem published by the Dublin University Review on "The two Titians" with a subtitle "A political Poem." The two Titians are for Yeats allegories of Ireland and the British Empire. His essay in the same Review on the poet Samuel Ferguson very much political in intent came out in the next issue which was highly criticized by a reader as 'the rather petulant intrusion of political polemics in almost every page of Mr Yeats article.' (Murphy, 139).

Ireland and politics remained with him and it got an added boost up when he met Maud Gonne first time in 1889 when in an afternoon in the sitting room in 3 Blenheim Road in London, she spoke about Ireland with passion and even violence which left a lasting impression on Yeats and with Ireland and mysticism, a third theme entered in his life, love.

This brought him back more to mysticism and his love for India. His collection Crossways (1889) included three poems on Indian themes. "The Indian to his love" has only a decorative Indian setting.

The second poem "The Indian upon God" displays his understanding of Indian spiritual idea of the divine immanence in all creatures.

The third is a brief poetic drama "Anushuya and Vijaya" describes :

> A little Indian temple in the Golden Age. Around it a garden; and around that the forest. Anushuya , the young priestess , kneeling within the temple.' Kathleen says that the temple setting is that of Shakuntala , the play by Kalidasa, the translation of which by Monier Williams was already available in UK (p. 335) but there is no temple setting in Shakutala, it is an hermitage and she meets Dushyanta in a shady, leafy bower in the hermitage.
>
> But this India provides evidence of Yeats's having fallen in love with India of poetry, and is little more than a charming setting for a young man's love at first sight, for Maud Gonne, whom Yeats describes 'as a classical impersonation of the Spring, who walks like a goddess and her luminous complexion like that of apple blossom through which the light falls.

We have Yeats's own word for this poem where Vijaya is entangled with two women, Anyshuya and Amrita. Yeats explains :

> The little Indian dramatic scene was meant to be the first scene of a play about a man loved by two women, who had the one soul between them, the one woman waking when the other slept, and knowing but daylight as the other only night... I am now once more in 'A Vision' busy with that thought, the

antitheses of day and night and of moon and of sun." (*W. B. Yeats, Collected Poems* (London, 1950), 2nd edition, pp. 523-524).

Naresh Guha suggests that this is a slight modification of the Indian conception of the higher and the lower selves expressed through the images of two birds sitting on the same branch, one bird eating the fruit while the other watches, (The Mundaka Upanishad 3.1. dwa suparna sauja sakhaya samana vriksham parishwaswajate). The Personal Self weary of pecking here and there, sinks into dejection but when he understands through meditation that the other bird , who is just watching- the Impersonal Self-is indeed the supreme *atma*, dejection disappears. (Guha, Naresh, *W.B.Yeats : An Indian Approach*, Calcutta : Jadavpur University, 1968, p. 41)

It is impossible, as says Kathleen, to give a precise date of Yeats turning again towards India but a significant turning point may well have been Yeats's reading of Kabir. (p.336). It is a little conjectural but at the same time the analogical study of Yeats and Kabir by Kathleen, a very distinguished English poet of her time cannot be ignored, who spent all her life in understanding the perennial philosophy. She makes two points in establishing her point of view :

(i) A little collection of 'versions' by Robert Bly of poems by Kabir and the reference of the chestnut- tree in one of Kabir's translated poems. Bly confesses that 'chestnut -tree' was his own addition.

(ii) Robert Bly created his version with the help of Tagore and Evelyn Underhill's version of 'One hundred Poems of Kabir.' Two copies of this book of translation of Kabir by Tagore and Evelyn were in Yeats's library and there can be little doubt this is the book, according to Kathleen, Yeats had read, for in it are several unmistakable and important similarities with many poems of Yeats with Kabir.

The reference of chest-nut tree is from Bly's translation as Tagore in his translation does not mention name of any tree but elsewhere writes of the Banyan. (p. 336). Chest-nut tree of the poem "Among School Children" has been derived from one of Kabir's poem which Yeats read in Tagore's translation.(Naito, Shiro, *Yeats and Zen : A Study of the Transformation of His Mask*, Kyoto,Yamaguchi

Publishing House, 1990, p.17.) Raine herself records this suggestion in her book that Yeats makes an effective use of the tree symbol from Kabir's poem. :

> The unconditioned is the seed,
> The conditioned is the flower and the fruit.
> Knowledge is the branch, and the Name is the root,
> Look and see where the root is :
> Happiness shall be yours when you come to the root,
> The root will lead you to the branch

The leaf, the flower and the fruit. (Jeffares, Norman *A., One Hundred Poems of Kabir* Trans. Rabindranath Tagore. London : Macmillan, 1915, p. 86.)

Yeats's poem also emphasizes the root :

> O chest-nut tree, great rooted
> blossomer
> Are you the leaf, the blossom or the bole?

(*The Collected Poems of W.B.Yeats*, Dublin : Gill and Macmillan, 1933, p. 245.).

Upanashadic argument is that a human being is born into this world with a 'physical self' and also with an *atma* 'true self' which is also the all pervading 'ultimate self' or godhead. *Atma* is referred to as *hamsa*,swan, an Upanishadic term used by both Kabir and Yeats.

This atma or *hamsa* is trapped within its body and within the domain of *maya* and its goal is to free itself from these bonds and be reunited with the 'Beyond' or all pervading 'ultimate self.' Yeats first encountered a sample of Kabir's poetry in translation, which was published in 1914.The brief fable of the *hamsa*, swan in the 12th song in that book must have resonated strongly with Yeats, for its symbolism of the soul as a swan on a journey beyond the physical human world. It seems to have influenced his conception of "the wild swans at Coole" published in 1916.

Kabir had written, *Hamsa, puratan baat :*

> Tell me, O Swan, your ancient tale
> From what land do you come, O Swan?
> Where would you take rest, O Swan, and what do you seek?

The swan is a world-wide emblem of the soul which ultimately renounces his body on his way to be one with the Supreme Soul as says Yeats :

But now they drift on the still water,

Mysterious beautiful :..
...when I awake some day

To find they have flown away? (The *Collected Poems of W.B.Yeats,* London, 1955, p.148).

In another poem no 77, in Tagore's English translation.

Kabir speaks of the destination of the swan or the soul : *chal hansa waa desh jahaan* : but surprisingly Tagore translates *hamsa* as heart and not swan : 'O My Heart : let us go to that country where dwells the Beloved, the ravisher of my heart!

O bodiless one! Do not sit on your door step;
go forth
There it is ever moonlight and never dark…

It is in this land, Kabir says, woods of spring are a-bloom and the fragrant scent 'He is I' is borne on the wind.

There is no doubt that Yeats was impacted by Kabir's ideas of Vedantic oneness, more as a romantic oneness between the Supreme self and the physical self, his imageries, and symbolism of Swan, lotus, tree, and dancing tree were useful to him for his artistic purpose. Yeats says :

O Body sways to music, O brightening glance,
How can we know the dancer from the dance?
(Among School Children)
This par excellence image of dancing tree is not
there in Kabir but about dance there are many
images in Kabir : *nirgun age sargun nache*

Before the Unconditioned the Conditioned dances :

Thou and I are One' this trumpet proclaims.'
Or *'nacho re mero man matta hoi'*
'Mad with joy life and death dance to the rhythm
of this music.

(Jeffares, Norman A., *One Hundred Poems of Kabir Trans. Rabindranath Tagore.* London : Macmillan, 1915, p. 38-39)

It is not surprising that Yeats has not taken the name of Kabir any where in his writings because his interest in India was not that of a philosopher but that of a poet. Therefore he accepted ideas and symbols which were useful to him for his artistic purpose and hence names were not important to him. Whenever he borrowed or liked an Indian idea he tried to find an equivalent or a parallel for it with some Irish or European ideas.

The same thing happened with Tagore. In his *Autotrophies* of 592 pages, he takes the name of Tagore only once and that too about his gift of 7000 pounds to Tagore's school. But when he read first time Tagore's Gitanjali in English translation, he was deeply moved by these poems , recorded his impressions later in the introduction he wrote for Gitanjali in November,1912 :

> I have carried the manuscript of these translations about with me for days, reading it in railway trains, or on the top of omnibuses and in restaurants, and I have often had to close it lest some stranger would see how much it moved me. These lyrics---which are in the original, my Indians tell me, full of subtlety of rhythm, of untranslatable delicacies of colour, of metrical invention---display in their thought a world I have dreamed of my entire live long. The work of a supreme culture, they yet appear as much the growth of the common soil as the grass and the rushes.

But before that on 10th July 1912, in a speech at a reception to Tagore at the Trocadero Restaurant, London Yeats said that :

> I know of no man in my time who has done anything in the English language to equal these lyrics.

On 25 November Yeats write to Edmund Goose suggesting that : Tagore should be elected to our committee' 'for he is worshipped as no poet of Europe is. All these have become a part of history but a history of friendship rather than of a creative literary partnership as says R. K.Dasgupta (Rabindranath Tagore and William Butler Yeats : The story of a Literary Friendship, Delhi University,1965).

There is no doubt that the introduction to Tagore's Gitanjli by Yeats or essays by Ezra Pound and Andre Gide on that book are of a great deal of critical value for us as they give some perspectives. But nourished by different cultures, particularly Yeats, having a Celtic mind and a different poetic sensibility, his initial adulation of Tagore, though, was undiluted, his criticism of Tagore at a later stage was strong and highly Western in approach. However, it never crossed the line of civil decency.

"From about 1912 through 1915', says Richard Ellmann, Yeats felt his blood stirred by Rabindranath Tagore", particularly his two qualities appealed to him :

(i) His poems belonging to a supreme culture yet seemed 'as much the growth of a common soil as the grass and rushes';

(ii) 'He brought together purity and passion in a way which seemed to Yeats un-European.' (Ellmann R., The Identity of Yeats, OUP, 1984, p.183)

Ellmann says further that eventually Tagore proved a disappointment to his admirers in England as he grew prolix and revealed a want of English style. Yeats, like most Westerners, abandoned Tagore without having understood him.

From the very beginning of his western career the stereotypical figure of Tagore as Latter-day Wise Man from the East, the prophet did lingering harm to him.

Nirad C Chaudhuri says that in England Gitanjali was taken as a counter thesis to the English life and its spirit in the Edwardian age and it was only a stop – gap antithesis in the absence of a better and more real one. The literary alternative to Tagore came from the post war poets and novelists and above all from the Bloomsbury group and then with the loss of psychological topicality of his message the initial exuberance faded away very soon and the Western man's disillusion dawned in and criticism started.

The first hint of the gap between Tagore and Yeats emanated when Tagore in a letter to Rothenstein on 14th February 1913 said about Yeats that he was not satisfied with some of the corrections that was made without his knowledge in the printed version of English Gitanjali.

The gap became a little wider when a malicious rumour spread more in India and less in England that Yeats had been chiefly responsible for the success of English Gitanjali which was discounted by Rothenstein in his memoirs, "Yeats did here and there suggest slight changes, but the main text was printed as it came from Tagore's hand."

(Dutta and Robinson, Rabindranath Tagore, pp.183-4). However the miasma of doubt that had been spitefully created could never entirely be dispelled as Tagore wrote to Rothenstein in 1932. But this kind of a false propaganda produced quite a lot of heartburning in Yeats and he openly started talking about Tagore's poor English. In a letter to Purohit Swami in 1938 he asked him not to write further in English and said that the mess Tagore made with his poems should be avoided by Swami. (Letter of August 17, 1938 of Yeats to Swami included by Shankar Mukashi- Punekar in his book on Yeats, p. 267). This was, in fact, a clash of ego between both of them.

But the intellectual clash could not wipe out their literary friendship and one can see its manifestations in many cases. When Robert Bridges wanted to refine the English of one of the Gitanjali poems so as to include it in his wartime anthology of great poetry, "The Spirit of Man", London 1916 Tagore bluntly refused. Only when Yeats intervened, at the request of Bridges, did Tagore yield. In 1917 Yeats wrote to Tagore :

> 'Is there any likelyhood of your autobiography (My Reminiscences) being published in English? I believe it would be very successful if it came out at the close of the war and thus it would help your fame more just now than any other book you could publish.' (Selected Letters of Rabindranath Tagore, Eds Krishna Dutta and Andrew Robinson, CUP, 1997, p.171).

To Yeats's eternal credit, he wanted Tagore to present to the world his full Bengali personality – not merely the simple image projected by Gitanjali. He informed this in a letter on 24th April, 1918. (Ibid, letter no131).

From 1918, there was no letters between Yeats and Tagore for over ten years, though both of them met in London in 1920. Yeats was disappointed by the poor quality of poetry translations after 1913 – though he remain receptive to some of his prose – and Tagore was aware both of the poor quality of the translated poetry and no doubt of Yeats's reaction. (On Yeats and Tagore, see Dutta and Robinson, Rabindranath Tagore, London, 1995, pp. 3-4). However Tagore, in a letter to Rothenstein in 1932 requested him to thank Yeats once again on his behalf for the help which he rendered to his poems in their perilous adventure of a foreign reincarnation and assure him that he never underrated the value of his literary comrade ship (Selected Letters of Rabindranath Tagore, (eds.) Dutta and Robinson, p.419).

But in his contribution in the form of a letter to Tagore (dated 7 September, 1931) published in *The Golden Book of Tagore* in 1931, Yeats wrote :

> 'I... want to tell you that I am still your most loyal student and admirer'. 'Your poems came to me as a great excitement; and of recent years I have found wisdom and beauty or both in your prose... *The Home and the World*, your short stories and your reminiscences.'

(Ramananda Chatterjee (ed.), Golden Book, p. 269.)

Despite rejecting most of the English translations of Tagore's poetry and calling his poetry verbose, mystical and monotonous, Yeats remained interested in Tagore in both his prose and personality and regretfully wrote :

> 'I have always so much regretted that no chance has arisen to renew our old friendship. I have heard of you from time to time from English and Indian friends, and I have a book with your remarkable pictures in it.'

(Yeats to Tagore, June 1935, VBQ, 30, No 3, 1964-5, p.176).

In reply Tagore revealed his deepest feeling about Yeats :

> 'Your letter seems to come from a remote age reminding me of those days of my acquaintance with you intense and intimate....I often remember a meeting

> with you in that chamber of yours quaintly unique, that seemed to me, I do not know why, resonant of an old world silence, and though I find it difficult distinctly to recollect the subject of our talk the feeling of it lingers in my mind like the aroma of a rich and rare wine.'

(Selected Letters of Rabindranath Tagore, eds, Dutta and Robinson, p. 455).

In spite of this kind of deep personal friendship there was some kind of intellectual differences between both of them on issues like mysticism and modernity. Yeats mysticism was different and that what he said in an interview with Abinash Chandra Bose that his mysticism was based on intellect and Tagore's on spiritual experience. He aimed at clear logical expression but Tagore was vague. In fact, Tagore interspersed Vaishnava philosophy of love between Krishna and Radha in his mysticism as the search of the human soul for God. This puzzled Westerners who could not decide whether the poems were meant as love lyrics or as religious poetry or both. This idea at a later stage emerged modified and expanded as a full –fledged philosophy of life in Tagore's Religion of Man. Yeats mysticism, as says Mary Logo, emerged in 1925 as the cosmology of A vision, the cyclical astrological view of history which is a compendiam of all Yeats's mystical, magical and personal ideas about life. (Mary M. Lago, The Parting of the Ways : A Comparative study of Yeats and Tagore, Indian Literature, Sahitya Akademi, 1963).

But the real bone of contention between Tagore and Yeats was Tagore's rejection of Western modernity. There is no evidence that he ever cared to know or understand the essential greatness of Yeats's mature poetry. His *Adhunik Kavya* written in 1932, which is a strident document of how one of the greatest poets of the modern world failed to respond to the complexity of the modernist poetry in English. But at the same time it would proper for us to say that Tagore found unity of beings in the realization of the spirit, *atma.* Hence, while defining modernity, he had no hesitation to declare in Beijing in 1924 that :

'The impertinence of material things is extremely old. The revelation of spirit in man is modern. I am in its side, I am modern.' This 'other modernity' of Tagore is an unique phenomenon of his thinking and creative process. But at the same time we must say , he was unkind to T S Eliot and even Yeats as one does not find any evidence that he ever cared to know or understand the essential greatness of Yeats's mature poetry. Hence one can conclude that their literary friendship was deep and brought them nearer to each other but their strong intellectual conflict was deeper. However I would not like to take it just a lip service by Tagore, who fought for truth and justice all through his life, when he said in his condolence message, sent on receiving the news of Yeats's death in 1939 : I shall cherish the fact to the end of my days that my life has been linked with the memory of one of the greatest poets of modern Europe.

□□

Chapter Twelve

Tagore's Understanding of Universality and Cosmopolitanism and how these Constitute his Modernity

> I am a poet of the world, 'I try to capture its melody, wherever it rises
>
> (Aikatan, Harmony)

This chapter focuses on the nature of universality and cosmopolita-nism with reference to Rabindranath Tagore's social and political thought and his creative philosophy. It primarily alludes to the critical analysis of universalism and cosmopolitanism and also nationalism done by Isaiah Berlin and Ashis Nandy and also Martha Nussbaum and Amartya Sen and their attendant explication of Tagore's views on these concepts.

Today Tagore's thought is affirmed and treated honourably by all, with the gradually fading out of the former ideological bias of east and west, or of tradition and modern.

Martha, Amartya, Isaiah and Ashis they all argue on this issue of cosmopolitanism but differently. Nussbaum thinks that Tagore's understanding of universality (here Nussbaum uses both the notions, universalism and cosmopolitanism, interchangeably) is of an abstract Stoic and Kantian sort based on some moral reasoning; in discussing Tagore's political philosophy, Isaiah Berlin invoked the allied notion of internationalism. In fact, Berlin's essay is devoted to developing a sophisticated account of Tagore's vision of internationalism. Amartya Sen has almost a similar idea but he is, at the same time, convinced that it is, indeed, to Tagore's everlasting credit that his great cosmopolitan vision never sacrificed the richest possible sense of tradition. His actual words are, "The main point of cosmopolitanism, which is taken to be the world-citizenship claim, need not militate against valuing elements in one's own tradition" (Sen, 'Humanity' 112).

The universal reach of reason is quite consistent with the values of tradition and inheritance but at the same time universal reach of reason and moral life do not pay sufficient heed to the play of inheritance and tradition in the constitution of human condition. It is particular cultural traditions that can provide the bases for understanding and morally relating to others and ultimately for developing a vision of universality.

Tagore's one of the central preoccupations in his writings was to raise his voice against violence which he thought was a crime committed against humanity and hence his notion of humanism was not only based on any porous (universal) notion of reasoning but it was also bounded (particular) reasoning and for him it was very ease to weave them together as for him both bounded and porous are complementary to each other. The best example of his description of violence with full of pain and suffering is to be seen in his letter to the viceroy in1919 while relinquishing his knighthood or in his travelogue in which he describes the pilot's relishing description, while flying from Iraq to Iran, as how to kill through aerial bombing.

The cosmopolitan attitude here is not derived from a conception of reason that in its universality always tends toward abstractions; rather, it is dependent upon reason's articulation of the universal through an engagement with the local. "When we understand this truth in a disinterested spirit, it teaches us to respect all the differences in man that are real, yet remain conscious of our oneness", (Creative Unity, 171-172).

Ashis Nandi, by referring to the 'real' (quotes mine) tradition of India, says that Tagore looks back to what he sees as the real tradition of India, which is to work for "adjustments of races, to acknowledge real differences, between them, and yet seek some basis of unity. "It is this solution—unity through acknowledgement of differences— that India has to offer to the world." (Nationalism 1985 p. 64)

Tagore's conception of cosmopolitan universality, as Sarindranath Tagore says, does not merely yield postmodern toleration of alterity, but aspires to dissolve instances of otherness altogether by enriching one's own tradition through hermeneutic absorption and assimilation (S. Tagore, Tagore's conception of cosmopolitanism : A reconstruction).But one should be very guarded to make a statement like this because in this kind of an 'assimilation' and 'absorption' there is always the risk of mixing it with the American notion of the 'melting pot' or a synthesis or amalgamation of diverse identities. Tagore always believed in the confluence of cultures and human unity. He never believed in a monolithic structure of one culture or an alchemical unity of cultures but in the creation of bridges among cultures for better understanding of human beings so that an edifice of human unity could be established. Tagore's seminal statement in this respect is, 'Perfection of unity is not in uniformity, but in Harmony, (Creative Unity 171–72).

In this regard Tagore was very definite in his thinking, while he was talking about Asian Universalism Tagore said that :

> "Each country of Asia will solve its own historical problems according to its strength, nature and need,"

Tagore, during a visit to Iran in 1932, said further, "But the lamp that they will each carry on their path to progress will converge to illuminate the common ray of knowledge...it is only when the light of the spirit glows that the bond of humanity becomes true." (English writings of Tagore, ed : Sisir Kumar Das), pp. 480-488, 511-520.).

One thing should be made very clear before proceeding further that all these conceptual terms like humanism, universalism, cosmopolitanism, nationalism or internationalism are not universal terms which can give the same meaning in context of any time (kala) and or any space (desa). If these terms are the product of a specific culture, then its merits must ultimately be assessed by measures arising out of that culture. Tagore's views on these subjects may look contradictory but at the same time contradictions are complementary to each other, which is an age old philosophical concept of India and China known as "complementariness of the opposites" and hence for Tagore it is easy to hint at the transnationality of the nationalist imagination, accept universalism without denying particularity and not discuss cosmopolitanism without weighing it with tradition as he says :

> I have come to feel that the mind, which has been matured in the atmosphere of a profound knowledge of its own country and of the perfect thoughts that have been produced in that land, is ready to accept and assimilate the cultures that come from other countries ('The Way to Unity').

He, in his Hibbert lectures, describes India as an idea and not a mere geographical fact and the idea of India as he describes in his acceptance speech of the Nobel Prize, which he received after eight years of its declaration in 1921, is the spirit of unity of all races and, by quoting Upanishad he gives this philosophical message, which he says is the message of the East to the West :

> He who sees all beings in his self, and his self in all the beings does not hate any one, and knows the truth.

In 1922 in Pune in the Kirlosker Theatre he gave a lecture on Indian Renaissance, elaborating the same idea as was mentioned in his acceptance speech, the Bengali version of that is titled : 'shikkhar milan'. He said that :

> A man who is alone or one is meaningless because there is no unity in one. The one with many is truly one because in that one, one can see the unity and this unity gives the message of truth.

Two very important philosophical traditions that were important to Tagore's intellectual development were the Vedanta (broadly the Upanishadic texts and philosophical commentaries of the Advaitic (non-dual) philosophy by Sankara and a school of Vedanta philosophy which admits the truth of, or what is known as the principle of *bhedabheda.* It may generally be taken to indicate a belief that *bheda* or 'distinction; and *abheda* or 'unity' can co-exist and be in intimate relation with each other. Substance and attribute, universal and particular, whole and parts may seem to be different from, or even opposed to, each other, but really there is no incompatibility between them, for they can be reconciled in a unity which pervades the difference and is its very being.

This view is sometimes described also as *parinama vada* or 'theory of development' implying that reality yet maintains its identity throughout. (M. Hiriyanna, Indian Philosophical Studies, 1 (1957), pp. 95-96).

These schools of thought, though divergent in many respects, agree on one tenet : that the phenomenal world of everyday cognition is ontologically interconnected.

This point is finely illustrated, through different routes, in Sankara's doctrine of *adhyasa* [imposition] and the Buddhist theory of dependent *pratitya-samutpada* [origination], both of which point to the interconnected reality of the phenomenal world. Tagore's social and political insights are extensions of this fundamental non-atomistic metaphysical orientation which is so beautifully described on an ontological level in a line of a poem by him :

> The Infinite plays its tune within the Finite and
> hence the music is so luscious.

Infinite expressing Himself in the finite is a miraculous revelation and mysterious expression and a thing of wonder and joy. The self and the Unknown Infinite are fused into a single unified field and one ultimately realizes one's oneness with the total universe. In *Sadhana* Tagore elaborates this point further,

> Thus the state of realizing our relationship with all, of entering into everything through union with God, was considered in India to be the ultimate end and fulfilment of humanity.

Sugata Bose has made a candid revelation that "(humanism), universalism, cosmopolitanism and internationalism are words and concepts jostling for interpretive space in new global, interregional and transnational histories." Most of the scholars use these concepts interchangeably e.g., Nussbaum makes the following statement that Cosmopolitanism shares some aspects of universalism namely the globally acceptable notion of human dignity that must be protected and enshrined in international law. Different universalism in Sugata Bose's connotation of the phrase shares significant common ground with the meaning of vernacular cosmopolitanism as evoked by Homi Bhabha or local cosmopolitanism as enunciated by Engseng Ho or rooted cosmopolitanism as described by Anthony Appiah while diverging in subtle points of emphasis or "new" cosmopolitanism as explained by Louise Blakeney Williams and intuitive cosmopolitanism of Uma Dasgupta (Homi Bhabha, *The Location of Culture*, (2004); Engseng Ho,*The Graves of Tarim : Genealogy and Mobility across the Indian Ocean*(2006), Anthony Appiah, *Cosmopolitanism : Ethics in a World of Strangers* (2006), Louise Blakeney Williams, Overcoming the "Contagion of Mimicry" : The Cosmopolitan Nationalism and Modernist History of Rabindranath Tagore and W.B. Yeats (2011) and Uma Dasgupta, Tagore's vision for the future, Santiniketan Ashram Sammilani International Magazine, 2011) all discuss in their way the notion of cosmopolitanism though not very much different from each other approaching the issue in the bigger perspective of universalism.

At least two meanings of universalism is in currency, one which is a part of India's ethos of the continuity of thought and, another, since the colonial times :

The age old conception of universality is about which Tagore says that it is for the sake of our humanity, for the full growth of our soul, that we must turn our mind towards the ideal of the spiritual unity of man.' ('The way to Unity', English Writings...vol iii.p. 465). The Unity gives man the message of truth. It is in this sense that a unity is said to underlie the seeming diversity of the universe and therefore the issues of immanent and transcendent values and aspirations for the worldly and religious orders are to be viewed within this unitary framework where immanent and transcendent are dialectically united and one becomes that which one loves. While talking with Einstein Tagore said the same thing, "when our universe is in harmony with Man, the eternal, we know it as truth, we feel it as beauty." In the meditative Upanishadic times we are told that this earth is a human family (vasudhaiva kutumbukam) and the divine spark is the guiding principle and we are the divine spark. Under this concept the whole world (consisting of Universal Self, Nature and the self) is a family and is very different than the cosmopolitian concept of Diogenes of Sinope , who said : "Asked where he came from, he answered : "I am a citizen of the world (kosmopolitês)." This can be, if not narrow, but a broad view of particularism and does not in any way prove one's identity as a member of a family but just a citizen of the world (state). The concept of the world as a family is also different from the present creation of the Western civilization of a global order or a global village, a point in the relentless process of westernization of the globe. The terms and conditions for living and participating in the life of this village are laid down by the west for their own benefit and if the terms and conditions are not followed one cannot stay in that village.

The second conception of universality is related to enlightenment. The emergence of enlightenment thought extolled reason and science as the best means of improving society and of ending political despotism and the tyranny of "blind faith and superstition". There is no reason for anybody to belittle this complex intellectual enterprise which is the basis of the current conceptions of modernity which was adopted by India during the colonial time because of a false perception that westernization is modernization. This became a big deterrent in the understanding of our realities and our modernity.I shall take up the issue of modernity a little later.

The post- structuralist theory developed an important critique of the coercive aspects of enlightenment thought but did not critically comment on its presumption that sacred is superstitions and regressive and that secular is progressive. The forking of sacred and secular, non-reason and reason, non-modern traditions and forward looking modernity, spirituality and materialism, though created a new meaning of western universalism, but at the same time brought a division between humanity that progressive west is civilized and regressive east is backward. Progressive west is universal and the regressive east is particular. This kind of a notion of cultural uniqueness goes against the concept of human unity so assiduously nurtured by Tagore by introducing the notion of universal humanity :

> Oh my mind, awake heroically on the shores of the
> ocean of universal humanity.

In order to contest the universalist boasts of Europe Tagore on February 10, 1937, composed his poem on another continent, "Africa", towards the end of his long and creative life in literature. Sugata Bose says that even more than the empathy for Africa's history of 'blood and tears', what marked the poem was a searing sarcasm directed at the false universalist claims of an unnamed Europe. Even as the "barbaric greed of the civilized" put on naked display their "shameless inhumanity", church bells rang out in neighbourhoods across the ocean in the name of a benign God, children played in their mother's laps, and poets sang paeans to beauty."

The sanctimonious hypocrisy of the colonizer stood in stark opposition to the wretched abjection of the colonized. This is what is known as homogenised universalism about which African writer Chinua Achebe in his essay on "Colonialist Criticism" says that in the nature of things, the work of a western writer is automatically uniformed by universality. It is ony others who must strain to achieve it. Fredric Jameson's statement which is no doubt inadequate and slanted, describes the third world literary works as national allegories, which gave nothing to do with universal cosmopolitanism. And so Chinua Achebe says that he should like the word 'universal' banned altogether from the discussions on African or to add Indian literature until such time as people cease to use it as a synonym for the narrow, self-serving parochialism of Europe, until their horizon extends to include all the world.

The colonizers did not simply erect walls around their notions of cultural difference, they were keen to be players in broad arenas of cosmopolitan thought zones and wished to contribute to the shaping of a global future. Their universalism flowed from a sense of exclusiveness or exceptionalism resulted from Eurocentric interpretation of enlightenment where rationalism, science, equality, freedom, human rights and industrialism are accepted as the unique by-products of European civilization and which created a homogenised universalism which was very much different from Tagore's universalism which grew with its strong basis of particularism or with the help of knowledge and learning of one's own culture or a deep understanding of the tradition and a humanistic insight.

Louise Blakeney Williams used the adjective 'old' and 'new' with cosmopolitanism and said that the 'old' cosmopolitanism or universalism of the 18th century, which proposed the national differences be minimized in favour of one uniform enlightened culture, was the product of enlightment project. Tagore thought that a homogenized universalism, itself a product of the uprootedness and deculturation brought about by British colonialism in India, (Nandi : 'Illegitimacy…', preface) and did not blame the enlightment project to that extent.

Tagore undoubtedly was a powerful critic of worshipping the Nation as God and was horrified by the crimes committed by modern nation-states. Yet he loved the land that had nurtured him and never abandoned a basic anti-colonial or anti-imperialistic stance and even gave up his knighthood for the heinous crime committed by the British in 1919 by killing the unarmed peaceful people in Jalianbala Bagh in Amritsar, India. However he simply did not want Indian patriots to imitate European nationalists. It is not without reason that Mahatma Gandhi in his obituary comment on Rabindranath Tagore in 1941 lauded the poet as "an ardent nationalist". The large ethical claims made by votaries of a brand of cosmopolitanism that is dogmatically opposed to patriotism need to be put to the test on the ground of the history of colonial empires. Cosmopolitanism would serve as a weak pillar of any theory of human justice if it ruled out as illegitimate most modes of anti-colonial resistance.

Tagore never thought that universalism is contrary to nationalism and that they pull on opposing direction.

It is a balance between universalism, nationalism and the traditional world that Tagore hoped to achieve in his universal nationalism and hence one can conclude that Ashis Nandi or Nussbaum or others were wrong when they did not consider Tagore as a nationalist, They claim that he was a patriot and anti-imperialist because he loved his country and did not want the British to rule it, but he was a universalist rather than a nationalist because he advocated the creation of a culture common to all people, instead of separate national cultures, and because he did not want independence if that also meant adopting the form of nation-state, (see Nandy, *The Illegitimacy of Nationalism*; Martha Nussbaum, "Patriotism and Cosmopolitanism," in Joshua Cohen, ed., *For Love of Country : Debating the Limits of Patriotism* (Boston, Mass., 1996).

Ashish Nandi recognises Tagore's universal nationalism as unself-critical Indian nationalism as a response to western imperialism which was limited by its time and its origin. Chittaranjan Das, (quoted in Hay, *Asian Ideas*, 253) condemned Tagore for his "anti-nation" idea and his "nebulous conception of universal humanity." If Tagore's ideas on nationalism are not very well understood, it may be because they appeared in many different places. While Tagore devoted an entire book and a novel, *Home and the World* to the subject, he also wrote articles, which were published in a variety of books and journals, as well as many letters about.

Nationalism. The views of Tagore, therefore, have to be pieced together from a variety of sources and writings. Nevertheless, it is clear that Tagore had consistent theories of nationalism that did not change significantly after the first decade of the twentieth century. Tagore argued that India had always been varied in religion and lifestyle because she accepted "alien races as factors in her civilization," and hence any concept of national identity denying diversity or a unitary sense of national identity, Tagore feared would lead to cultural homogenization, or as he puts it further by referring to the view of nationalists of those days, that the "notion that the culmination of national unity was reached by pounding all differences into an undifferentiated mass" was an attempt to suppress differences and was an imitation of Anglicization, and was "as wrong as murder." The real tradition of India is to work for an adjustment of races, to acknowledge the real differences between them, and yet seek some basis of unity (Tagore, Nationalism, reprint, 1985, p.18). The basis for this tradition has been built in India at the social level, not the political, through saints like Nanak, Kabir, Chaitanya and others. It is this solution – unity through acknowledgement of difference – that

India has to offer to the world, (ibid. p. 64). If one says that India's unity is a social fact, not a political agenda then it becomes easy to understand that for Tagore universal nationalism is an inclusive plural concept of a nation which goes beyond the idea of exclusive nationalsism and where the whole earth is a family.

In India's history of living within the differences Tagore saw an ideal of unity that he hoped that the world would accept as India's and Asia's contribution to the Modern Age where the scientific facility had brought the human races closer but not without their baggage of psychological barriers. He insisted that the psychology of the world had to change in order to meet the new environment of the new age. Europe was at the time conceiving of a League of Nations which was ultimately formed in October 1919. Tagore wrote enthusiastically that this was a momentous period for India and Asia to restore their spirit of cooperation in culture and heal the suffering peoples of the modern age from the divisive politics and materialistic greed which were vitiating even the citadels of peace and harmony. He insisted that the psychology of the world had to change in order to meet the new environment of the new age. Europe was at the time conceiving of a League of Nations. Tagore enthusiastically signed the "Declaration of the Independence of the spirit" sent to him by Romain Rolland. The other signoteries were Bertrand Russel, Albert Einstein, Stephen Zweig, Benedetto Croce, Hermain Hesse, Upton Sinclair, K. Coomaraswamy and many other celebrated authors, scientists, thinkers and others. It was a momentous declaration of the spirit of that age which was seeking an answer to violent and ethnic nationalism, exclusive materialism of the west, and as how to look at this world as a whole :

> We serve Truth alone which is free, with no frontiers, with no limits, with no prejudices of race or caste without dissociating ourselves from the interests of Humanity. We shall work for it, but for it as a whole. We do not recognise nations. We recognise the people – one and universal.

The copy of the declaration was prepared by Romain Rolland and sent to Tagore on 10th April 1919 just immediately after the war.

His reply was similar to his idea of universal humanism :

> When my mind was steeped in the gloom of thought, that the lesson of the war had been lost, and that people were trying to perpetuate their hatred and anger into the same organised menace for the world which threatened themselves with disaster, your letter came and cheered me with its message of hope. The truths that save us have always been uttered by the few and rejected by the many and have triumphed through their failures. It is enough for me to know that the higher conscience of Europe has been able to assert itself in one of her choicest spirits through the ugly clamour of passionate politics and I gladly hasten to accept your invitation to join the ranks of those free souls, who in Europe have conceived the project of a Declaration of Independence of spirit.

As said earlier all these terms universalism, cosmopolitanism, internationalism are used interchangeably by scholars and also used as binary opposite to nationalism which is, in fact, not what Tagore thought of these terms and nationalism. In spite of the fact that there are many like Loise Blankey Williams who used the adjective 'new' with cosmopolitans, and also called it 'rooted' or 'realistic' cosmopolitans,which means those who respect the variety of traditions and nationalities, but also believe in universal values that all people in all countries should accept. and that is what Tagore's cosmopolitan universality is. As said earlier cosmopolitanism is the progressive alternative committed to dialogue and consent . It creates a space for us to think about justice and cooperation but it also recognises that we not only exist 'unavoidably side by side' but also that we live 'unavoidably one after another'.

This may provide the key to the construction of the 'different modernity' for which Partha Chatterjee is looking, by suggesting a better way to negotiate between the modern and traditional, West and East, than either adopting one side or the other, or restricting one to the public and the other to the private sphere (Chatterjee, "The

Disciplines in Colonial Bengal," in Chatterjee, *Texts of Power*, 27). The idea of modernity rooted in the soil is first floated by Tagore and Gandhi. While marking our modernity in the continuity of Indian tradition both Tagore and Gandhi warned us in the beginning of the 20th century about the danger of developing a colonial mentality or mental colonisation. Tagore said in those days that true modernism is freedom of mind and not slavery of taste. He observed, "You must apply your Eastern mind, your spiritual strength, your love of simplicity, your recognition of social obligations in order to cut out a new path for this great unworldly car of progress shrieking out its loud discards as it runs."Extending this idea of a different or other modernism he said in Beijing in 1924, "The impertinence of material things is extremely old. The revelation of spirit in man is modern. I am on its side, for I am modern."

In another essay Tagore said, "Once you did solve the problems of man to your own satisfaction and evolved your own art of living- all this you must apply now to the present situation and out of it will arise a new creation and not a mere repetition, a creation which the soul of your people will own for itself and proudly offer to the world as its tribute to the welfare of man."

By redefining the terms of discourse in terms of the creative expression of Asian autonomy and individuality in the pursuit of 'true modernity' in all fields, Tagore and Gandhi were setting, as it were, a fresh agenda to understand our modernity.

In Western terminology, modernism is a breaking away from established rules, traditions and conventions, and implies fresh ways of looking at man's position and functions in the universe, and inheres in some cases remarkable experiments in form and style. In 1784, Immanual Kant, in a short essay, 'Enlightment', speaking in the same vein, was talking about the way the present was different from the past. In this difference he was trying to draw out the meaning of enlightment, or the definition of modernism. For Tagore any great art is the expression of both the tradition and the actual. To be uprooted from tradition is tantamount to alienation from one's own self. It is interesting to note that in the west with the emergence of post-modernism the discussion on cosmopolitanism became intimately intertwined with debates on global heterogeneity and multiculturalism and that what Tagore anticipated in his cosmopolitan universality and related to that in his concept of modernism based on his denouncement of universalist metanarratives of enlightment based on discursive matrices such as progress, science, technology, reason embodied by contemporary nation-states.

In India, modernism as a phenomenon or value is not an absolutely unrelated one without reference to the past or the future. It absorbs in it traditional values as well as new innovations and is indicated by the term 'continuity'. It is essential to do that because the spirit of India, as says Tagore or as the writers have observed over the ages, is not to reject anything. Everything has a place here as an alternative. India lives with many alternatives which become part of the continuity of thought and creativity and hence the choice which Gandhi or Tagore offered to us was not tradition versus modernism, but the choice of both versus the forced acceptance of one. This is the Indian way of thinking. Our thinking is not logo-centric and exclusive, but symbolic or inclusive and hence India has no problem to live with many life choices and this is possible because as said by Tagore, one has the freedom of mind, and also as he mentions in his essay on 'Modernity in Literature', accepts element of universality as well as permanence and expresses the profundity of aesthetic joy.

But for all practical purposes, one can say that whatever is western is modern. This kind of an idea is based on a counterfeit concept very cleverly designed by the colonial masters that westernization is modernization. There is no doubt that the largest corpus of ideas, thoughts, modes and methods, etc., of our life in the present and recent times are admittedly western by origin, yet the fact remains that in the process of our becoming modern something was happening within ourselves, that, in spite of our acceptance of Western modernization, we were doubtful about its value and results, and were constantly searching for our own modernity. The West develops through substitution and it writes itself again and again. India develops through accommodation. It is, as says Tagore, like a sea of great humanity where all are merged in one body. Here new ideas may supplant older ones, but the older ones linger on. They are allowed to co-exist with what is new. Here one does not reject to create one's modernity.

When Tagore said that modernity is freedom of mind and not slavery of taste he was actually hinting at a critical openness that allows one to retrieve, rediscover and redefine elements of culture in a creative way, by a return of pride in one's roots, while looking ahead and hence when in the modern times Tagore could still write :

> Thou hast made me endless
> Such is Thy pleasure

Yeats could not but talk of a particular historical strain in the western modernist movement :

> Things fall apart; the centre cannot hold.

Tagore's poem speaks of the spiritual bond between the self and the universal self and rejects any kind of narrow approach related to humanity. This universalist idea, as a part of historical processes of long duration that strengthened Tagore's notion of modernity, which one may call different modernity, which was in a way related with his cosmopolitanism or cosmopolitan universality and by itself a civilizatory cosmopolitan notion and force. Yeats' line of the poem reveals that Europe with all its materialist advancement and prosperity seemed to be haunted by a TS Eliot – Wasteland feeling of inner desolation so prominent in her poetry and art - What Heidegger was to call the feeling of homelessness? The mood of despair, agony, resignation, listlessness and ennui surfaced as the dominating mood of modernism. But this kind of notion termed as the spirit of an age is rejected by Tagore because in his view the essence of art is unchanging but in the later phase his frequent use of the word modern was not deprecatory and the retrospective preface of his novel *chokher Bali* is an instance. The gist of his essay on Modern Poetry (1339 B.S.) indicates his acceptance and at the same time negation of western modernity. In a letter to Amiya Chakravarty (23 Feb 1939) he hesitantly speaks about his moving between two worlds and speaks about the pressure of the current movement in the curves and cracks in his track; but his statement is tempered by the assurance that he has not moved house and soon we discern his magisterial voice of cosmopolitan universality which eclipses the second voice of western modernity. The self-assertion of wholeness soon seems to dominate.

I shall like to bring the arguments of Amartya Sen to understand Tagore's view on western modernity. Sen is impatient with "contemporary attacks on modernity (especially on a 'modernity' that is seen as coming to India from the West)". The attackers consider modernity a European cultural phenomenon—defined by peculiar notions like individualism, progress, secularism, and democracy—and they question its universality or suitability for the non-Western world. While at home with concepts like "reason" and "heterodoxy", Sen considers the notion of modernity "befuddling" and "irrelevant as a pointer of merit or demerit in assessing contemporary priorities". To those who see a problem with importing modernity in India (including Ashis Nandy), he responds with characteristic precision :

> The point is that there is no escape from the necessity to scrutinize and assess ideas and proposals no matter whether they are seen as pro-modern or anti-modern. For example, if we have to decide what policies to support in education, health care, or social security, the modernity or non-modernity of any proposal is neither here nor there. The relevant question is how these policies would affect the lives of people... It is in a way to show one's faith in the continuity of an epistemological tradition of the world over.

To those protective of the Indian masses against the "corruptions" of the West (Gandhi, for instance), Sen, like Tagore, "cannot bear to see the people eternally treated as a child." Instead, as Tagore said, it should be that "whatever we understand and enjoy in human products instantly becomes ours, wherever they might have their origin." For Sen, "the need to resist colonial dominance is, of course, important, but it has to be seen as a fight against submissive compliance, rather than as a plea for segregation and localism. The so-called 'post-colonial critique' can be significantly constructive when it is dialectically engaged—and thus strongly interactive—rather than defensively withdrawn and barriered." This gives us the true meaning of Tagore's modernity. In his essay '*tatah kim*' Tagore is critiquing western way of thinking and using nature as a political metaphor to raise the voice of resistance against the western civilizational values but at the same time saying in his novel 'Home and the World', "I do not think that it is the spirit of India to reject anything, reject any race, and reject any culture. The spirit of India has always proclaimed the ideal of unity. Tagore's desperate search was for *ananda*, the ananda (an idea of sublime bliss) which can be realized only in the unity of mankind and he lived, although, all through his life in this state of ambivalence as well as resoluteness.

Both the notions of universalism with a difference and cosmopolitanism springing from vernacular roots are dramatically at odds with the dominant discourse and debates within the charmed circle of contemporary British and North American analytical philosophy.

❑❑

Chapter Thirteen

Tagore's Idea of India in the Context of Post-Colonialism

The critics are not in agreement whether the term should be used with or without hyphen : i. e. 'Post-colonial' and 'postcolonial' have different meanings. The hyphenated term 'Post-colonialism' marks a historical period as is suggested by phrases like 'after colonialism', 'after independence', 'after the end of empire' whereas the term 'postcolonialism' referring to all the characteristics of a society or culture from the era of colonization and its aftermath, the anti-colonialism to the present time of global imperialism. However both these terms are also used interchangeably.

One thing should be kept in mind that there is no essential 'political disjunction' between anti-colonialism and post-colonialism. In many ways the latter may be viewed almost an extension of the former–'a decentred anti-colonial network' fighting :

(i) The challenge of eurocentricism and enslavement not only of lands but minds and debunking the western notion of universalism and orientalism;

(ii) Global imperialism to rejuvenate native culture and its symbols, indigenous intellectual traditions and histories of popular protest and create counter modernity;

(iii) the neo-colonial avatars within the society to undo the ideological heritage of colonialism;

(iv) as critical insiders the gender and caste bias, and communal predisposition and making people hear the unheard voice of the subalterns

(v) the bureaucratic state violence termed as political action inspired resistance and protests in the colonial times in the action and writings of Tagore and Gandhi in India and in the post colonial period the dynamics of violence in the Algerean war of independence aroused Sartre, Frantz Fanon, Althusser, Lyotard, Derrida and many to write against it.

European intellectuals became aware of the challenges to European control and dominance from the Philippines, Cuba, Puerto Rico, China,Morocco and South Africa. They were influenced by the Bolshevik Revolution (1917) which ideologically and openly opposed traditional European imperialism and colonialism and established global networks such as Communist International, or The Third International or Comintern founded in Moscow in March 1919, for the purpose of undermining the imperial system. Post colonial studies developed from those earlier moments but it expanded in the course of time by infusing in it the other ideological modes of resistance against imperialism.

The Subaltern Studies Group (SSG) was begun by the historian Ranajit Guha in India in 1980s and it was further enriched by amalgamating the perspectives and insights of Critical Studies pioneered by Birmingham Centre for Contemporary Cultural Studies and led by Raymond Williams, E. P. Thompson and above all Stuart Hall. Cultural Studies scholars allied with post colonial and subaltern theorists in Australia such as Bill Ashcroft, Gareth Griffiths, Helen Tiffin and Ranajit Guha.

This interesting academic ensemble was further stimulated by feminist scholars, chiefly Gayatri Chakravorty Spivak. The SSG collectives borrowed the ideas of Antonio Gramsci (1881-1937) and adopted his terminology especially 'hegemony' and the 'subaltern'. They found in the Italian's writings (mainly The Prison Notebooks) "theoretical modes of understanding applicable to the developing world, to feudal incrustations and religions backwardness, to weak and wavering bourgeoisie seeking ways to constrict hegemony"(Sil, 2008, p. 22).

Postcolonialism created a space for writers and activists to register their resistance and protest against colonial brutality and their nefarious planning of destroying the culture of the subjugated by the culture of the subjugators and at the same time it brought a real change of mind and planning in the study of literature, history and social sciences of the colonial people and after their achieving independence.

Meenakshi Mukherjee rightly observes :

> Post-colonialism is not merely a chronological label referring to the period after the demise of empires. It is ideologically an emancipatory concept particularly for the students of literature outside the Western world, because it makes us i) interrogate many concepts of the study of literature that we were made to take for granted, ii) enabling us not only to read our own texts in our own terms, but also iii) to re-interpret some of the old canonical texts from Europe from the perspective of our specific historical and geographical location .

When Tagore in a letter to Rev C.F. Andrews said that my India is an idea and not a geographical expression :

(i) he was in fact trying to deglamorize the imperial notion of creating an empire.

(ii) and the notion of nationalism giving importance to the territory of a country and related violence:

(iii) and to stress the equal and common human destiny the idea of human unity because of the very nature of its existence, and also because it inhabits a contiguous and inseparable geographical space.

If India is an idea, what is that idea?

Certain key themes configure Tagore's idea of India. Rather than the glorified version of India produced in geographical or political nationalism.

(i) The idea of the humanity of our God or the divinity of man the eternal. In simple language it is the Divinity in Man.

Tagore in his Hibbert lectures spoke about the religion of Man in which the infinite became defined in humanity and came close to human beings so as to need his/her love and cooperation. This is also known as realization of the soul or the unity of the finite with the Infinite. This is called Universal Humanism. The idea of India is the idea of Universal Humanism.

Nothing is greater than the person; he is the ultimate goal.

(ii) Man must reveal in his own personality the Supreme Person (Jivan Devata) by his disinterested activities. This is what Tagore calls surplus in man. What distinguishes Tagore from other great poetical genius of his time is the unity of inspiration described so insightfully in his poetry :

> The Infinite wants the finite's intimate comradeship
> And the finite wishes to lose itself in the Infinite.

But Tagore did not link the pursuance of what he perceived to be a higher ideal with any degree of national superiority.

(iii) 'This Infinite Personality of man is not to be achieved in single individuals, but in one grand harmony of all human races. The darkness of egoism which will have to be destroyed is the egoism of the people.'

(iv) Tagore, as a "counter–modernist critic of the imperial West" (to borrow the phrase coined by Ashis Nandy) held that in the nineteenth century, the West believed in "freedom of personality." At that time there was a possibility of cultural dialogue between the East and the West. But the modern West seemed to be engrossed in the "fetish of nationalism", bringing with it "dehumanization, de-spiritualization, deformity and doom." This has led to a separation between the two hemispheres, as Tagore sarcastically holds :

> We in the East believe in Personality. In the West you have your admiration for power. But that does not mean by this kind of a statement Tagore is trying to prove the superiority of the East over the West.

(Personality is described as the inner unity of his ideas and creativity/action and the unity of the individual with the universal or as said above the Infinite Personality).

Tagore had faith in the Enlightened West, which, he thought, would redeem the East from its dark dungeons of superstitions. But this belief was thwarted when Tagore observed :

> But how short was that twilight of a vanishing age, of chivalry, of idealism higher and greater than one's own nationality... you do not realize what terrible menace you have become to man. We are afraid of you.

Tagore said in his acceptance speech of the award in1921 that the spirit of unity of all races is the message of the east to the west and quoted Upanishads to establish his point :

> "He who sees all beings in his self, and his self in all the beings does not hate any one, and knows the truth"

(v) In the unity of beings one realizes the spirit, soul or *atma*. Hence, while defining modernity, he had no hesitation to declare in Beijing in 1924 that :

> 'The impertinence of material things is extremely old. The revelation of spirit in man is modern. I am in its side, I am modern.' This 'other modernity' of Tagore is an unique phenomenon of his thinking and creative process—

Revelation of Spirit in man is the core philosophy of Tagore. Tagore's was not the lone voice during those days. Jose Ortega Y Gasset, (1883- 1955) considered to be the greatest Spanish philosopher of the modern time, developed a philosophical system known as 'ratiovitalism' ("I am I and my circumstance" : This *circunstancia* is oppressive; therefore, there is a continual dialectical interaction between Yo the person and his or her circumstances and, as a result, life is a drama that exists between necessity and freedom and it is more explicative then the Descartenian (Rene Descartes1596- 1650, Father of modern philosophy) statement "*Cogito ergo sum*" (latin phrase (French : *Je pense, donc je suis*; English : I think, therefore I am),)had said clearly that modernity brought two common elements Disorientation and Dehumanization in poetry and then affirmed that artisans are recognized by their tools. The poetical tools of the Bengali poet Tagore resembled the universal propositions of philosophy. Rabindranath is not in need of anything historical and sumptuary, particular to his time or his land.

> With a little of sun,
> With sky and clouds,
> With mountain and thirst,
> With storms and river banks,
> With a door and frame of window from
> which to look out,
> and above all, with all a loving favour
> for God, He produces his songs.

This lyric poetry thus consists of universal things which are and have been everywhere and transforms it into a bird eager to sing from every branch. Then Ortega includes a sentence of Tagore :

> 'In the creation of God, nothing has an end. All which is true remains.'

When Tagore said that modernity is freedom of mind and not slavery of taste he was actually hinting at a critical openness that allows one to retrieve, rediscover and redefine elements of culture in a creative way, by a return of pride in one's roots, while looking ahead and hence when in the modern times Tagore could still write :

> Thou hast made me endless
> Such is Thy pleasure
> (First song of English Gitanjali or Song offerings)

Yeats could not but talk of a particular historical strain in the western modernist movement :

> Things fall apart; the centre cannot hold;
> (W.B. Yeats, The Second Coming)

Yeats' line of the poem reveals that Europe with all its materialist advancement and prosperity seemed to be haunted by a TS Eliot — Wasteland feeling of inner desolation so prominent in her poetry and art - What Heidegger was to call the feeling of homelessness?

Tagore's poems speaks of the spiritual bond between the self and the universal self and rejects any kind of narrow approach related to humanity.

(vi) Tagore envisioned India as standing for man's existential search for the highest ideals of truth, where truth is perceived not only as an objective law but as a state to be realized by man through :

Detachment,
Self-effacement and
Compassion.

(vii) He saw wisdom rather than wealth, as the higher human goal, and Buddha and the state of sannyas (renunciation) as the highest ideals of the land.

(viii) Tagore conceived of identity in terms of relationship rather than confrontation.

(ix) India committed to a civil society and Tagore believed that historically India's strength lay in her 'social civilization' whereby her people learnt to live in relative harmony by ignoring the successive invasions and conquest. To him society was an 'end in itself' without an 'ulterior purpose', whereas, he held, the Nation state made individuals bend their personal wills to the 'National will' with impersonal goals.

He put his faith firmly in education to find freedom from this predicament and mentioned India was always a knowledge society and spread this message.

(x) Lastly as said by Tagore, "I love India not because I cultivate the idolatry of geography, not because I have had the chance to be born in her soil, but because she has saved through tumultuous ages the living words that have issued from the illuminated consciousness of her great sons :

> *Satyam, jnanam, Anantam Brahma*, *Brahma* is truth, *Brahma* is wisdom, *Brahma* is infinite :
>
> *Santam, Sivam, Advaitam*, peace is in *Brahma*, goodness is in *Brahma*, and the unity of all beings.

Tagore's "A Vision of India's History" is a synoptic sketch of the main of Indian history, is an attempt to write 'living history' not the living past. In his "A Vision of India's History" Tagore opts for a mythico-symbolic reinterpretation of India's history and tries to locate the essence of history in the epics and *Puranas*Mythical histories) of India. Tagore holds that the Western critics are ready to judge us with a sneering sense of superiority when comparing India's history with their own. They never take into consideration the enormous burden of difficulty which Indian civilization has taken upon itself from its commencement. Tagore, thereby, indicates the cultural compatibility that India as a civilization has been preaching since its inception, opposing it to the antithetical notion of Western nationalism : an ideology which has derived its theoretical and material consolidation from eighteenth century.

Tagore was very critical of the existing notion of history of his times. He said, these histories do not answer the question, where were the people of India? As if people of India did not exist, only those who maimed and killed alone exist.

Tagore's vision of the past encapsulates two themes :

> The interrelationship of communities, and the crisis
> of his times.

The history of India has been the history of the struggle between first Aryans and non-Aryans (racial strife) and later by Brahmins and Kshatreiyas (within the Aryans). After the racial streife unity was sought not by exterminationof all inherent differences but by toleration of these distinctive differences within the bonds of adjustment. He (Rama of Ramayana) who strove to bring about the reconciliation between Aryans and non-Aryans is worshipped to this day as an Avatara (incarnation of God).

The struggle between Brahmins and kshatriyas was between confirmmity and order insocial organization and creative spirit of man, which seelks freedom and love for its self expression. It was the pull of two opposite principles : self preservation of Brahmins and and self expansion of the kshatriyas or principle of stability and principle of movement. Brahmins represent the static ideal of society which spans into elaboration of the different forms of ritualism and set up sectarian barriers between clan and classes. Kshatriyas developed the principle which was for expansion and inclusion.

Due to diversity of their duties and profession the Brahmins and the kshatriyas formed two separate clans, one representing wisdom and the other courage. The rigidity of Brahminism was against unity and the moving spirit of life unites.

In Tagore's view the two were interrelated, because the crisis had been caused by overmuch skepticism and superciliousness on the part of one people towards another.

The assumption of civilizational superiority by the West was founded on its understanding of history as an account of the triumph of man over nature, of man over man, and of the mechanical over the abstract. This history was a narrative that prioritized only one set of values, concerning on the political dominance of the vocal minority over the silent majority, a position that Tagore wanted to disclaim.

According to Louise Blakeney Williams, Tagore believed in the 'cyclic' theory of history which rejected all kinds of teleologies and periodization. Stressing Tagore's fascination with diversity, and his assumption that all ages manifesting "the values of a superior tradition were equivalent and interchangeable", Williams holds that in this outlook of history, the key distinction was between superior and inferior traditions of values, rather than that which occurred earlier or later in time, or that which was from the West or the East. Because of this, and because history would not witness the triumph of one dichotomy over another, a nation did not have to exclude any part of its past, any group of people, or any features of other nations from its identity.

Hence Tagore outlined a history of the evolution of consciousness undeterred by racial conflicts.

From the many instances of Tagore's symbolic/poetic reconstruction of India's history one deserves mention. He views that in ancient India a dichotomy arose between the Brahmin cult of Ritualism (represented in the myth of Bhrigu) and the religion of love (embodied in the figure of Krishna, a Kshatriya.) Tagore holds the mark of Brahmin Bhrigu's kick, which Vishnu carries on his breast, is a mythrelic of the original conflict.

The story of the Ramayana is to be interpreted, as Tagore put it in a Vision of India's History, not as a matter of historical fact but in the plane of ideas and in fact as a marvellous parable of reconciliation, the historical questions asked need not be straightforward, and may even be highly speculative, such as Rabindranath Tagore's interesting but bold conjecture that the mythical version of King Janamejaya's ruthless serpent sacrifice may quite possibly stand for an actual historical event involving an attempted extermination of the entire Naga race by the dominant powers in ancient India. Whether or not it is easy to satisfy our curiosity (it may not always be possible to settle a debate regarding what actually happened), truth has an obvious enough role in exercises of this kind. In fact, curiosity is a demand for truth on a particular subject.

Some critics claim that this abandonment of history altogether for the preference of a historical constructions of myth, is truly the indigenous understanding of the past, since it not only subverts the "master narratives authorized by imperialism", but also has an authenticity because it is located in the domain of pre-colonial and pre-modern societies.

In many ways, Tagore's historical concept was similar to that of Tolstoy. Berlin says that like Tagore, Tolstoy was aware that conventional historical narrative omits the "inner" events, while inscribing 'political'/public-events; yet 'it is they, the "inner" events, that are the most real, the most immediate experience of human beings'. (Berlin, 1994, p.33) and thus created 'War and Peace' a historical situation that was in many ways profoundly unhistorical.

Under the post colonial perspective the main thrust of post-colonial writings is to 'establish or rehabilitate self against either European appropriation or rejection (Chris Tiffin, 1988. p. 172) There is no doubt that writers of countries like Africa, Australia, India, which have well developed metaphysical systems and resources to fall back to challenge the European perspectives and the Western modes of their representation by their conscious deployment of myth as mythical history but in the case of Tagore it was more than the exposure of European historical perspectives but to develop an all embracing universal perspective of history by rejecting the dichotomy between the East and the West. In the post colonial thinking both historians and literary theorists believe that the opposition between history and myth may have been true in the past, especially in the days of positivistic historiography , but is not tenable now. The two have a fluid relationship, because they overlap and interpenetrate.

Chapter Fourteen

Tagore : At Home in the World

I

The theme of the conference 'Tagore : At Home in the World' can have different significance. It may denote that Tagore looks at this world metaphorically sometimes as the West or else philosophically as Western modernity linking it with so called progress or otherwise ideologically as antithetical to tradition.

As for the metaphorical meaning of the theme for Tagore the World is just like a home, comfortable and congenial i.e. the world or the West and the home or the East are not in opposition but are in harmony with each other.

It can also mean philosophically that the world or the West is happily at home or is at ease in a different cultural environment i.e. in the writings of Tagore Western modernity and traditional India are properly blended together and Tagore handles this issue as says Ashis Nandi (The Illegitimacy of Nationalism, 1994, p. 1) within the format of India's 'high' culture, within her classical Sanskrit tradition, leavened on the one hand by elements of European Renaissance and modernity and on the other by India's own diverse folk or little traditions.

But did Tagore really look at these two sets of opposition as binary opposites or did he attempt to reconcile these contradictions by negotiating these two sets of opposite as one whole and gave new modes of meaning of East West relationship and Western modernity and Indian tradition?

There can be a third ideological purport of the theme. In his own novel *ghare baire,* or 'the Home and the World' (1919) Tagore describes the clash between the traditional Indian and the Western ways of life, between nationalism and universal humanism and the past and the present and gives his own meaning to Indianness and nationalism. The heroine Bimla once said, "I could not think of my house as separate from my country" or in other words it means that for Tagore the home is India. While the entire novel centres on the *sadeshi* movement (the denotative meaning of *sadeshi* is home rule but the common meaning is the nationalist movement, which began more as an economic than a political one, having as its main object the encouragement of indigenous industries), the author of the novel is not advocating it but rather warning the audience of the dangers of such a movement.

II

The paper will take up the following three issues related to the theme :

(i) The East West relationship : conflictual or complementary,

(ii) Western modernity and Indian tradition of continuity,

(iii) The issue of Nationalism

The theme has also a *fourth meaning* that it actually reveals Tagore's integrated vision of life where the home (self) and the world (Universe) are one and the same.

III

Nirod C. Choudhuri has said in his book "Thy Hand, Great Anarch!" that "historically he is the greatest product of the interaction in India of the 19th Cen., between European and Hindu life and civilization, and it remains equally significant in his life as in his works. In one sense, he may be regarded as the victim of the interaction, and in another as its prophet and even that image – fantasized in age very soon lost its tenor.

His own life was caught in the conflict which this interaction brought about and his writings stand for its achievement.

Although Tagore had crossed over the sea even in early manhood he never learned to regard the English people as anything but 'they', (author's quote) and taken in the mass, as a very unpleasant 'they'."

During his short second stay he took a positive dislike to English life. In a letter to his neice, Indira, Bibi /Bob Tagore, by quoting the *swayambar* of Indumati from *Raguvamsa* of Kalidasa clearly displayed his apathy towards the egocentricity of the Western women (Selected Letters of Rabindranath Tagore, Ed by Krishna Dutta and Andrew Robinson, 1997, p. 33) :

> Suddenly with the blasts of conch shell and bugle sound Indumati, in bridal finery supported by Shundada, enters and stands between the rows of the suitors. What a superb picture! Then she is introduced by Shunanada to the princes one by one, and to each of them Indumati makes a courteous *namashkar*, and passes on. How beautifully she does it! Though she has her individual power to reject each one, at the same time she is so respectful that her gesture seems like reverence. This is far superior to the haughty vanity of an English miss.

Tagore once said, "I want nothing else if only I can remain unknown to the entire civilized world and sitting in a corner of my country collect her love like a bee to fill my hive." On one side he had this truly unsocial nature and on the other side he had to come to England and Europe again and again for recognition and appreciation and this duality became the supreme tragedy of his existence, though, it did not affect his writings and in fact they, the other, the West had a place in his thinking.

For the Western world also the orient was the 'other' and our literature, philosophy were located in the context of Indian culture, especially religious philosophy. West developed a myopic vision of Indian thought as religious, spiritual and transcendental. The other, an inalienable entity external to one self is both a source of terror and an object of desire for the West.

Sartre's famous statement 'hell is the other' carries a strong echo of Hegel, who always defines one's identity as identity against the other either to be appropriated or to be destroyed.

By defining the identity of the self in this manner, however a European finds himself entrapped in his own contradiction. The Western mind knows well that if he succeeds in completely subjugating the 'other', the identity of his own self becomes dubious. He wants to become whole by destroying the other but without the other, he becomes nothing.

The Western view is linear and binary and so Huntington writes about the clash of civilizations between Western and Muslim civilizations each forcefully confronting the other and hence they are confused by Tagore's own description of his Bengali family as the product of a confluence of three cultures : Hindu, Mohammedan and British.

The spirit of India believes in the ideal of unity – it does not reject – comprehends all with love and sympathy. For Tagore the 'other' was never a source of reference to define one's own identity as it was for the Europeans because here the self is always self- referential.

Let us not forget that just three years before he wrote 'Gitanjali; he had written the famous novel 'Gora' which gives a most vivid account of the most anguished debates which were raging within the Hindu society at the beginning of the 20th century, no less passionate and self searching than what Thomas Mann was to depict later in his famous novel 'The Magic Mountain' concerning the dark and troubled state of European civilization. Two novels about two destinies.

Thomas Mann broods over the threatened collapse of the civilized values, which constitute the identity of Europe. Tagore, on the other hand, reflecting over the crisis of Hindu identity which is being threatened precisely by those 'civilized values' of Europe which were being forced on a society that had no choice but to accept or reject them. This is the message of Gora and Tagore's approach to Western civilization and the realization of India's identity. Gora in his journey from communalism, sectarianism, religious conservatism to the ideals of humanism says at the end of the novel :

> I am Bharatiya. Within me there is no conflict
> between communities, whether Hindu or Muslim

> or kristan. Today all the castes of Bharat are my caste. For me there is nothing bigger than my country- I am not beyond the pain and happiness, knowledge and ignorance of the total India, (Gora, tran. Sujit Mukherjee, 1997, p. 475).

This is India's vision of human unity. This includes the entire world in it and rejects, as said earlier, any kind of narrow nationalism. Tagore says it clearly that we have missed the character of India as one related to the world. India has always sought to find the oneness of existence through the multifariousness of the universe. Here the spirit is to acknowledge the whole world as one's family as conceived in the Vedic discourse : *vasudhaiva kutumbukam.* This is definitely different from what the Greek philosopher Diagenes of Sinope has said in 412 BC, 'I am a citizen of the world' because it does not in any prove one's identity as a member of a family.

This idea of *vasudhaiva kutumbukam* is India's all-embracing age old vision of human unity. This includes the entire world in it and rejects any kind of narrow nationalism. Tagore says it clearly that we have missed the character of India as one related to the world. India has always sought to find the oneness of existence through the multifariousness of the universe.

Tagore posits the idea that the history of the growth of freedom is the history of the perfection of human relationship and hence i) freedom and ii) unity of mankind are the two voices of Tagore which were two very important aspects of India's civilizational values.

IV

Let me here present my first thesis by rejecting a well-entrenched view about Tagore that his main contention was to bring a synthesis between the West and the East for a true resurgence of India and a well-meaning message of spirituality to the West.

On the contrary his theory was that there is no other way open to us in the East, but to go along with Europeanization and to go through it. Only through this voyage into the foreign and strange can we win back our own selfhood. Going through does not mean acceptance but understanding it. Tagore further justifies this view while giving the Nobel Prize acceptance speech on 26th May 1921 at Stockholm (The English Writings of Tagore, vol iii, ed by Sisir Kumar Das, 1996, 966. On 13th November 1913 the Nobel Prize for Tagore was declared, however, Tagore could not be present at the Nobel Award Ceremony on 10th December 1913, but sent a telegram accepting the Prize, which was received by the British *charge d'affairs* in Sweden on his behalf and on 29th January 1914 at a special ceremony in Calcutta Lord Carmichael, Governor of Bengal, delivered the medal and citation on Tagore. There is no reference available of Tagore making a speech on that occasion. However, in a function after about eight years at Stockholm on 26th May 1921he made a speech, which is recorded in the archives of Swedish Academy as his Nobel Prize Acceptance Speech). In his Acceptance Speech Tagore said :

> I do not think that it is the spirit of India to reject anything, reject any race, and reject any culture. The spirit of India has always proclaimed the ideal of unity… Now, when in the present time of political unrest the children of the same great India cry for rejection of the West I feel hurt… We must discover the most profound unity, the spiritual unity between the different races. We must go deeper down to the spirit of man and find out the great bond of unity which is to be found in all human races... Man is not to fight with other human races, other human individuals but his work is to bring about reconciliation and peace and restore the bonds of friendship and love.

The voyage into the foreign creates a space where one can talk to another tradition, feel it, touch it and then realise one's own power, own self. It is a radical departure from an approach arising from colonized consciousness, where the encounter was always conceived between the spirituality of the East and materialism of the West. And so he could in the essay 'East and West 'included in the book of essays 'Creative Unity' end it with a rebuttal of the imperialist notions of incompatibility voiced by Rudyard Kipling :

> It is true that they (East & West) are not showing any real sign of meeting. But the reason is because the West has not sent out its humanity to meet the man in the East but only its machine. Therefore, the poet's line has to be changed into something like this. Man is man, Machine is Machine and never the twain shall wed (English Writings of Tagore, vol ii, ed. Sisir Kumar Das, 1996, 536).

The idea of the East as some shadowy, threatening 'other' with which the West is in sharp conflict, and the essentialising of East and West into two simple and contrastive categories has a long history and can be traced back to the time of Herodotus but that history is now a past history (Herodotus, the Greek historian (440 BC), who never visited India but wrote about India and surprisingly not at all in a laudable term. At the most one can say his description of India was imaginary, Herodotus, The History of the Persian wars, George Rawlinson, tran. 1862).

By using the term 'buffered' and 'porous' Charles Taylor (A Secular Age,2007, 40-41), asserted that one remains a bounded and buffered self if one remains suspicious of the porous self of the enchanted world or the enchanted East. Buffered self always has an anthropocentric identity which makes one blind and insensitive to whatever lies beyond this ordered human life and its instrumental-rational project and makes one a part of the complex modern-European concept of 'civilization' and blind and insensitive to the porous self, who is open in his thought and lives in freedom and also outside with nature and even beyond.

Imitating our poet-philosopher Tagore, one can add that "where knowledge is free" and "where the clear stream of reason has not lost its way in the dreary desert sand of dead habit", there and then the buffered self is demolished to allow the porous self to enter and flower.

This is the meaning which Taylor (A secular Age, Harvard University Press, 2007) accepted when he said that recognizing the otherness means accepting the inner meaning of his (self) experience, thought and culture as making sense of itself from its self-interpretation, and not receiving it from a foreign judgment.

The concept of human unity so assiduously nurtured by Tagore is now at the centre of philosophical discussion in the West. Emmanuel Levinas, in fact, proposed a model for thinking the self-other relation in his book "Totality and Infinity" (1961) which Derrida revisited in his own essay "Violence and Metaphysics" (1967) which states that the philosophy seeks to grasp the other and so doing reduces the 'absolute alterity' of the other to the self-same. However, Levinas sees this operation in the work of Husserl in his 'Cartesian Meditations' which constitutes the other in terms of the self-same as an alter ego and here the ambivalence of the Western mind becomes visible because the alter ego is not the self-same.

In fact both Emmanuel Levinas, the most celebrated philosopher of the contemporary world, while discussing the issue of the self and the other, says, 'The foundation of ethics consists in the obligation to respond to the other.' 'In being for the other only the sense of responsibility (goodness, mercy, charity) calls forth.' For Jacque Derrida, another very celebrated philosopher, says, 'the foundation of ethics is hospitality, the readiness and the inclination to welcome the other into one's home.' Levinas's and Derrida's theories of ethics – responsibility and hospitality- no doubt, reveal a new consciousness emerging in the West about its relationship with the East but the view of the West is still just a broad view of particularism. It holds out the possibility of an acceptance of the other as different but of equal standing. This is no where nearer to the Upanishadic idea of oneness, as referred to by Tagore in his acceptance speech delivered on 26th may 1921 at Stockholm :

> *Yastu sarvani bhutani aatmanyevanupashyati!*
> *Sarvabhuteshu chatmanam tatonavijugupsate!!* (Isopanishad)
> One who perceives all the beings in his own self and own self in all the beings does not hate any one anymore.

This notion of complete identity, though a reality for India and Tagore, it is still a distance hope for the West.

The present Western concept of 'multiculturalism' and the slogan that 'The World is a village' are not simple concepts or statements but are cleverly employed for use as handy political weapons to hoodwink the minorities or to surreptitiously invite other countries to the war, an unholy war, against terror. It is not an invitation to be a member of the village but to conscript one as a part of the unholy war. If one refuses to be conscripted one cannot be a member of the village. These concepts can never come anywhere nearer to Tagore's concept of human unity. Tagore says, "When the science of meteorology knows the earth's atmosphere as continuously one, affecting the different parts of the world differently, but in a harmony of adjustments, it knows and attains truth. And similarly, we must know that the great mind of man is one, working through the many differences which are needed to ensure the full result of its fundamental unity. When we understand this truth in a disinterested spirit, it teaches us to respect all the differences in man that are real, yet remain conscious of our oneness; and to know that perfection of unity is not in uniformity, but in harmony", (Creative Unity pp. 171–72). Tagore always conceived of the self as an individual, as a part of humanity and also one with the Universal Self. This threesome way of reckoning brings the humanity in one nest and is the higher unity, which is different from corporate globalization or what Tagore called the "mere political or commercial basis of unity."

A meeting of races for Tagore is unity of man. (Tagore, The Voice of Humanity', in English Writings, vol iii, 523 also see Tagore, A Vision of India's History, Reprint, Calcutta : Visva-Bharati, 1962, pp. 31-32).

V

On the issue of modernity and Indian tradition of continuity both Tagore and Gandhi warned us in the beginning of the 20th century about the danger of developing a colonial mentality or mental colonization. Tagore said in those days that true modernism is freedom of mind and not slavery of taste. It is independence of thought and action, not tutelage under European school masters. ('Nationalism' English Writings, vol iii, p. 446) He observed, "You must apply your Eastern mind, your spiritual strength, your love of simplicity, your recognition of social obligations in order to cut out a new path for this great unworldly car of progress shrieking out its loud discards as it runs." (Ibid, p. 439)

In the same essay Tagore said, "Once you did solve the problems of man to your own satisfaction, you had your philosophy of life and evolved your own art of living. All this you must apply now to the present situation and out of it will appear a new creation and not a mere repetition, a creation which the soul of your people will own for itself and proudly offer to the world as its tribute to the welfare of man." (Ibid, p. 439)

By redefining the terms of discourse in terms of the creative expression of Asian autonomy and individuality in the pursuit of 'true or other modernity' in all fields, Tagore and Gandhi were setting, as it were, a fresh agenda to understand our modernity. Tagore even went further to define other modernism in 1924 in Beijing and said, "The impertinence of material things is extremely old. The revelation of spirit in man is modern. I am on its side, for I am modern."

One can realize that the ethic of 'authenticity' or 'expressive individualism' of modernity has shifted the place of the spiritual in human life, at least as lived by many, even during Tagore's time. Tagore had the impression that the present age suffered from a threatened loss of total meaning. So the need for meaning, for Tagore, could be met by a recovery of transcendence or by our own depth sense. In one such attempt, which has had a great impact on the history of modernity, 'Nature' becomes and always was in Indian tradition, not just the ensemble of natural reality, but a profound source in us where man and nature are in mysterious harmony and this model of unity with nature, as Tagore explains, became the revelation of spirit of man and revealed to us Tagore's attempt to gather together the scattered moments of meaning into some kind of whole. So deep is Tagore's love of nature that to him every aspect of nature becomes a symbol of beauty. He does not love nature for its own sake, but because he views it as an attribute of the divine; not for the abundance of joy that it brings into life, but for the intimations it gives of a higher spiritual life. To him even a blade of grass or an atom of dust brings a message from unknown. In fact for Tagore nature and man or society are revelations of the divine spirit.

It is generally understood in the West that the nation as a political institute is the product of European Enlightment and Industrial

Revolution, which resulted in the decline of religious modes of thought and rise of western mode of secularism and also face-off between modernity and tradition and also humanism and spirituality. Tagore always looked at it as one and the same.

VI

In Western terminology, modernism is a breaking away from established rules, traditions and conventions, and implies fresh ways of looking at man's position and functions in the universe, and inheres in some cases remarkable experiments in form and style.

In 1784, Immanual Kant, in a short essay, Enlightment, speaking in the same vein, was talking about the way the present was different from the past. In this difference he was trying to draw out the meaning of Enlightment, or the definition of modernism.

All the major moderns of Europe, James Joyce, Ezra Pound, Stravinsky, Picasso—all have built on romanticism but at the same time tried to break away from it—breaking away from established rules, traditions and conventions and, as already said, imply fresh ways of looking at man's function in the universe.

For Tagore any great art is the expression of both the tradition and the actual. To be uprooted from tradition is tantamount to alienation from one's own self. Tagore's everlasting credit is that his great cosmopolitan vision never sacrificed the richest possible sense of tradition.

May I now here present my second thesis that for Tagore what India needed was to regain her selfhood through a process of decolonization of the self itself, which no outside agency but only their own tradition could have set in motion. West sought to colonize India's sense of time and establish that its present being merely a corruption of the past.

In India, modernism as a phenomenon or value is not an absolutely unrelated one without reference to the past or the future. It absorbs in it traditional values as well as new innovations and is indicated by the term 'continuity'. It is essential to do that because the spirit of India, as says Tagore or as the writers have observed over the ages, is not to reject anything. Everything has a place here as an alternative. India lives with many alternatives which become part of the continuity of thought and creativity and hence the choice which Gandhi or Tagore offered to us was not tradition versus modernism, but the choice of both versus the forced acceptance of one. This is the Indian way of thinking. Our thinking is not logo-centric and exclusive, but symbolic or inclusive and hence India has no problem to live with many life choices and this is possible when as said by Tagore, one has the freedom of mind, and also as he mentions in his essay on 'Modernity in Literature', element of universality as well as permanence and profundity of aesthetic joy.

But for all practical purposes, one can say that whatever is western is modern. This kind of an idea is based on a counterfeit concept very cleverly designed by the colonial masters that westernization is modernization.

There is no doubt that the largest corpus of ideas, thoughts, modes and methods, etc., of our life in the present and recent times are admittedly western by origin, yet the fact remains that in the process of our becoming modern something was happening within ourselves, that, in spite of our acceptance of western modernization, we were doubtful about its value and results, and were constantly searching for our own modernity.

The West develops through substitution and it writes itself again and again. India develops through accommodation. A belief was created during the colonial time and still continuing in the post-colonial time that progressive West is universal and the regressive East is particular. This kind of a notion of cultural uniqueness goes against the concept of human unity so assiduously nurtured by Tagore by introducing the notion of universal humanity :

> Oh my mind, awake heroically on the shores of the
> ocean of universal humanity.

It is, as says Tagore, the spirit of Bharat which is like a sea of great humanity where all are merged in one body (*bharat tirtha*).

Here new ideas may supplant older ones, but the older ones linger on. They are allowed to co-exist with what is new. Here one does not reject to create one's modernity. When Tagore said that modernity is freedom of mind and not slavery of taste he was actually hinting at a critical openness that allows one to retrieve, rediscover and redefine elements of culture in a creative way, by a return of pride in one's roots, while looking ahead and hence when in the modern times Tagore could still write :

> Thou hast made me endless
> Such is Thy pleasure
> (First song of English Gitanjali or Song offerings)

Yeats could not but talk of a particular historical strain in the western modernist movement :

> Things fall apart; the centre cannot hold;
> (W.B. Yeats, The Second Coming)

Yeats' line of the poem reveals that Europe with all its materialist advancement and prosperity seemed to be haunted by a TS Eliot – Wasteland feeling of inner desolation so prominent in her poetry and art - What Heidegger was to call the feeling of homelessness?

Tagore's poems speaks of the spiritual bond between the self and the universal self and rejects any kind of narrow approach related to humanity. This brings us to the issue of nationalism.

VII

Tagore said in his essay on 'Nationalism in India' (Nationalism,1917) that those of us in India who have come under the delusion that mere political freedom will make us free have accepted their lessons from the West as the gospel truth and lost their faith in humanity.

Tagore, once in his letter to C.F.Andrews, very clearly said that 'I love India but my India is an idea (*chinmaya*) and not a geographical expression (*mrinmaya*)', (Tagore to Andrews, in letters to a friend, 22nd July 1920, 119). He further says, therefore, I am not a patriot —I shall ever seek my compatriots all over the world. (Ibid). He would further elaborate that the word nation is not in our language. India has never had a real sense of nationalism. Society is in the core of India's civilization. Politics is in the core of Western civilization and hence the importance which Europe gives to freedom we give to liberation of the soul.

While talking about nationalism he deviated both from colonialist historiography and the nationalist ideology and spoke of that vision of India's history where nation is spelled with a small 'n' which meant society which was relevant to humanity and avoided to use the term nation with a capital 'N' meant a nation-state or the 'Nation' of the West that has a self-destructive tendency, and turns violent and snatches one's freedom and spreads homogenized universalism and makes one selfish and exclusive- oriented person and also violent It will be interesting to note that every year 80% of the killing in the world is committed by the states. To name only a few of the gigantic evils perpetrated in the name of nationalism by the nation-states are, one, by the British colonial rulers in Kenya, who, for quelling the rebels against its colonial rule killed about 1,50,000 Kenyans in 1950s and the other was the genocide in Bangladesh by Pakistan in the 1970s claiming three million lives. Tagore's one of the central preoccupations in his writings was to raise his voice against violence which he thought was a crime committed against humanity.

The best example of his description of violence with full of pain and suffering is to be seen in his letter to the viceroy in1919 while relinquishing his knighthood or in his travelogue '*Parashya*' in which he relates the penchant description of a Christian chaplain, attached to a British air force division stationed at Baghdad, as how extremely easy to kill so many people dwelling in the desert by ferocious aerial bombing without any fear of repercussion. When asked for a message by the Christian chaplain he wrote :

> Man has accepted this dust-laden earth for his dwelling place, for the enacting of the drama of his tangled life ever waiting for a call of perfection from the boundless depth of purity surrounding him in a translucent atmosphere. If in an evil moment man's cruel history should spread its black wings to invade that realm of divine dreams with its cannibalistic greed and fratricidal ferocity then God's curse will certainly descend upon us for that hideous desecration and the last curtain will be rung down upon the world of Man for whom God feels ashamed.

VIII

Tagore was for non-parochial, inclusive nationalism relevant to humanity where the difference between home and what Bimala says country and the world melts away and borders between the two disappear or blurring of frontiers becomes a reality.

Tagore did not reject nationalism but formed his own understanding of it by studying what was authentic in his country's history. Tagore said, "We, in India, must make up our minds that we cannot borrow other people's history, and that if we stifle our own we are committing suicide, when you borrow things that do not belong to your life, they only serve to crush your life... I believe that it does India no good to compete with western civilization in its own field... India is no beggar of the West. (Anthony Soares, X, 1970, p. 106). Tagore was convinced that :

(i) It was essential for us to fight against social injustice rather than political freedom;

(ii) To work for an adjustment of races, to acknowledge the real differences between them where these exist, and yet seek some basis of unity. The basis for this tradition has been built in India at the social level, not the political, as explained by Tagore, through saints like Nanak, Kabir, Chaitanya and others. It is this solution—unity through acknowledgement of real differences between them where these exist that India has to offer to the world.

He made it clear that

(a) "Patriotism cannot be our final spiritual shelter; my refuge is humanity. I will not buy glass for the price of diamonds, and I will never allow patriotism to triumph over humanity as long as I live", (He says this as early as 1908, and puts his position about nationalism succinctly in a letter replying to the criticism of Abala Bose, the wife of a great Indian scientist, Jagadish Chandra Bose, quoted by Amartya Sen in his article on 'Tagore and his India', (1986). One can further refer to Nikhil of "The Home and the World" who refuses to change his views about patriotism : "I am willing to serve my country; but my worship I reserve for Right which is far greater than my country. To worship my country as a god is to bring a curse upon it." It is no wonder that his motto for Viswabharati was *yatra viswam bhavet eka nidam* where the world meets in a nest;

(b) to accept the concept of nationalism from the West would mean selling our own inheritance. He was opposed to the idea of the nation or of the Indian nationalists, who wanted India to join the bandwagon of nationalism, because it would have compromised India's history and identity as a culture and bring it under the shadow of the West (Anthony Soares X, ed. Rabindranath Tagore, 1970, 106).

(c) The idea of the Indian nation should at no cost supersede the idea of Indian civilization. Tagore was probably encouraged as further mentioned by Ashis Nandi(The Illegitimacy of Nationalism, 1994,7) by the entry into Indian politics of a person who openly declared that his
   (i) nationalism was intense internationalism and
   (ii) it was not exclusive because it recognized the eternal truth.

This new entrant was Gandhi who said that violent nationalism otherwise known as imperialism is the curse whereas non-violent nationalism is a necessary condition of corporate or civilized life and Indian freedom movement therefore was India's contribution to peace.

But there are many who find some kind of ambivalence in his idea of nationalism. They think that Tagore's critique of nationalism is a little lofty and far-fetched—and are layered in atavistic spiritualism and romantic idealism. Tagore could perhaps be faulted for impracticality; his vision for India was too sublime and unrealisable in an imperfect world. (Imagining 'One World' : Rabindranath Tagore's Critique of Nationalism, Mohammad A. Quayum, 2004). However, much of their query is how a person can practice anti-imperialist politics his entire life by rejecting the idea of nationalism and even patriotism? As said earlier Tagore believed in non-parochial inclusive nationalism or as said by many as unself-critical nationalism and also believed in patriotism which rejected violent nationalism hence it was easy for him to denounce imperialism all through his life so much so that in his last stirring lecture 'The Crisis of Civilization' at the age of 80 he did not hesitate to mention the impertinent challenge by the imperial ruler to our conscience. There was no politics in it. He was only talking about a universal struggle for political justice and cultural dignity and a protest against violence or any kind of narrow nationalism and spoke about a world embracing and inclusive nationalism which became the basis of Pundit Nehru for creating India's future as a liberal, secular democracy.

Tagore was sure that exclusive patriotism takes away your freedom with the help of which you can accept the total universe. It was possible for Tagore to reject the extreme form of nationalism and patriotism because for him Indian unity was primarily a social fact, not a political agenda.

Both Tagore and Gandhi created a moral universe and made it a part of politics and gave a bigger lofty meaning to nationalism. Tagore but at the same time spoke loudly about (i) living in freedom and (ii) reasoning in freedom and expressed this, as mentioned above, in his letter to the Viceroy of India after the Amritsar massacre. Tagore analysed the nature of brutality and opposed the attack on humanity. It was in 1919 but long before that Tagore was always very apprehensive of 'the naked passion of self-love of nations, 'drunken delirium of greed', 'vengeance' and 'burst in a violence of fury' and wrote a poem 'The Sunset of the Century" on the last day of the last century(19th) in a mood of outrage and disenchantment :

> The crimson glow of light on the horizon is not the
> light of the dawn of peace, my Motherland.

It is the glimmer of the funeral pyre burning to ashes the vast flesh,—the self-love of the Nation, —dead under it as own excess :

> The morning waits behind the patient dark of the East,
> Meek and silent.

Tagore knew it well that unity brought by a kind of nationalism which is based on hatred against somebody or another nation can be very temporary. In India people were united against the British by spreading hatred against them. But as soon as the cause of hatred vanished the artificial unity also fell like a pack of cards as could be evinced in the division of the country in 1947.

IX

Today the new reading of nationalism by Tagore looks so relevant. Post-colonial critics such as Ernest Gellner, Benedict Anderson and Tom Nairn have pointed out how nationalism cultivates the sentiments of irrationality, prejudice and hatred in people. In spite of the fact that Benedict Anderson (Imagined Communities : Reflections on the origin and spread of Nationalism,1991) defining the nation as 'imagined' and Ernest Gellner, (Nations and Nationalism, 1983) as 'invention' and 'fabrication', and Tom Nairn (The Break Up of Britain : Crisis and Neo-Nationalism, 1977) as a 'militant movement by the community', the phenomenon enjoyed and still enjoys profound political legitimacy in modern society and remains the most powerful force in twentieth century politics.

But the West is now seriously thinking if the nation-state has failed. Frantz Fanon has explained that although the objective of nationalism is to create a horizontal relationship and fraternity within its people, in reality the nation never speaks of the hopes and aspirations of the entire 'imagined community', and hierarchy, factional hegemony, inequality and exploitation remain a daily occurrence in its body, ("National Culture", The Post Colonial Studies Reader, eds. Bill Ashcroft, Gareth Griffiths, and Helen Tiffin, 1997, 170). In the novel *Ghare baire* Tagore has insightfully and shrewdly anticipated in Sandip's actions all these pitfalls of nationalism pointed out by later literary-cultural critics.

Today and the recent past, in the name of nationalism ethnic nationalism unfolded itself resulting in two world wars, costing millions of lives. Tagore's assertive denunciation of the Nation proved prophetic with the outbreak of two world wars;

In India nationalism has turned into ethnic politics which is creating all kinds of problem for India. The violent nationalism is used by the terrorist to spread terrorism and violence. On top of it in the name of nationalism one may find only death and conflicts in the 3rd world countries of Asia and Africa.

The countries of Africa fought against colonialism and racism but now the net result is that these countries are the dens of corruption, cruelty and impertinency. Now nationalism looks like a dark elemental unpredictable primeval power or what Tagore said long back *bhougolic apodebata* or territorial demon (quoted by Uma Dasgupta in her edited book, The Oxford India Tagore : 2009, Selected Writings on Education and Nationalism, Introduction xxiv. Tagore used this term *bhougolic apodebata* in a letter to Jagananda Ray, an early teacher of Shantiniketan school on 8 March 1921, Bengali Letters File, Visva-Bharati University).

In his classic autobiography, Errata : An Examined Life, George Steiner, one of the foremost philosophers of the 20th century, wrote :

> It is possible to suppose that the period since August 1914 has been, notably in Europe and Russia, from Madrid to Moscow, from Sicily to the Arctic Circle, the most bestial in recorded history (Steiner, 1997 : p. 103).

Steiner's epitaph to the essential tragedy of the 20th century may well serve as a postscript to Rabindranath's critique of nationalism. Indeed, it would be logical to infer that much of the cause for the human grief, pain and humiliation in the 20th Century, can be attributed to the conflicting claims of Nation States. Far from acting as an instrument for realizing collective or communitarian aspirations and welfare, Nationalism has tragically led to collective despair.

If the Enlightenment voices of Voltaire and Jefferson had heralded an end to 'judicial torture, to the burning of dissenters and books', 20th century European Nationalism paradoxically led to the Holocaust. As Steiner reflects :

> Perhaps there is no other instance precisely analogous to ontological massacre – this is to say, to the deliberate murder of human beings whose guilt minutely verbalized and set out by bureaucracy, was that of being" (Steiner, 1997 : p. 106).

What are the precise connections between the tragedies of the 20th century and the rise of different forms of nationalisms? What are the underlying roots or principles of nationalism that inevitably result in militancy and chauvinism? In his own time, at the height of anti-colonial protests in India and elsewhere, Rabindranath was chastised by many as a romantic who had reservations about the claims of nationalism. It is so interesting to realize now that Tagore's position on nationalism has become a potent reality.

His nationalism called for the acceptance of a radical social programme as described in his essay *byadhi o pratikar* or 'melody and cure', (in Samaj, Rabindra Rachanavali, vol xiii, 1961, p. 131) and launching a movement against the divisive forces of caste, poverty and alienation between the elite and the masses. He repeated again that only those with the 'vision of spiritual unity' would find a 'permanent place 'in the days to come, and further said that those with any 'intolerance of aliens' would be eliminated (bharatbarshiya samaj, in atmashakti and somuha, Rabindra Raachanavali, vol xii, 1961, p. 678).

X

William Radice makes (Rabindranath Tagore : Selected Poems, tr., Penguin, 1985, rev. 1987; new ed., 1995; Penguin India, 1995) an intelligent use of a line from Upanishad in respect of Tagore : 'He is far and he is near.' Radice says that 'Tagore's ideals of religion, his ideals of nationalism his culture which springs forth from his deep faith in man and in an ideal of wholeness are far from us but he comes very near us in his torments and exasperations.'

But this debate of proximity and distance is too elusive. We all know Tagore tends to transcend them all; after all his ultimate wish was to celebrate life and that is what makes a poet truly great. His modernity was different from that of the modern European, in so far as he never regarded the individual as the sole arbiter of his freedom unless it is sanctified by the presence of a supreme principle pervading in nature and the entire universe.

This brings us to the fourth issue related with the theme. This supreme principle or the unknown mystique is beautiful because it shines through the known and it is only in the unknown that we have perpetual freedom. Here the microcosm and the macrocosm, the inner (home/self) and the outer world coalesce together. This is the eternal voice of India and also of Asia and to understand this voice, Tagore would insist, that the study of the past is so imperative because it is through that we could understand our present. Asian soil, has mastered the trick of trapping eternity somewhere, somehow.

My last thesis is that the Asian identity is just not poverty and suffering but an endless quest for inner peace and spiritual freedom that binds mankind together. Today Asian and European traditions are seeking a sort of completion in one another not through a philosophical discourse or mutual cross-questioning but by creating a common space within which the voice of the one evokes a responsive echo in the other and hence important issues like :

(i) abandoning the narrow nationalism
(ii) paving the way for multiculturalism and
(iii) going for ecological oneness

have become very meaningful issues and a thing of concern for all of us of the East as well as the West.

This was Tagore's intense concern – concern for the relationship between the unity of the universe and uniqueness of man. This is his deepest message to mankind which has made him much relevant to people of the new millennium.

XI

To conclude let me assert that Tagore did not ignore the state but it was not a deciding factor for him. State and community (*samaj*) both were important for him and both were complementary to each other.

Tagore's concept of a nation was not nation-state nor was he thinking of a federation of nations- turning everything into one homogenized universal whole. On the contrary Tagore was thinking of an alternation, a universalism which grew with its strong basis of particularism or with the help of knowledge and learning of one's own culture or a deep understanding of the tradition and a humanistic insight. Tagore thought that a homogenized universalism based on an idea of cultural uniqueness itself a product of the uprootedness and deculturation brought about by British colonialism in India.

Tagore never thought that real universalism is contrary to nationalism and that they pull on opposing direction. The cosmopolitan universality envisioned by Tagore, therefore, would incorporate many opposites. Because he saw no difference between the best ages of the past and present, East and West, there was no reason why a balance could not be achieved between the modern and traditional, foreign and native, religion and science, elites and masses, and local and national governments, particular and universal, finite and infinite.

It is a balance between universalism, nationalism and the traditional world that Tagore hoped to achieve in his universal nationalism or better said as universal humanism and hence one can conclude that Ashis Nandi or Martha Nussbaum or others were wrong when they did not consider Tagore as a nationalist, they claim that he was a patriot and anti-imperialist because he loved his country and did not want the British to rule it, but he was a universalist rather than a nationalist because he advocated the creation of a culture common to all people, instead of separate national cultures, and because he did not want independence if that also meant adopting the form of nation-state, (see Nandy, *The Illegitimacy of Nationalism*; Martha Nussbaum, 'Patriotism and Cosmopolitanism,' in Joshua Cohen, ed., *For Love of Country : Debating the Limits of Patriotism* (Boston, Mass., 1996). On the contrary Tagore puts it; a culture could reflect 'universal ideas,' "without a loss of national identity. It was in fact a search of nation ness in *bharatvarshiya samaj* or of *bharatvarshiya samaj*. If one understands Tagore's view that India's unity is a social fact, not a political agenda then it becomes easy to understand that for Tagore universal nationalism is an inclusive plural concept of a nation which goes beyond the idea of exclusive nationalism and where the whole earth is a family.

Tagore, as many can think, suffered with some kind of irresoluteness and at the same time very definite about what he is saying. In his essay '*tatah kim*'(so what) Tagore is critiquing western way of thinking and using nature as a political metaphor to raise the voice of resistance against the western civilizational values but at the same time saying in his novel 'Home and the World', "I do not think that it is the spirit of India to reject anything, reject any race, and reject any culture. The spirit of India has always proclaimed the ideal of unity."

Tagore, as he sees the real tradition of India, says (already mentioned earlier) that it is to work for 'adjustments of races, to acknowledge real differences, between them, and yet seek some basis of unity.' It is this solution— unity through acknowledgement of differences— that India has to offer to the world.' (Nationalism, 1985, p. 64). This conception is the principal element of Tagore's idea of universal nationalism. His desperate search was for *ananda* (an idea of sublime bliss), which can be realized only in the unity of mankind and he lived all through his life complimenting the notion of exclusive nationalism with the inclusive plural notion of a nation and sought for human unity. Tagore says that people are greater than the nation, all those individuals all over the world who think clearly, feel nobly, and act rightly, thus becoming the channels of human unity. It is not an alternative system, it works like trees, and they spread their roots in the soil and their branches in the sky, without consulting any architect for their plans for an alternative system.

❑❑

Chapter Fifteen

The Idea of India : Rabindranath Tagore, Swami Vivekananda and Ramananda Chattopadhyaya

The idea of India is an age–old construct and did not come as a trend for establishing our big-time cultural and civilizational image during the British occupation of India. The idea was revived by the great minds of India during the freedom movement to scuttle the false propaganda by the British that before the advent of British there was no clear geographical picture of One India.

Where is Bharatvarsha?

Before I proceed further let me relate a passage of a dialogue from the novel *Aranayak* written by Bhibhuti Bhushan Bandyopadhyaya in 1939. The dialogue is between the narrator -writer and a tribal girl. The writer asks :

Have you ever been to a city ?
No babuji, she answered.
Have you heard of any cities ?
The writer enquired.
Gaya, Munger, Patna
Have not you heard of Kolkata ?
Yes, I have

Do you know where is that ?
No, babuji
Do you know the name of the country where we live?
Yes, we live in the district of Gaya.
Haven't you heard of Bharatavarsha?
Bhanumati shook her head.
She has not heard of it. She had never been out of Chakmakitola.
Where is Bharavarsha?

The question asked by the narrator-writer, where is Bharatvarsha? problematizes modern India's search for identity. Should we live with a regional identity or a national identity? Did we ever have a notion of a nation?

Image of One India

Before the advent of British, we had a psychological and geographical image of one India but then it was quite loose in its conception. It was loose because of the pluralistic structure of Indian society. But, at the same time a multilingual, multiracial, multireligious and multicultural India had some kind of an integrative framework of a nation governed by *dharma*. Whether India followed the polity of confederated republics or monarchial state, it was *dharma*, the religious, ethical, social, political, juridic and customary law which governed the life of the people. The king was only the guardian, executor and servant of *dharma*. It was with the British rule that the idea of a modern-state entered Indian society but then it was also opposed by many nationalist Indians like Bankim Chandra Chatterjee and others.

Religio-cultural Nationalism

Bankim constructed an idea of a nation based on *dharma* and explained it in terms of *manusattava* and *samanjasya*, humanity and harmony.

This religio-cultural nationalism, as said by historians like K.M.Panikkar, was responsible in uniting the people of India into one nation. He said, "What gave Indian nationalism its dynamism and ultimately enabled it to weld at least the major part of India into one state was the creation of a sense of community among the Hindus to which the credit should, to a very large extent, go to Swami Vivekananda." (SV : A Comprehensive Study, Swami Jyotirmayananda, p. 279)

Nationalism and Communality

This sense of communality is as old as the Indian civilization and is the force unifying the Indian people and their activities, social, religious, political and intellectual rather than any other political call for unity.

There is no doubt that India has a geographical identity – a geographical territory but the idea of a nation is more cultural and less political and hence in spite of the geographical changes, for example, Ashok's India was different from Akbar's India and Akbar's India was different from British India and present India is different from British India, the idea of India as a unified cultural space remains and which is described as *Sapta dwip Bharat desa* in the *Bhisma Parva* of Mahabharata or *Nuhu Sifir,* India of the ninth sky by Amir Khusro or India as a unified cultural space by Shankara Deva, the most distinguished medieval devotional poet of Assam.

India : Rastrapradhan or Samajpradhan or an Idea

This being the reason, India is not a nation- dominated *(rastrapradhan)* country as Tagore would say, where the core of the country remains encased in its nationhood but a society-dominated *(samajpradhan)* country, where the core of the country is spread all over the place among the people in diverse forms. He further said that I love India but the true India is an idea, and not a mere geographical expression (The Religion of Man). While writing a scholarly detailed article on Tagore after his death in the 'Modern Review' in the September, 1941 issue Ramananda Chattopadhyaya, in a way, endorses this view by quoting it in his article.

Swadeshi Samaj, Atmashakti and Swaraj

Tagore's concept of *swadesi samaj* is more important to him than the concept of nationalism. His theory was that before achieving freedom our priority should be to bring all round changes in the society and make it forward looking and ultimately fit to receive freedom of the country. This could be possible by developing *atmasakti* or self-reliance or self help. His idea of *samaj* as social upliftment and along with it *atmasshakti,* self-reliance and thereafter *swaraj,* self-rule, form a sequential progression to true national freedom wherein there is no scope for violence.

Through the pages of a Bengali journal started by Ramanandababu in 1900 from Allahabad, 'Prabasi', the creed of self-reliance, or what Tagore called *atmasakti*, was popularized from *Bangabhanga* days i.e. from 1905, which became the creed of the whole Bengal. The socio-political environment was full of *swadeshi* schemes -the detail of which was given by the Prabasi of kartik 1313 (1906) issue. This concept of *swadeshi samaj* can be interpreted as 'non-parochial inclusive nationalism' relevant to humanity.

Nationalism and Internationalism and Sarvodaya

Ramanandababu had almost a similar view and once told that "the utmost to which we might venture to pledge ourselves would be nationalism for all nations as a means to internationalism."Nation, for him is a welfare body, what Gandhi called *sarvodaya*, for all humanity. This idea he tried to promote through the pages of 'Prabasi' and Modern Review. After Surat Split (1907), Ramananda wrote an essay on nationalism where he spoke that nationalism was not a political party but a political idea. In his two journals, 'Prabasi' and Modern Review, he wrote prolifically on nationalism which would not only inspire a country to free itself from foreign subjugation but would also help to promote peaceful co-existence among different nations of the world. In other words nationalism would be the first step towards the path of internationalism.

In this respect Ramanandababu was much nearer to Gandhi than Tagore. Gandhi broadly shared Tagore views. For him too, the stronger the society, the less is needed to rely on the state to maintain its unity and stability. A country is the creation of its citizens for both Tagore and Gandhi, and it becomes theirs when and to the extent that they identify with and cares for each other.

The modern civilization undermined this unity and fragmented and dehumanized the individual and forced him to rely heavily on the coercive institution of the state.

Nationalism and Humanity

Tagore's inclusive nationalism is explained by Ramananda babu as humanity, which is a grand and beautiful edifice and nations are the sound and well made bricks with the help of which it is to be built(Welfare, 1925).

However, Gandhi was definitely more practical then Tagore and wanted people to concentrate on one's attention and energy on one's country and thereafter humankind at large. Gandhi's road map was from nationalism to internationalism and for Tagore both were to be accepted as a single unit.

Indian nationalism is the nationalism of an idea, the idea of an ever-ever land to which we belong as says Shasi Tharoor. This land imposes no procrustean exaction on its citizens : you can be many things and one thing. Interestingly in India's political arrangement there is no way for any person to be only Indian and nothing else; indeed, one could not be an Indian without being some other things at the same time. Indianness is a complex and multi layered identity, which encompasses other such identities without canceling them. India's great diversity, a pluralistic worldview and its multicultural and multi-religious reality form the basis of Indian identity. You can be a good Bengali, a good Hindu or Muslim and a good Indian all at once.

It is obvious that India, instead of developing itself as a homogenized monolithic structure of a Nation State to support a strong, interventionist, democratic, secular and centralized state with a uniform rule of citizenship, upheld a distinctively pluralistic idea of a nation.

Adjustments of races, to acknowledge real differences, between them, and yet seek some basis of unity

Tagore, as he sees the real tradition of India, says that it is to work for 'adjustments of races, to acknowledge real differences, between them, and yet seek some basis of unity.' It is this solution— unity through acknowledgement of differences— that India has to offer to the world.' (Nationalism, 1985,p.64), and yet seek some basis of unity (Tagore, Nationalism, reprint, 1985, p.18). The basis for this tradition has been built in India at the social level, not the political, through saints like Nanak, Kabir, Chaitanya and others. It is this solution–unity through acknowledgement of difference–that India has to offer to the world, (ibid, p.64).

Universal Humanism

If one says that India's unity is a social fact, not a political agenda, it becomes easy to understand that for Tagore universal nationalism is an inclusive plural concept of a nation which goes beyond the idea of exclusive nationalism and embrace the whole earth as a family. Margery Sabin in her article on Ramananda Chatterjee has explained this in detail that the distinctiveness of vision Ramanandababu brought to the monthly (Modern Review) was tolerance for variety; he allows multiple versions of the good in the journal's representation of what an invigorated modern India can include. Modern Indian nationalism thus emerges in Modern Review as pluralistic and cosmopolitan.

Cosmopolitanism, Swadeshi and Tradition

The next statement of Ramanandababu is a new idea of cosmopolitanism propagated for the first time by Tagore. Margery says that what Chatterjee has sponsored throughout his career – whether in art, politics, or industrial productivity – is cosmopolitan ism and in that it thrives on openness to the worldwide commerce of ideas as well as good, with Indians venturing out to acquire whatever is good from their indigenous culture (*swadeshi*) and tradition for strengthening their civilizational world view or the idea of cosmopolitanism. In simple words it is moving to universal without loosing the particular.

It speaks of cosmopolitanism as the ideology that all human ethnic groups belong to a single community based on a shared morality but in this concept both Ramanandababu and Tagore intertwine *swadeshi* (indigenous India) and *parampara* (indigenous

Indian tradition) of the country to which they belong. Amartya Sen while explaining this says that it is, indeed, to Tagore's everlasting credit that his great cosmopolitan vision never sacrificed the richest possible sense of tradition.

His actual words are, 'The main point of cosmopolitanism, which is taken to be the world-citizenship claim, need not militate against valuing elements in one's own tradition' (Sen, 'Humanity' p.112).

The authenticity of Tagore and Vivekananda's vision lay in its universality, even when they were addressing a country acquiring a modern national identity. Both Tagore and Vivekananda transcended nationalistic boundaries and became world citizens, in the sense that they were addressing both their regional/national interlocutors as well as those on the other side of the imaginary fence of nationhood.

Vasudhaiva Kutumbukam

Our idea of cosmopolitan universality is based on the Vedic mantra, *basudhaiva kutumbukam,* the whole world is a family. This concept of the whole world as a family is very different than the cosmopolitan concept of Diogenes of Sinope, a Greek philosopher of 412 B.C., who said, "If somebody asks from where I come from; I will answer, I am a citizen of the world."

One can easily notice that there is a vast difference between a member of a family and a citizen of the world – which is just a broad view of particularism, whereas being members of a family betrays warmth, closeness and togetherness as members of a family.

The concept of the world as a family is also different from the present creation of the Western civilization of a global order or a global village, a point in the relentless process of westernization of the globe. The terms and condition for living and participating in the life of this village are laid down by the West for their own benefit and if the terms and conditions are not followed, one cannot stay in that village.

Universal Humanism = Love for All

On the contrary the idea of India is love for all or universal humanism. This is the summum bonum of the concept of dharma or love for all. In 1893 at Chicago's World Parliament of Religions Vivekananda gave the message of love and fraternity, tolerance and universal acceptance and faith in all religion and said :

> I am proud to belong to a nation which has sheltered the persecuted and the refugees of all religions and all nations of the earth.

In this respect Ramnandababu in his article 'Nation building and the Critical Spirit' published in 'Welfare' in 1925 says that all the religions that we know of teach the lesson of love, and therefore religion ought to have proved of the greatest value to the internationalist as well as to the nationalist.

Dharma and Love

Sister Nivedita in her writings in the editorial columns of the Modern Review once said "*dharma* is the substance, the self-ness, of things and of men." (John Murray, 'Higher Nationality', 1913, London) and that is, in fact liquidating (nihshesh kara) oneself for love.

The acceptance of religious plurality is possible in the country because of our understanding of *dharma* as a socio, ethical category. The spirit of *dharma* is love for everything.

Shri Ramakrishna and Vivekananda

Please recall that night when a storm was blowing very hard and the rains were lashing at all and sundry and in that dark stormy dripping night came the disciple to meet the master. Master (Sri Rama Krishna) asked Naren (Swami Vivekananda) : Why have you come on this turbulent, squally night ? You don't want me, believe me. "You want to know, why do I come because I love you!" said Vivekananda to his Master.

Love, this is the locus of India's pluralistic existence and is a part of our secular polity. It is a part of our tradition and culture, of our identity as a civilization. This spirit of love which is the core of *dharma* is the unity of our socio-political and cultural existence. Tagore's religion of poet was love for humanity or human unity and freedom.

It is *dharma* which sustains every one and which creates love and respect for all leading to the Indian principle of communitarian polity. Indian polity holds that state is subject to the rule of *dharma* which is its duty to uphold and protect. Swami Vivekananda says that the voice of Asia has been the voice of religion. The voice of Europe is the voice of politics. (Quoted in Swami Gambhirananda, A Short Life of Swami Vivekanda, p.114).

He further said that :

> The Englishman can understand religion through politics, the Americans through social reforms; but we understand even politics and sociology through religion… (Quoted in V. S. Narvane, Modern Indian Thought, 1960, p.97

India for Social or inner Unity

The voice of India calls for inner unity or social unity based on dharma and never longed for political unity. European go for uniformity, its unity is political. India's unity is harmonious and spiritual. European civilization revolves round the state whereas the Indian civilization revolves round the society, its organization, and its activities. History of India, therefore, is the history for unity among diversities. This unity is achieved not only by exterminating the intrinsic differences but by toleration and adjustment, by following the path of virtue or *dharma* – a moral cum ethical construct.

The idea of India reflects that our democracy cannot survive without the support of an extra-political normative moral order, which is *dharma.* In the August 1947 issue of Modern Review, the then editor Kedar Nath Chatterjee, son of Ramanandababu, published the editorial entitled, "1947 : Dawn of a New Age" and quoted Jawaharlal Nehru that wherever flag of India will go – it will bring a message of freedom and comradeship to those people. A message that India wants to be friends with every country and that India wants to help any people who lack freedom.

The issue of the Other

This is the idea of India of universal humanity and resolves a very problematic issue of the other. Initially in the West the other was an inalienable entity external to one self and was a source of terror and an object of desire. The other was a white man's burden and even a great philosopher like Sartre, whose famous statement 'hell is the other', carries a strong echo of Hegel, who always defined one's identity as 'identity against the other', either to be appropriated or to be destroyed.

Today there is a change to be seen in the West. The distinguished French philosopher Levinas says that "the foundation of ethics consists in the obligation to respond to the other." For another very distinguished French philosopher, Jacque Derrida, "The foundation of ethics is hospitality, the readiness and inclination to welcome the other into one's own home." No doubt these ideas reveal a new consciousness emerging in the West about crossing the boundaries and looking beyond one's nation but it is still a broad view of particularlism. It holds out the possibility of acceptance of the other as different but of equal standing. This is nowhere near to the Upanishadic idea of oneness as referred to by Tagore in his acceptance speech of the Noble Prize delivered on 26th June, 1921 at Stockholm. He quotes, "One who perceives all the beings in his own self and his own self in all the beings does not hate anyone, any more" :

Yastu sarvani bhutani atmanevanupashyati,
Sarvabhuteshu chatmanam tato na vijigupsate

In the first issue of 'Prabasi' Rabindranath wrote a poem exemplifying this unity of all human beings by declaring that his home is in all lands, his country in all countries, and his close kindred in all homes there.

I shall raise two more points related to the idea of India and then I am done with my presentation.

Depressed Class, Ambedkar, Tagore and his Gora and Swami Vivekananda

The issue of the depressed class, the untouchables and the caste spirit, are great setbacks in all round development of India and in realizing the Idea of India. Annanya Mukherjee Reed in her perceptive article in 'Outlook' in May 2011 issue says that on the question of inequality and democracy, the parallels between Ambedkar and Tagore go very far : both viewed India's development from the perspective of inequality and saw 'chauvinistic nationalism' as a disaster; both wished for the 'annihilation' of caste rather than its reform; and both hoped to see resistance of the oppressed. Tagore wrote :

He more durbhaga desh jader karecho apaman
Apamane hote habe thahader sabar saman
Your breathern you have treated with disrespect,
You have denied them their simple human rights.
You have made them stand and wait before you,
And not given them a place in your affection.
You must share with them all, their ignominy.

To both Tagore and Ambedkar, the primary questions for India were those of inequality and social justice; the primary contradiction between the façade of formal democracy and the reality of structural injustice.

In Tagore's Gora untouchability is the main issue which could be resolved by universal humanism. Ramanandababu is very candid in this respect and says that to do away with untouchability to the extent that Mr. Gandhi wants though that itself would be to pullout one much of a remedy, it is the caste spirit which must be exorcised (Welfare, January 1925).

Swami Vivekananda while talking of depressed classes of India first castigates the rich and says, "You, the upper classes of India, do you think you are alive? You are but mummies ten thousand years old and it is you who are the real walking corpses... of India! You represent the past tense, with all its varieties of form jumbled into one. You are the void, the unsubstantial nonentities of the future. You merge yourselves in the void and disappear, and let New India arise in your place. Let her arise–out of the peasant's cottage, grasping the plough; out of the huts of the fisherman, the cobbler and the sweeper. Let her spring from the grocer's shop. Let her emanate from the factory, from marts and from markets. Let her emerge from groves and forests, from hills and mountains. These common people have suffered oppression for thousands of years – suffered it without murmur, and as a result have got wonderful fortitude. They have suffered eternal misery, which has given them unflinching vitality."

John Kenneth *Galbraith, the first US Ambassador in India in the Nehruvian era once said, whatever you say about India is true but the opposite is equally true. This is very much reflected in this issue of the depressed class and class spirit. Right from the hoary past stories like Satyakam, Javala and Rishi Gautam,*

Valmiki and tenets of Buddha dharma and later on the sayings of medieval poets strongly spoke against the caste spirit and went for love for all humanity and harmony in life.

Shastra and Loka and Patanjali

Tagore's seminal statement in this respect is, "Perfection of unity is not in uniformity but in harmony."

The best example of this harmony, one can find in the coexistence of *loka* and *shastra* or folk/tribal and classical in the making of India's composite culture. In India *loka* and *shastra* are always complementary to each other. The very interesting example is the legend representing the conversion of a pre-Hindu mother goddess located at Kamakhya into the pan-Indian *shaktidevi.* In the Indian context, the *loka* and *shastra*(folk/tribal and elite) contrast is contrary to the western contrast between great and little tradition. India does not believe that non-literate cultures are 'knowledge blanks' which need to be filled in with the modern knowledge of different discipline and dominant cultures.

Cultures are never 'blanks'. In some matters, e.g., in the ecological management practices used by tribals are for superior to anything we could teach them. The tragedy is that modernism has imposed a single perspective in dealing with human culture and today this kind of fixed perspective is challenged by the indeterminacy of experience. The search for one truth in many is at odds with the relativist experience of anthropology.

In the introductory chapter of Mahabhasya written about 2500 years ago, Patanjali clearly pronounces, *prayukta Lokarthah* and accordingly, *loka* is the authority of word, and its meaning and their relationship, and not the classical rules. *Loka* is one of the important guides of human behaviour and *lokamata* or the views of common people constitute a significant part of polity (*nripanaya*) of a country and even the essence of Veda (*nigama nichoda*) and the views of the wise (*prajnavana*).

I really feel proud to be born in a country like India where the elite and the common, *shastr a*and *loka,* stayed together. Tagore, Vivekananda, Ramananda Chatterjee or even Amartya Sen and many others proposed to give priority to education to resolve many of our social problems and challenges which India has faced in the modern times. Ramanadababu's insistence on education as a higher priority than the non-cooperation, that Gandhi was advocating among students, was a bold step message of that time. This was a dynamic feature of Ramanandababu's response to Gandhism throughout the 1920s. Ramanandababu was convinced that a really liberal and national education will develop a critical spirit in our midst. He writes in 'Welfare' that the critical spirit will show what obstacles we are to overcome, what pitfalls we are to avoid, and in general what dangers we are to be beware of.

Tagore spoke of human unity and freedom and his philosophy of education is to lay emphasis on harmony, balance and total development of personality both intellectual and spiritual. Swamiji was against sectarianism, ritualism and his religion was service to humanity or what Shamita Basu says 'Dialogic Hinduism' and accommodate many of the enlightenment values of rationalism, the spirit of scientific enquiry, and the tenets of universal literacy. It is because of critical insiders like Tagore, Swamiji and Ramanandababu that the idea of India is still a deep, vibrant and strong impression of total India.

Chapter Sixteen

Celebrating Tagore's 150th Birth Anniversary and 60 Years of Japan's Cultural Relation with India

India is celebrating 150th birth year of Rabindranath Tagore and Japan is celebrating its 60th year of cultural relation with India.

India has a long history of cultural relations with Japan first through Buddism which entered in Japan in 538 AD but it did not come to Japan on a popular level, but was only accepted by the imperial court and then disseminated in the country from the top.

In the modern times the cultural relation between Japan and India dates back to 1902, the year which marks a historical meeting between two great intellectuals, Tenshin Okakura and Rabindranath Tagore in Calcutta. Tenshin, the forerunner of Japan-Bangla relationship, was deeply impressed by the revivalist movement of culture and an art, going on at that time in Kolkata.

This relation with Japan was further enhanced by the five visits of Rabindranath to Japan (1916,1917,1924, 1929 twice). Since then there have been an intimate and lingering cultural and artistic ties between the two countries. These encounters had brought into contact a remarkable group of intellectuals and artists of Japan and Bengal. After his second visit he brought back to India with him some rare Japanese paintings and a talented artist, Yokoama Taikan who was also advised by Okakura to visit Tagores in Calcutta earlier in the begining of the 20th century.

In his second visit to Japan Tagore visited Taikan's studio and also the studio of the great artist of post-first world war Japan Shimomura. Taikan showed Tagore by unfolding the scroll of his masterpiece, 'River' which was so similar to many lines of Tagore's masterly world picture in his Balaka poem :

River of Immensity
Thy waters unknown and silent
Rapidly and uninterruptedly glide into Eternity

On his return from Japan, the poet gave many valuable talks on Japan and influenced his artist-nephews Gaganendranath and Abanindranath Tagore, who illustrated the Jivansmriti, reminiscences, of Rabindranath with sketches in the Japanese styles initiated by Taikan. The Master-painter, Yokoyama Taikan spent time at the studio of Abanindranath and Gaganindranath Tagore and stayed with them in Tagore's ancestral home at Jorasanko, Calcutta. Both the brothers were pioneers in many ways - in adopting Indian styles of painting after training in western art, and then absorbing many strains of Japanese styles.

Both the nephew added new element to the exhibitions organized by the Indian Society of oriental arts, Calcutta during those days. In the chronicles of the society one can trace the influence of the techniques of sino-Japanese art on the new school of Indian art.

During that visit Tagore sent his associate Acharya Kshitimohan Sen to the oldest Buddhist monastery of Koyasan, near Kobe where he worked with the school of monks of the Singon or mantra-yana sect introduced to Japan from China by the Japanese monk scholar Kobo Daishi. There are still preserved rare texts and paintings attesting to the fusion of Hinduism with Mahayan Buddism.

Tagore also met during that visit Dr. J.T.Takakusu, who took the poet to his grand publication centre- the 'pitaka Niketan', named after the poet's Shantiniketan. The poet wrote admirable pen-pictures of the social and cultural life of Japan, in his Japan-Jatri, (Letters from Japan) to immortalize his first two visits to Japan.

During his first two visits in 1916 and 1924 Tagore was a little depressed by seeing Japan's contrast between traditional beauty and imported ugliness which made Tagore quite unhappy throughout his stay there.

Though his unbounded joy could be seen in coming in contact with the art and Japan's love for beauty of which Tagore was a great admirer since his young days. He was enchanted by the Japanese women who came in large numbers in his lectures in the model school in Karuizawa and the women's University in Tokyo. Few of them spoke English but with a rare grace they brought before the poet their lovely silk pieces and fans to receive on them in japanese ink his poetic messages. The poet obliged them by writting in ornate Bengali script short Bengali poems and epigrams on their fans and silk pieces some of which were later published in Bangali as 'fireflies'. Here are some examples in English translation :

Mind's underground moths
grow filmy wings
and take a farewell flight
in the sunset sky.
The butterfly counts not months but moments,
and has time enough.

or

From the solemn gloom of the temple
children run out to sit in the dust,
God watches them play
and forgets the priest.

On the way to Tokyo by train, nearly two weeks after his arrival in Kobe in 1916, he was greeted at the station in Shizuoka by about two dozen Buddhists who had come to pay their respect.

None could speak a world of English, so they stood with joined hands in a reverent attitude before the carriage window while their leader requested Rabindranath to place some incense in a burner; after which they all bowed solemnly and stood in silence as the train pulled out. At that moment, Tagore said later, 'for the first time I had the feeling that I was really in Japan, and I was so happy that tears of joy came to my eyes.'

After he reached Tokyo he saw the ugly Japan of western technological imitation. Later he told : 'The contrast is so striking that it is difficult to understand how a people with such an inherent love for beautiful things can copy of our western ugliness and feel that they have got something which is worth having.'

Among those who saw the photographs of Tagore next day flashed practically in all Japanese newspapers was a seventeen year old boy still in school, Yasunari Kawabata. In 1968 he became the 2nd Asian to win the Nobel Prize for literature. Soon after the award, lecturing on ' The existence and discovery of beauty', Kawabata said of Tagore :

"I remember even now the features and appearance of this sage-like poet, with his long, bushy hair, long mustache and beard, standing tall in loose-flowing Indian garments, and with deep, piercing eyes. His white hair flowed softly down both sides of his forehead; the tufts of hair under the temples also were long like two beard and linking up with the hair on his cheeks, continued into his beard, so that he gave an impression, to the boy that I was then, of some ancient Oriental wizard."

Kawabata did not hear any of Tagore's lectures in 1916, but speaking in 1969 he singled out a remarks by Tagore at that time.

"It is the responsibility which every nation has to reveal itself before the world... (Japan) has given rise to a civilization which is perfect in its form, and has evolved a sense of sight which clearly sees truth in beauty and beauty in truth."

" We may rejoice' Kawabata commented, ' and yet at the same time be saddened, by the thought that (our) very ancient 'The Tale of Genji' fulfils the "responsibility of a nation" to which Tagore referred, much more brilliantly than any of us can do today, and will very likely continue to do so in the future."

On 13th June, the high point of his official reception in Tokyo he told the prime minister, president of the imperial university, minister of education, eminent Buddhist scholars and more than 200 other dignitaries assembled at the Kaniji Buddhist temple :

> "I sincerely hope that the Japanese people will not forget the old Japan."

Tagore, who was by the time came to be known as a world poet was apprehensive of the fact that though having undergone massive industrialization, Japan had emerged as an Asian superpower, it is now misusing its western borrowed technology to demonstrate the ugly face of nationalism.

The Sino-Japanese war and the Japan-Russia conflict had resulted in overwhelming victories and Tagore was deeply pained by the ruthless Japanese exploitation of the Chinese.

At the same time Tagore appreciated the Japanese strides in technology and its challenge to European categorizations of Asia as irrational. Tagore also had a deep respect for Japanese culture that had been deeply influenced by Buddhist. These dualities and conflicts weighed on his mind as he responded to Japan during his 1916 and also during other four visits.

The reception very soon cooled down during his 1919 vist. Japanese peopel felt that the nationalism that Tagore forcefully decried as wastern in origin and inimical in spirit to Japan was serving well in Korea and China. Tagore was shocked whien he received a letter form Yone Naguchi, a very eminent poet of that time, an associate of Yeats and Ezra pound, whom Tagore knew and respected, arguing vociferously for Japan's spiritual and moral role in sending its ary to china and depredating Korea. Naguchi's hope was to enlist Tagrore's support forom India. A shocked Tagore responded in his letter which ended with the following line, "Wishing your people whom I love, not success, but remores."

On Tagore's two subsequent visits in Japan, in 1924 and 1929, the response was cooler and cooler still.

But his faith in Japanese culture, its love for beauty and love for nature still was a great source of his empathy with Japan, its writers, poets and thinkers but in his visits to Japan which was by then far removed from his dream of 'The Land of the Cherry blossoms' he saw the imperialistic nationalism of the west being adopted by Japan and solemnly warned Japan against its tendency to imitate the western diplomacy of exploitation and pleaded :

> Of all the countries in Asia, here in Japan, you have the freedom to use the materials you have gathered from the west according to its genius and your need. Therefore your responsibility is all the greater; for in your voice.

Asia shall answer the questions that Europe has submitted to the Conference on Man.

Here Tagore was hinting to the League of Nations after the First World War but the visionary poet was not listened to and the rest of it is history, a bloody history.

It will be interesting to note that because of his complete apathy towards violence that he was so much against nationalism based on the concept of a nation-state which does not hesitate to kill in the name of sovereignty of a nation and rather goes for universal humanism and unity of mankind.

Today the new reading of nationalism by Tagore looks so relevant because of disastrous consequences of the prevalent nation of nationalims which we witnessed in the two world wars and now in the ethnic politics in India and else where, in terrorism and in the African countries, who fought against colonialism and racialism to regain their freedom dand the spirit of nationalism but now the net result of that is that these contries have become dens of corruption, cruelty and insolunce.

The West is now seriously thinking has nation-state failed? Post colonial critics such as Ernest Gallner, Benedict Andrson, Tom Nairn or Frantz Fanon have pointed out how nationalism cultivates the sentiments of irrationality, prejudice and hatred in people.

Now nationalism looks like a dark elemental unpredictable primeval power which Tagore called *bhougolick opodevata*. Tagore but at the same time spoke loudly about

(i) Living in freedom and

(ii) Reasoning in freedom

In his speech to the Students of the Private Colleges of Tokyo and the Members of the Indo-Japanese Association, at the Keio Gijuku University he said that,

"I have travelled in many countries and have met with men of all classes, but never in my travels did I feel the presence of the human so distinctly as in this land. The ideal of "maitri" with men and "maitri" with Nature.

And the true expression of this love is in the language of beauty, which is so abundantly universal in this land." He further said :

"And this has made me all the more apprehensive of the change, which threatens Japanese civilization, as something like a menace to one's own person. For the huge heterogeneity of the modern age, whose only common bond is usefulness, is nowhere so pitifully exposed against the dignity and hidden power of reticent beauty, as in Japan."

"While I agree with them so far as to say, that the spirit of the race should harmonize with the spirit of the time, I must warm them that modernizing is a mere affectation of modernism, just as affectation of poesy is poetizing.

True modernism is freedom of mind, not slavery of taste. It is independence of thought and action, not tutelage under European schoolmasters." This is what Ms Ruini Ko Kora also said that overcoming the western modernism is possible through circular temporality open cosmoplitanism & flexible mind.

Today we all are realizing that how true Tagore was about the nation of nationalism and its violent and disastrous effect.

Tagore's search was rather for an alternative Japanese culture that emphasized the twin aspects of human tolerance and the sense of aesthetic beauty. It was in this binary that he located Japan.

In fact, it was in the power of control of emotions and capability to forgive, that Tagore located Japanese heroism. In his Japan Jatri (Japan Travelogue) Tagore wrote that : " I have seen in the conduct of the Japanese their wonderful self-control, and what seems to be a sense of forgiveness, or at least of mutual understanding... It is not easy. It has required strenuous discipline and centuries of civilization... I shall have to confess that the Japanese possess a monopoly of certain elements of heroism - a heroism which is one with their artistic genius. In its essence, it has a strong sense of movement; in its form, it has that perfect proporation which comes of self mastery. It is a creation of two opposing forces, that of expression and repression.

It is this opposition- of mastery over the self and its aesthetic expression that Tagore saw as central to the form of the Haiku.

Tagore quotes two major Haiku poems to make his point and in each case analyses the symbolic significance of the details, The first poem :

An old Pond
A frog jumping

The sand and water is read as a symbolic reference to the spark of a new idea in the stasis of the human mind. Tagore sees the density of the silence indicated, while the dynamism of motion in the backdrop of such a density assumes great importance. The other poem :

A rotten branch
A crow
Autumn
Symbolizes the presence of death to Tagore.

Tagore's own renderings of the Haiku are few but significant. The first poem situates his perception of the alternative heroism in Japanese self-control :

Brave warriors
I have seen
Victorious
I have never seen
Such quiet courage
To hold the victorious flag
With such silence

The second poem is more in the nature of a prophecy that locates a victorious Japan. which combines the scientific progress with its humanitarian values :

On the shores
Reddening clouds herald
The end of dark night
The Bird of the East
Sings the Praise
Of the great East.

Tagore was quick to realize that overall progress could not be exclusively spiritual. It had to take into cognizance science and technology. He confessed; "Do I think that Eastern throught, the Eastern outlook can be reconciled with the mechanism of western civilization? I think it can and must be. In the East we have striven to disregard matter to ignore hunger and thirst... But that is no longer possible, at least for the whole nation".

In his third Haiku he talks about India's willingness to learn from Japan in this regard :

The saint
In saffron
Once taught
Your nation
Today he goes
To your door
As a disciple

To learn a different education

This last Poem is significant on many counts. First, it outlines Tagore's awareness of, and willingness to receive scientific knowledge. But more importantly it indicates his vision of cultural dialogue and mutual cooperation between nations.

He also wrote, "If Japan has borrowed anything from India, they have made it their own. A nation which is dynamic can absorb the qualities of another nation. One which is static considers it a great load because its own existence lies heavy upon it."

Time has come now for us to learn from Japan. This is the message of Tagore which is to be highlighted during these celebrations of 60 years of Japan-India cultural relations.

❑❑

Chapter Seventeen

Medieval Indian Bhakti Poetry of Conversion and Subversion and Tagore's Gitanjali : Continuity of a Tradition

Medieval devotional i.e. bhakti poetry is poetry of conversion of the total India into an alternative way of showing love for the divine and also of subversion and interrogation. Bhakti literature questions the social and religious norms, and brings gods (Vishnu, Shiva, Rama, Krishna) from the temples to make them members of the human family by crossing and subverting the boundaries of hierarchies.

Bhakti has only one meaning love - love for the divine. It *is* a celebration of life with the divine in you and hence more than life-negating it is a life-accepting movement. Everything pertaining to worldly love is offered to God, as Tagore says, "What we can give to God that we present to our beloved; what we can offer to our beloved, that we give to God. From where shall we get anything else otherwise? God becomes the beloved and the beloved God".

But surprisingly Western Indologists, particularly, one of the most distinguished Indologists, the founder of the Asiatic Society, Sir William Jones, by following their hidden agenda, described the ancient period as the golden period in Indian history and the medieval period as the dark age. It is not difficult to see why they did this—the British wanted to represent themselves as the saviours of India, that they were the ones who rescued India and brought to it the benefits of Western civilization and led Indians back from darkness to the bright path of modern civilization.

When one goes through the content of the second Anniversary Discourse in 1794 to the Asiatic Society of Bengal, where Sir William Jones, in search of the history of India, makes a comment that he would go to remote antiquity but restrict his researches downwards only up to 11th Century, one realizes that Edward Said's attempt to view Western Literary approaches to the East in terms of political discourse cannot be ignored completely.

Jones' statement has two hidden political meanings :

(i) That pre-British India had no history. It was the dark period of India of religious beliefs and with the advent of British the darkness faded;

(ii) In the process Jones tried to obliterate a part of the history of India, medieval bhakti period, which was, in fact, the golden period of Indian literature and as a result created historigraphical inversions by wiping out a portion from its history to suit his hidden agenda.

The darkness of religious beliefs is an expression which tallies with the notion of the conventional historians that medieval India is all 'dark ages' comparable to the 'dark ages' of Europe. But we all know that medieval India with its multiple flowerings in different field of human expressions like architecture, sculpture, painting, music, dance and most and above all poetry is the golden period of Indian art and specially literature.

But the worst thing the Indologists (particularly William Jones and Thomas Warton) planned was to introduce the theory of savageology in the context of India. Accordingly savages may be opulent in their imagination but they do not know how to cultivate it so that it receives the blessings of reason and hence savages rest content with their past as they need no present. In the process the Indologists attempted to wash out India's cultural memory by popularizing the so called notion that 'westernization is modernization' and tried to eliminate India's past as well as its present.

This view encouraged a debate in India between the advocates of 'tradition' (*purana*) and the advocates of 'modernity' (*nutana*) throughout the 19th century and many great writers discovered the universal, everlasting values in our ancient texts, Vedas and Upanishads and in the medieval devotional poets like Kabir, Nanak, Dadu,Vasavanna and *Vaishnava* poets like Chandidasa, Jnandasa and also in the Indian folk songs and folk religious expressions like *Bauls* of Bengal a message of humanism.

Tagore with the help of Kshitimohan Sen took the lead in recapturing the essence of bhakti and folk religion and restructured the Upanishadic notion of 'there is only one pervading the world' into bhakti's divine love between the two- Lord and the Devotee. Devotion is possible only when there is the lord and the devotee. Tagore said boldly that a man who is alone or one is meaningless because there is no unity in one. The one with many is truly one because in that one can see the unity and this unity gives the message of truth.

This debate exposed the easily detectable and obvious fault lines of Western modernity known as the notion of the Whiteman's burden and their understanding of orientalism as explained and criticised by Edward Said.

In India, modernism as a phenomenon or value is not an absolutely unrelated one without reference to the past or the future. It absorbs in it traditional values as well as new innovations and is indicated by the term 'continuity'. It is essential to do that because the spirit of India, as says Tagore or as the writers have observed over the ages, is not to reject anything. Everything has a place here as an alternative. India lives with many alternatives which become part of the continuity of thought and creativity and hence the choice which Gandhi or Tagore offered to us was not tradition versus modernism, but the choice of both versus the forced acceptance of one.

This is the Indian way of thinking. Indian thinking is not logo-centric and exclusive, but symbolic or inclusive and hence India has no problem to live with many life choices and this is possible if one has the freedom of mind as boldly explained by Tagore that :

> True modernism is freedom of mind, not slavery
> of taste. It is independence of thought and action,
> not tutelage under European school masters.

He further mentioned in his essay on 'Modern Poetry' that the joy of natural and detached way of looking at things belongs to no particular age; it belongs to every one whose eyes know how to wander over the naked earth.

It is over a thousand years since the Chinese poet Li-Po wrote his verses, but he was a modern, he looked upon the universe with freshly opened eyes : To quote Li- Po :

Why do I live among these green hills?
The question makes me laugh, I don't answer. My mind is still.
I live under another sky and on another earth—
In a world that belongs to no man.
The peach tree blossoms, the stream flows by

In the unity of beings one realizes the spirit, *atma.* Hence, while defining modernity in his own terms, Tagore had no hesitation to declare in Beijing in 1924 that :

> The impertinence of material things is extremely old. The revelation of spirit in man is modern. I am in its side, I am modern.

In this way Tagore created his other modernity by stressing on freedom, objectivity, continuity of a tradition particularly bhakti and spirituality and prepared the basis for his Nobel Prize winning book of poetry, Gitanjali.

When in every language of the world the western modernity made its presence felt.

Tagore's views, questioning the very basic postulates of Western modernity, made an impact on the scholars who drew the attention of the world to its fault lines. Elie Wiesel and John Beverley argued that modernity's fault lines had produced a narrative impulse to bear witness—their examples, holocaust narrative and the Latin American *testimonio* (emergence of the Latin American subaltern literature of personal experience of discrimination, violence and ethnic hatred). These kinds of violence are the result of modernist individualism, crash consumerism and secularism but in the post modernist period religion has staged a grand come back and entered in literature as a spiritual revival. In other words, even though the "grand narratives" of religion might be in decline, religious or spiritual elements appear to punctuate literature. It is in this overall context that the need for a new philosophy and social ethics becomes urgent and imperative.

It was not only William Jones, a distinguished Indologist, George Abraham Grierson (1851-1941) when came into contact with the insightful depth of medieval Indian literature especially Hindi devotional poetry he was absolutely bewildered and in his response said that all of a sudden like the flash of lightening, a new idea surfaced over the darkness of old religious beliefs... No Hindu knows from which source this new idea materialized and also no one could with certainty establish the reason of its manifestation.

It is in this context Hazariprasad Dwivedi (a great Hindi scholar brought to Visva-Bharati by Tagore as head of Hindi Bhawan) alludes to Grierson, to convincingly assert, that it was not all of a sudden like a flash of lightening that things started happening but for hundreds of years the clouds gathered for rains to take place and more than that the unique thing that happened during that time was the crossing of boundaries of hierarchies to interconnect the tribal and folk conventions and regional distinctions (*pravritti*) with the erudition of *Shatra*-oriented or classical epistemology of *Acharyas* (learned pundit) and concrete *Pauranic*(mythical) imaginative narrations and establish the complementariness of these two traditions of *loka* (folk/trival) and *shastra* (classical/elite) and also their interdependence on each other and a literature of love for the divine. It was not only crossing but interrogating and even sometimes subverting the boundaries of hierarchies.

The emergence of bhakti poetry simultaneously in several new languages can be seen as reflecting fundamental changes in India in the social, aesthetic and philosophical connotations of basic concepts like Time, Language and Self.

Let me take up all the three one by one :

> Time : In India besides eternal, mythical, linear and also cyclic progress of time, the most dominant notion of time is of the 'inverted' process of human evolution, from satyayuga to kaliyuga, from a luminous age to dark age (samkhya view).

The emergence of bhasha literature and bhakti movement (pasyadana of Jnaneswari) express a strong hope for a better future for every human being and as a result an accentuated sense of the future and the past being distinct from the present moment developed with the new languages and presented in bhakti literature.

Language :

> In a similar way, the bhakti era made radical revisions of the concepts of the languages and the self. The main thrust of bhasha culture was towards humanizing these and other related concepts. Devabhasha (divine speech) Sanskrit was discarded by literatures in favour of matribhasha, mother tongue. God is like one's mother tongue, he is everywhere accessible.

He is not seen as beyond language, as ineffable (*anirvacaniya*). By this time, Sanskrit had become the second language, i.e. a language of culture, an inter-provincial lingua franca, the preserver and carrier of traditions.

The *bhakti* poets were all against the imposition of the elitist Sanskrit language on their bhasas (mother tongues) and hence poets like Kabir in the North showed his displeasure by saying :

> Sanskrit is standing water of a well.
> Bhasa is flowing water of a river.

In their view, god lives inside us as a mother tongue does, and we live in God as we live in language–

To lose this first language is to lose one's beginnings. Thus the poet-saints required and created poetry and a poetics of the mother tongue. They empowered language, the mother tongue, and toned down the influence of Sanskrit, known as the language of gods. So the Marathi poet Tukaram says that. 'If Sanskrit is the language of gods, what then is my language? Is it the language of thieves?'

Self :

> The impersonal philosophic conception of the relation between Brahman and Atman (the Universal Principle and the Self) proposed by

Shankaracharya was replaced by a more personal and intimate relation between the divine and the human, whereby a saint poetess like Meera could claim the cowherd god, Krishna, as her only mate (mere to girdhar gopala dusro na koi). I have already mentioned how Tagore by discarding the One of Shankaracharya accepted the Two of bhakti. Hence Tagore creates his concept of Jivan Devata (the god of life) which evolves in three stages, i) as the 'beloved lady'; ii) as his inner being (antaraatma); and ultimately iii) Goddess of life who is the Infinite Being and gives his core philosophical notion as enumerated in

Gitanjali :

> The Infinite wants the finite's intimate comradeship
> And the finite wishes to lose itself in the Infinite.

In other words Tagore is speaking about the idea of the humanity of our God and the divinity of man, the eternal.

The medieval *bhakti* movement was in fact initiated by the common people, mostly belonging to lower caste, poor, involved in low professions but always ecstatic in their love for God. Just to cite one example from the Kannada *vachana* texts of Basavanna (1134-1196), the leader of the Virasaiva religious movement of medieval Karnataka :

> The rich/will make temples for Siva/What shall I/a poor, do?
> My legs are pillars/the body the shrine/the head a cupola/of gold.
> Listen, O lord of the meeting rivers/things standing shall fall/but the moving ever shall stay.

Indian temples are traditionally built, as explained by A.K. Ramanujan, in the image of human body. The temple in brick and stone carries the primordial blueprint of the human body but in time the human metaphor faded and temple became a static standing thing of brick, stone and mortar and its moving originals were forgotten. The Virsaiva movement was a social upheaval by and for the poor, the low-caste and the outcaste against the rich and the privileged; it was a rising of the unlettered against the literate pundit and demonstration of the common man's perception of the mundane world as something real and concrete not as illusory or transient.

Bhakti poetry was first written in the sixth and seventh century AD in Tamil and appeared in Tamil speaking areas in South but by 16th century it became a pan Indian movement and proliferated in every Indian language from east, to west and north. *Bhakti* poetry is, in fact, like a stream of flowing oil, *tailadhara*, from vessel to vessel, from verse to verse, from mind to mind, from god to devotee. It was a revolution that took the imagination of people by storm.

Shaguna Ramanathan says,

Bhakti (devotion) *is* love, faith and humility, as opposed to common forms of discourse that serve to delimit a field, mark off its boundaries, legitimise norms and perspectives. Discourse is the practice of power through language that keeps a society stable, but there comes a point when such a world is felt to be radically insufficient. The heart, disturbed by love, moves towards a point outside the given boundaries and challenges common discourse. Then devotional poets like Kabir, Nanak and Meera and many others cross the boundaries of rules and authority and wander from place to place, as they sing of the love of God and domesticate godhead.

Playing a crucial role in the background was a strong tradition of Tamil, Prakrit and Sanskrit love lyrics mostly of 1st century AD. These lyrics were neither sacred nor religious.

Some had a moral thought or religious belief cleverly injected into them but their core was of the earth, earthy. The celebration of life in these songs was of stylised romance.

With adult free love their main theme, they were to be found in Hala's *Gatha Saptasati* (between 200 BCE-200CE), Tamil *Sangam* poetry and Sanskrit *Subhashitas,* mostly in poems that have a double meaning. Some examples are :

> Here sleeps my mother-in-law, like a log;
> Me here, all others there,

O night-blind traveller do
not come and fall into my bed,
Gatha Saptasati, 7.67

Having chased the wild boar
In jungle dark –even your dogs are tired–
Don't go, sir. There that is my place, where
bamboos tall attract
The chubby elephant.
Kuruntokoi (6th or 7th cen CE)

Most of the poems celebrate love among humans, apparently unaware or unmindful of the hand of divinity and indifferent to the voice of the ascetic.

With the passage of time, this erotic poetry became weary. By about the sixth century AD, this staleness showed itself as the inevitable consequence of monotony in theme and treatment. Poets churned out types rather than poems of any individuality. There was no freshness of approach and poetry became rigid by following a set pattern. A theory of 'fitting language' (*tinai*) was vigorously exercised, which further enhanced the inflexibility of the poems. For example, any reference to a parrot or a peacock in a poem depicting love on the plains or sea-shore would be frowned upon, as those birds belonged to the hilly region. Cerebration began to displace creativity.

Loss of royal patronage was another reason that led to the devaluation of this poetry.

The Vedas were on the decline, Jainism and Buddhism discredited the notion of God, in fact there was a general sense of confusion all around.

It was in this atmosphere that the idea of God as a personal Being, ready to respond when devotion was intense, captured the imagination of the people.

To look upon God as akin and near to the human was something substantial. It was an exciting idea and the situation could lend itself to ecstasy. It was not necessary to evolve a new form of poetics to celebrate love between the god and the devotee.

It was easily derived from the lyrical love poetry of the *Gatha* tradition and Tamil love poetry but then meaning started emerging differently.

The earthen lamp was the same which lit the room of the hero and his beloved in love but now the light pointed towards the sky presenting a new meaning – a transcendental meaning. This divine love emerges from sensuous love but it turns ultimately into sublime love. In the small circle of love, one experiences the expanse of the divine.

It seems to follow that, when a human falls in love with the Divine, the language of love cannot be any different from that which is applicable to mortals. In *bhakti* poetry the entire erotic tradition becomes a new signifier with *bhakti* as the signified.

One can give an example from a Tamil poem of the Ninth century AD, written by ManikkaVacakar (9th Cen) :

> I shall wear the *Kornai* bloom
> And feel the rounded arms of Siva
> In embrace; and have him,
> And feel dazed in love.
> In pure ecstasy I shall stand apart,
> Only to pine for his lips so red
> Pining within, I shall search,
>
> Only to think of his feet, says Manikka Vacakar.

The signifiers of love poetry are enlisted for a new signification (*bhakti*). The changes are subtle, only a name (Siva) or a context (feet) can change a profane poem into a sacred one.

The signature line (*bhanita* i.e. the name of the poet in the poem) is used to differentiate between worldly love and divine love (*madhurya* or *prema bhakti*).

Now, God is no more inaccessible out of bounds – now he is brought from the temple to stay in the house because *bhakti* poetry is the poetry of sharing, touching, seeing the many in one. The *bhakta*(devotee)and the god he worships become one. But in reality the god does not come to stay with you. It only hints at living truthfully , with God residing in you (Nanak) – and also at the harmony of life which only love can bring. This is the mystic union with the Lord.

In traditional cultures like India, context-sensitive facts rule and bind life. The dream is to be free of context and create an alternative paradigm, to reject the current discourse and subvert its value-systems. Hence Krishna, one of the gods of *bhakti* movement is black and not fair. The colour white indicates purity, fair play, power and authority and black is the opposite of that but, in reality; black Krishna possesses all that is divine. He is not a Brahmin of the elite class but is of the cowherd caste, almost a commoner. He is not connected with order, harmony, and the light of the heaven. He is rooted in this earth where, despite in their own, discourse-governed rules are not the most important thing. In fact, by breaking those rules men reach the transcendental state of reality which is the state of freedom from worldly bondage. As soon as Krishna starts playing his flute the message of love is floated on a flower-scented breeze and all self-control is lost. The *Gopis,* the married cowherd women, tear themselves away from home and husband and come running to Krishna, the illegitimate lover (*jara*).

Paradoxically, in the discourse-governed world unruliness becomes the rule. Faith breaks the boundaries, stands outside discourse and addresses it in a wholly new and strange way.

It is the faith of complete surrender (*atmanivedana*) for union with the non-containable and non-finite, the 'other', the transcendent which the phenomenal world is insufficient to satisfy. Hence a longing for completeness is the starting point of the devotional mystical way. It is a reversal of Gita's model of *swadharma* (follow your own duty), *nishkamakarma* (follow it desirelessly) and *atmasamarpana* (self-dedication). Now the devotee starts with atmasmarpana, self-dedication to the lord and it is possible only in a state of equableness, harmony and balance or *samadarshanah*. It needed courage to fiddle with the model of Gita and create one's own.

Bhakti is the last of the great Hindu anti-contextual notions. It defies all contextual structures, caste, ritual, temples, sacred space, sacred time, the Vedas and the *Sastras* (systematized knowledge). The Vedas are heard. Both sight and hearing are senses of distance. But the favourite *bhakti* sense is the sense of touch. The devotee's heart or hand's touch, not just the feet of God, but his entire body.

This impulse of touch and merging breaks the barriers and

distinctions between caste and caste, between touchable and untouchables, between male and female and between sacred and profane.

And within this movement, women defy more structures : gender, and all that goes with it (notions of modesty, marriage, dependence on men).

Once again *bhakti* shows us how close the independent, defiant women of the oral tales are to women in the *bhakti* movement. Akkamahadevi (12th Cen) of Karnataka and Lal Ded (14th Cen) of Kashmir, both gave up family life, wandered about without clothes and the necked body covered only with their tresses, defying social norms of the male governed society and spread the gospel of *Jnana* (knowledge) and worship of Siva. In one of her vachanas Akkamahadevi says :

> To the shameless girl
> Wearing the white Jasmine Lord's
> Light of morning;
> You fool,
> Where's the need for cover and jewel?

Akkamahadevi uses the mystic symbolism of the Virsaivas and Lal Ded employs the old Buddhist symbolism of river and ferry in her many songs. They were all socially ostracized but they cared less and established themselves as the precursor of a social movement of great magnitude by intertwining sacred with the love for life.

To sum up, Tagore was totally against idol worship and hence he followed the path of non-iconic (*nirguna*) bhakti of Kabir, Dadu and others.

The recurring images of beloved longing for the lover's company, or keen to give oneself up in the hands of the lover or constantly searching for him/her in nature, or beloved's pensive expectation and so on, are intertwined with the emblematic web of the finite reaching out the infinite and inversely Infinite seeking unity with the finite and so Tagore says, He is in so many ways, in so many forms, giving Himself (Sadhana : Realization in Action).

This notion binds Tagore with non-iconic bhakti poetry specially with Kabir and others as he said in 'The Religion of Man', 'I became aware of some underlying deep idea which is the obvious meaning of these love songs'.

Tagore also finds in the bhakti poetry the real tradition of India, which is to work for the adjustment of races, to acknowledge the real differences between them, and yet seek some basis of unity. Tagore further says in his essay on 'Nationalism' that 'the basis for this tradition has been built in India at the social level, not the political, through saints like Nanak, Kabir, Chaitanya and others.

Tagore got the cue from the medieval poets to speak about India's unity as a social reality. It was not a political agenda for him. His ideas of *samaj*, social upliftment and then *atmasshakti*, self-reliance and thereafter *swaraj*, self-rule, create a sequential progression to true human unity wherein the love for all of the medieval bhakti poetry becomes the dominating factor of a new world without violence, and of peace and fraternity.

Chapter Eighteen

Tagore's Concept of Community Development, Village Reconstruction and Community College Movement

In this paper I shall discuss Rabindranath Tagore's concept of community development or village reconstruction work and draw out the basic difference between Tagore's concept of community development and the community development programme of the Government of India introduced in the first five year plan. I shall also speak about Tagore's concept of community development in the context of the community college movement which has been growing in India ever since it began in 1995 with the opening of the Pondichery University Community College.

Tagore's ideas of community development or rural reconstruction were largely influenced by the ideas and forces with which he came into contact in early childhood. The influence on Tagore's thought of the Hindu Mela, which was founded in 1867 by Tagore's family, can hardly be exaggerated. The ideas which inspired the organisers of the mela were :

(i) Revival of crafts
(ii) Cultivation of literature and music
(iii) Physical exercise and
(iv) Self-help etc.

These ideas gave Tagore a clue to the social philosophy which he developed in later life.

Already in the early 80's of the 19th Century, in some of Tagore's writings and utterances, we got a glimpse of the thesis which he was to propound in mature years. In one of his essays on Nationalism in 1883 he said :

> We may get many things from the British by begging but never self-reliance. What is obtained by begging can never last. What is achieved by our own efforts has permanence.

In another paper in 1884 (*hate kalome* : In actual practice) he remarked :

> It is the small work which is the most difficult of all; an imposing programme is often but an evasion of real work. Our sphere of activities lies near us and around us in our homes and in our neighbourhood.

Here is a clear indication of the ideal on which his work of rural reconstruction was to be based. In the early 90's the task of managing the ancestral property devolved on him, gave him an opportunity to come into close contact with the people of rural Bengal and enabled him to form a true picture of villages and their people. The more he saw of the poverty and suffering of the village people, the more restless he became to do something for them. He even said :

> It seemed to me a shameful thing that I should spend my days as a Zamindar, concerned only with money making and engrossed in my own profit and loss account.

This first- hand experience of village life left a deep mark on his mind. Since then he harboured a strong feeling to do something for them. This inner craving to do something for them never weakened and continued to prey upon his mind up to the last days of his life.

His manifesto about the community development or the upliftment of the village community was revealed in 1904 in an essay 'Swadeshi Samaj'(Indigenous or Indian Society), which was the first comprehensive statement of his social philosophy. The salient features of his manifesto are :

(i) The source of Europe's strength lies in the state; our well-being depends on the society. Our mind is no longer in the society. The system of social duties, which was carefully built up through the ages, is now breaking down;

(ii) Villagers are deprived of the services of the well-to-do classes and who are now drained of their wealth which is consumed in urban centres;

(iii) Scarcity of drinking water. Tanks, which were looked after by the rich, now left for the centre, are now contaminated;

(iv) The widening gulf between towns and villages produced some curious anomalies;

(v) Wealth was regarded as a social trust. It was the task of the wealthy to look after social work. They were the pillars of rural society. Old values have now changed. The pursuit of wealth calls or tempts the upper classes away from the village;

(vi) Country fairs which were invaluable means of public education have become fairs of ugly amusements;

(vii) It has all along been the tradition in India to cultivate human relationship on an extensive scale;

(viii) An essay written in 1905 'Luxury's Noose' (*samaj*) Tagore deplored the general tendency to luxury. There was a time when our country cared little for wealth. Indeed in a characteristic way she lent a peculiar dignity and beauty to poverty. To eat alone was a greater shame for us than to use humble banana leaves for sharing our food with others. (*samuha*, appendix to the essay *swadeshi samaj*).

He analysed the causes of the disintegration of village life and made concrete suggestions for its reconstruction. As a sequel to the essay on '*swadeshi samaj*' prepared a complete scheme to give practical effect to the ideas he has expressed in it. The whole scheme centred on the reorganization of village life through concerted efforts. The salient features are :

(i) The revival of cottage industries to mitigate the poverty of the masses;

(ii) Intimate cooperation between rural workers and villagers as among the villagers themselves;

(iii) Curtailment of expenditure at socio-religious ceremonies;
(iv) The creation of a corps of volunteers to strive to establish harmonious relationship between Hindus and Mohammedans;
(v) Appointment of a people's representative as the leader of the society.

In *'abastha-o-byabastha'* written in 1905 Tagore went on to enlarge upon his idea of constructive work which he had already put forward in *'swadeshi samaj'* :

> Let us not ask for any favour. Let us instead concentrate our attention on ourselves and we shall soon discover that what God has given us is enough for us constitutes the only tangible asset that we possess.

Tagore laid great weight on the need for collective enterprise in villages. The use of labour-saving machinery was indispensable, but it would be possible only if collective cultivation were introduced through the initiative of union executives. In Gora, his novel published in 1910 have some unforgettable pages on rural life.

In April 1914 he acquired the site in village Surul, about a mile and a half from Shantiniketan (abode of peace) on which now stands the Institute of Rural Reconstruction Sriniketan (abode of well-being). Rabindranath invited Leonard Elmhirst from England to lead the Sriniketan Institute of Rural Reconstruction. He had met Leonard Elmhirst during his travels in America in 1920-21 when Elmhirst was graduating in agricultural studies at Cornell University. Early in 1915 he was associated with Bengal Social Service League and delivered three lectures bearing on the question of rural uplift. He chalked out a programme for the society which included the following items :

(i) Education to illiterate;
(ii) Promotion of public health;
(iii) Arrangements in villages for good drinking water;
(iv) Establishing of cooperative credit societies;
(v) Organization of public help in times of feminine etc.
(vi) Restoring balance between city and village – it is the

> blind pull of urban forces, which in its turn is an inevitable concomitant of a profit civilization, and is responsible in the breakdown of village societies. The balance can be restored by corresponding readjustment in our values and our outlook.

What he wrote in *swdeshi samaj* in 1904 he endorsed it in 1939 in a speech in Sriniketan which was possibly the best and most authentic accounts on his first experience in villages. He emphasised on three points :

(i) Life must be developed in all its varied aspects;
(ii) The people must be induced to exert themselves;
(iii) Rural life must again be made cheerful

An all-round regeneration of village life with the active co-operation of the people so that life in the village may again radiate with joy — this then was Tagore's ideal in rural reconstruction. No regeneration could be real unless it was all round. Administrative machinery is devoid of true feeling because it lacked the throb of life. It is inadequate. Tagore has invoked several times the spirit of service and sacrifice. In a unique way he combines his humanitarianism with his individualism and also his sense of realism. Self-exertion is the condition of growth. He once said :

> The real service is to awaken the mind and to call forth its latent energies. (1940 address at Sriniketan)

Tagore thought rural problems must be tackled in a scientific spirit. It needs expert handling – he first wanted investigation of the economic problems of Sriniketan villages. Whatever you want to give them give with respect and infuse self-confidence in the villagers. All through his life he was an ardent advocate of rural uplift work. It was far more important in his eyes then the "pure politics." There was a remarkable consistency in his ideas on rural reconstruction over a period of some 50 years. In *swadeshi samaj* he appeared in the main as an advocate of the rehabilitation of the village society. He said that the greatest task before the rural workers is to teach the villagers to stand on their own legs, and collectively look after general welfare (A letter to a worker in Kaligram). His village reconstruction work had two principles :

(i) Without trying to impose ideas from outside, the workers should slowly build up their programme on the basis of the experience gained in the field. There is nothing like drawing on one's own resources.

(ii) Tagore decided that approach to the rural problems should be integrated and not piecemeal.

These two general principles formed the base on which Elmhirst and his workers started building up the programme. This does not necessarily shut out outside assistance altogether. The specific function of the external agency should be to find out the special problems of the village, to find out a solution for them at the research centre and to communicate the technical knowledge, thus gained, to the villagers for their use. In substance, therefore, external assistance was to be limited to transmission of technical knowledge alone.

There are some basic differences in Tagore's concept of community development and the community development programme of the Government of India introduced in the first five-year plan and that is :

(i) lack of emotional appeal. Tagore links up the voluntary work with the emotion of love or religious veneration and as a result a course is undertaken in a mood of seriousness and respect for the welfare of the people whom we love and respect. His theory was that "the best way to offer service to God was to serve man because God is intimately manifest to man as man." Tagore would further say, "God as revealed in humanity in general and in particular in the underprivileged classes should receive our service." If one equates service to man as service to God then the antagonism between religion and what may be called positivistic humanism can be reconciled. In a poem in Gitanjali Tagore said, "My heart can never find its way to where thou keepest company with the companionless among the poorest, the lowliest and the lost." Tagore's religion was service to man. This idea was the basis of self-less voluntary work which he called *Viswa karma* (universal work) and the social worker *Viswa karma* whose main approach is to serve the community not the individuals. In other words what is good for community is good for the individual. When the relationship between community or society and the individual is understood it provides inspiration to the individual to develop his power without sacrificing his individuality and yet at the same time, to be able to serve his community. And b) not receiving any benefit himself. I remember what Father Alfanso (one of the founding fathers of community college movement in India) once said that the unemployed teachers are trained and given the proper vision that if they set their eyes and heart on salary they can never be true community college teachers. However, in Tagore's scheme of rural reconstruction the material aspect was not left out – it received explicit emphasis. Tagore always thought "true happiness depends more on the habit of the mind than on the size of the purse." For Tagore the task or rural reconstruction was to rebuild man. (City and Village, p. 25). His thesis was that a lighted lamp is for us the end, not a lump of gold."

(ii) Tagore decided that approach to rural problems should be integrated and not piecemeal. "No regeneration could be real unless it was all-round."Community Development programme of Government of India is also multipurpose in character and it is at the same time shaped as a self help programme. Tagore would say that the best way of helping others is to help them to help themselves.

Though Tagore would stop us from begging anything from the British and develop self-reliance but that did not mean that Tagore wanted us to shut out outside assistance altogether but what he desired that the external assistance was to be limited to transmission of technical knowledge.

In Tagore's concept of community development there is an added element of joy and happiness. He found the life in villages dull and dreary, no joy. For Tagore joy was both an end in itself and a means to an end. We live for the sake of joy. At the same time each of us gives our best only when there is joy within. A well-known song which is sung at the functions of Sriniketan runs as follows :

The sun shines, the rain pours down in showers,
The leaves glisten in the bamboo grove,
The smell of the newly tilled earth fills the air,
Our hands are strong, our hearts glad,
as we toil from morning till night to plough the land.

These lines not only show Tagore's sympathy for the peasant, but his desire to lend dignity to his work and to lighten the burden by introducing joy and music into it. He would say, "The Poverty problem is not the most important, the problem of unhappiness is the great problem." (City and Village, p.24).

For Tagore, the two experiments, pedagogic at Shantiniketan and agricultural at Sriniketan or cultural and rural were vitally linked. What he tried to work out in Shantiniketan and at Surul, Sriniketan, was an integrated programme in which culture of the mind and the culture of the soil went hand in hand. Tagore never wanted that Shantiniketan should grow as a cultural oasis in the midst of an arid waste of decaying humanity. It never seemed right to him. How to build a living and fruitful network of communication between the two had long troubled him.

It is a pity that this very real concern of his has somehow failed to receive due appreciation from his people. Is it because it was overshadowed, partly by his own glamour as a poet and partly by Mahatma Gandhi's mystic cult of the charkha?

Tagore's active concern with this problem was prior to the Mahatma's, dating from the nineties of the 19th century when he had first come face to face with the grim tragedy of the village economy while looking after his family estates in north-east Bengal. Though he lacked the Mahatma's singular power of dramatizing every issue into a national crusade, his practical approach to the actual problem was both more realistic and more comprehensive. He believed in the intelligent application of scientific technique as necessary for the development of Indian agriculture and of small scale rural industries. This belief, rather than the magic of charkha, has been amply vindicated by what has happened in many parts of India today. On the other hand, he shared the Mahatma's gospel of self-help and his faith in the dignity of manual labour, however seemingly low. Indeed had the Mahatma watched Leonard Elmhirst and his boys carrying latrine buckets to empty them into manure pits, he would have hugged them with delight.

It would be interesting to note that Tagore dedicated his book 'The religion of Man' to Dorothy Whitney Straight, daughter of an American millionaire, who later married Leonard Elmhirst and also endowed Sriniketan with a permanent fund to put Sriniketan on its feet financially.

The last point of discussion is community colleges. The community college is largely a phenomenon of 20th Cen. American higher education. Community colleges are comprehensive institutions that provide

(i) General and liberal education
(ii) Career and vocational education
(iii) Adult and continuing education

One can cite O'Banion's six principles of the learning community College :

(i) Creating substantive change in individual learners,
(ii) Engaging learners as full partners in the learning process,
(iii) Creating and offering as many options for learning as possible,
(iv) Assisting learners in forming and participating in collaborative learning projects,
(v) Defining the roles of learning facilators by the needs of the learners,
(vi) Documenting improved and expanded learning for its learners, the only way the learning college and its facilators succeed.

In America community colleges are people's colleges, they give equal access and opportunity especially to people who come from different parts of the world. Flexibility and cost effectiveness are the hallmark of these colleges. It is useful in Indian condition where there is rampart unemployment among the graduate youths.

The community college movement which started in 1995 by Father Aphanso has since been growing in India. Father Alphanso adapted the US community college system but added elements that make it applicable to our local indigenous people. Infusing self-confidence, self esteemed, self motivation in the students coming from socially, economically, educationally backward groups. The primary objective of the Jesuit Father, Alphonso was to start the community college movement in India for training the "backward people" described by most as the poorest of the poor of India's people and today there are 153 community colleges across 17 states. It is now a national phenomenon empowering individuals, who were devoid of the conventional education system, through skill development with the help of local industry and community.

"Do not go my love" is a poem by Tagore which is made into a song by Richard Hageman and sung in the shoreline community college sets the mood of these colleges, which are on one side, provide education for livelihood and, on the other side, these colleges are based on the whole philosophy that merit is an opportunity and excellence is developing the latent potential in the individual person by giving him/her the right type of opportunity at the right time in his/her life. The slogan of Leap Outreach Programme in Loyala College, Chennai 'Fit for life and fit for job' reflects that life is not one sided but a comprehensive whole where work and aesthetics go together.

The difference of perception between Tagore's rural reconstruction programme and community colleges' philosophy is that Tagore's programme was dedicated to community farming and development of the village economy and on the contrary the rationale behind community colleges is to enhance skilled labour force, but at the same time to empower individuals to improve the quality of life for individuals, communities and the nation. Tagore harboured a strong feeling to do something for the poor people of the villages but at the same time he would say, "It is not enough to try to remove wants. You can never remove them completely from the outside; the far greater thing is to rouse the will of the people to remove their own wants. Today the Ministry of Human Resource Development has borrowed some of Tagore's ideas, immortalized as the objectives of Visva-Bharati, in drafting the guiding aims of the promised new institutions formally referred now as 'Innovation Universities'. These guiding principles, as given below, if added into the philosophy of Indian community colleges, it would definitely give a true and comprehensive conceptual vision in the development of community college movement in India :

(i) Boundary-less pursuit of knowledge for the greater good of man;
(ii) To study the mind of man in its realization of different aspects of truth, from diverse points of view;
(iii) To strive for spiritual realization, amity, cooperation, and comprehension of ideas of thinkers from different cultures;
(iv) Harmonizing the cultures of India.

If these ideas become a part of community college philosophy, which primarily promotes job oriented, work related, skill-based and life coping education, it would definitely turn into an alternative holistic education system and a true man making education.

❑❑

APPENDIX

(i)

An Introduction Written for the Book by Dr. Kalyan Kundu on Tagore and Mussulini Published by Oxford Books

Krishna Kriplani, one of the most distinguished biographers of Tagore, first quoted what Tagore said before his departure to Italy on 15 May 1926, 'It is for me to study and not criticize from outside. I am glad of this opportunity to see for myself the work of one who is assuredly a great man and a movement that will certainly be remembered in history' and then commented that the idea that Duce was 'a great man' was a delusion which Tagore temporarily shared with many shrewd and seasoned politicians of that time.[1] After Tagore's Italian tour when he met Romain Rolland in Villeneuve, Signora Salvadori in Zurich, Modigliani in Vienna and Firnande Luceir, wife of Gaetano Salvemini in Paris and many others, he could realize how the Italian propaganda machine had duped him and made him appear to be a defender of Fascism. Tagore could apprehend the sinister design of Mussolini and wrote a long letter to Charles Freer Andrews, which was later published in the Manchester Guardian on 5th August 1926, explaining his visit to Italy and condemning Fascism in no uncertain terms. He especially wrote in that letter to the Manchester Guardian, 'It is absurd to imagine that I could ever support a movement (Fascism) which ruthlessly suppresses freedom of expression, enforces observances that are against individual conscience, and walks through a bloodstained path of violence and stealthy crime.'[2] He also wrote to Romain Rolland, 'I have to pass through a purification ceremony for the defilement to which I submitted myself in Italy.'[3] But there were many in Europe and England like the expatriate Salvemini who were sarcastic in their treatment of Tagore and did not accept whole-heartedly what he said about Mussolini in the Manchester Guardian. In India also many comments were published in a leading Bengali journal, Prabashi, which were full of wild disbelief regarding Tagore's criticism of Mussolini and the reasons for it.

Tagore remained ever indebted to Mussolini for his generous gift of a large number of classics in Italian to Visva-Bharati without realizing that it was to encourage and influence the poet to accept the Italian government's invitation to visit Italy -all part of Mussolini's heinous ploy. But the unfortunate part of the episode, that which raised the suspicion in the minds of many, came when Guglielmo Salvadori suggested to Tagore in a letter on 16 July 1926 that he return all these books to Mussolini and Tagore ignored the suggestion.[4] Carlo Formichi, the prime mover of Tagore's Italian tour and a villain of the piece, was both adored and hated because of his knowledge of Sanskrit and Indian culture and his allegiance towards Mussolini and fascism. But whether he had respect and regard for Tagore is a big question particularly when firstly, after Tagore's first speech in Milan Formichi, called it "cheap sermons of love and peace" and said that this "humanitarian sermon was absolutely out of place".[5]

Secondly, Formichi sent a rejoinder to Tagore's letter to the Manchester Guardian criticizing Mussolini and Fascism and made a determined attempt, with the help of concocted facts and lies, to show that Tagore had spoken in favour of Mussolini and his politics. What truly surprises me is that Mahatma Gandhi also visited Italy four years after Tagore's visit and lauded Mussolini's many economic and social reforms but he was never targeted and the way besieged by criticism as was Tagore.[6] However there was a single but very crucial difference between the two of them. Gandhi heeded Romain Rolland's advice and did not become a state guest of Mussolini whereas Tagore accepted the offer to be a state guest and that changed the attitude of the liberals towards both of them. However Tagore redeemed himself considerably by that letter to the Manchester Guardian and when Amartya Sen said in an interview for the Italian newspaper "LaVoce Republicana' that 'in Italian Fascism there could have been the seeds of a new anti-imperialism." Dimmed by that illusion , Tagore accepted to be exhibited by the regime during a brief official visit in Italy.[7] But when Tagore decided to write a letter of gratitude to Mussolini four years after his visit to Italy in 1930 at Formichi's behest (whom Tagore met that year in America), it would have proved completely suicidal and Tagore would have remained beyond redemption, but thanks to his son Rathindranath's advice - the letter was never sent.[8] However Dr Kundu, quoting Mario Prayer and Sofori, maintains that the letter was actually sent but there is no evidence yet to confirm whether or not Mussolini ever saw this letter.[9]

I have always thought that both Tagore and his love for Italy and Mussolini and Jawaharlal Nehru and his love for China and Zhou Enlae turned out to be their *hamartia* which made them the tragic heroes of that part of history which was related to the Italian and Chinese episodes in their lives.

Having this kind of attitude towards Tagore's Mussolini episode, when I chanced to read Dr Kalyan Kundu's latest book "Meeting with Mussolini : Tagore's Tours in Italy : 1925 and 1926", I was not only amazed by his deep and well researched and evaluative study of the subject but also by his objectivity in discovering the truth and nothing but the truth about the whole episode. I have no hesitation in saying that there is no book on Tagore-Mussolini episode like this one. It includes details such as an almost day by day record of Tagore's tour in Italy in 1925 and 1926 as well as news reports, interviews etc. -as much as he could gather from various sources. It incorporates detailed conversations between Tagore and all the main characters in this drama in which Mussolini is himself a major player.

There are references of Tagore's Italian tours in the biographies of Dutta Robinson, Krishna Kripalani and also Prabhat Mukhopadhyay. Understandably there are no critical studies of this episode in those books. They all followed the conventional line. However, there are some important papers on the subject which are :

(i) Rathindranath Tagore, "On the Edges of Time", pp.136-140, Visva-Bharati, 1958.

(ii) Prasanta Chandra Mahalanobis : "Our Founder-President in Italy, 1926", Visva-Bharati Bulletin, Visva-Bharati Quarterly, October 1926.

(iii) Nirmal Kumari mahalanobis : "Kobir Sange Eoropey," Mitra O Ghosh, Kolkata, 1969.

(iv) Carlo Formichi : "India e Indiani" relevant section translated by Mario Prayer and published in *Rabindravikshya.*

(v) Giuseppe Flora : Rabindranath tagore and Italy; facing history and politics

(vi) Besides these there are other articles some are in Italian and some are in English by Mario Prayer.

Guiseppe Flora's article follows more or less the conventional tale but it is a well researched appraisal of the subject set against the European political context. Dr Kundu mentions that in his introduction.

Dr Kundu is the first scholar, to give a lot of importance to the Italian news published in the Italian Press in connection with Tagore's tour particularly because of other scholars' constant and persistent blaming of Italian papers for publishing distorted news about Tagore during his tour in 1926. Dr Kundu has made the Italian material an important part of the book so that the truth could be revealed.

Dr Kundu says that he has no concrete evidence of what Tagore said in his interviews (especially at those times when Tagore's secretary was not present) but from the published report he found nothing offensive or any way of telling which part of Tagore's interviews had been edited on grounds of anti-fascist element.

But at the same time we cannot forget that all the liberals and friends of Tagore - Romain Rolland, George Duhamel, J.G. Fraser, Forel, Bovet and others - spoke with one voice when he met them after crossing over to Switzerland, about the garbled and distorted versions of his speeches and interviews which were being headlined by the Italian press to boost the fascist regime. It was only when Tagore was convinced that the Italian propaganda machine had made a dupe of him that he wrote the letter to Charles Freer Andrews which was later published in the Manchester Guardian. At the same time it is difficult for me to believe that Dr Kundu's conclusion arrived at after a painstaking study of all the Italian material, is not worth considering.

Dr Kundu also does not agree with the general perception of Carlo Formichi and Giuseppe Tucci as fascists trying to use Tagore for political ends. Dr Kundu's purpose in the book is to show Formichi and Tucci's actions in a newer light before imposing any indictment on these two very distinguished Orientalists. It is true that both the professors were fascists and they never hid that fact but they had a high regard for Tagore which cannot be ignored. One thing we must remember, as explained by Dr Kundu, is that Formichi came to know about Tagore through Kalidas Nag before Mussolini came to power (See the letter of 8 May in the Chapter 'Italy 1925'). He had a genuine admiration for Tagore's literary works, and a passion for visiting India also. Tagore in 1921, while touring Europe, was also searching for visiting professors for his University and Formichi's name was on the card. But he failed to meet Formichi in 1921.

In 1925 when Tagore actually met Formichi he invited him to join Visva-Bharati. So it was Tagore, concludes Dr Kundu, who invited Formichi not, as popularly believed, Mussolini who sent Formichi to Tagore's University.

When Formichi failed to raise sufficient funds to buy Italian books and resources for Visva-Bharati (basically as a matter of prestige as other European visiting professors before him had donated books and resources to Visva-Bharati) he approached Mussolini for financial support. In 1926 Mussolini was passing through a difficult time in his political career. The murder of two prominent socialist activists had raised a hue and cry in the European left wing press condemning the fascist's policies. Mussolini took the opportunity to divert political attention by inviting Tagore to Italy. He unhesitatingly accepted Formichi's proposal with unusual generosity.

Dr Kundu's conclusion is that for Formichi and Tucci's safe existence they had to be loyal to Mussolini and for that they had sometimes to play a duel role. This can be seen as their predicament, giving rise to some complex psychological tension, through which they passed at that time. I have no reason to disagree with this opinion except that the relation with Tagore was more of love but sometimes of disgust also but at the end it was abiding respect and adoration for Tagore's creativity and scholarship.

Tagore's esteem for Mussolini was untarnished for a few years more. He even wanted to patch up the difference in 1930, four years after the incident, as mentioned earlier in this preface. It was only after Italy invaded Abyssinia (now Ethiopia), that Tagore completely changed his opinion about Mussolini and wrote a poem "Africa" on 10 February 1937 which was, as Sugata Bose explains, a searing and sarcastic criticism directed at the false Universalist claims of an unnamed Europe (Italy). Even as the "barbaric greed of the civilized" put on naked display their 'shameless inhumanity', church bells rang out in neighbourhoods across the ocean in the name of a benign God, "children played in their mother's laps, and poets sang paeans to beauty."

I would like to end by saying that in Dr Kundu I found a true Tagore scholar with a deep research- oriented mind. He gave a very objective and honest account of the Tagore-Mussolini episode which still remains an enigmatic chapter in Tagore's life history.

Notes and References

(i) Krishna Kriplani, Rabindranath Tagore–A Biography, Reprint 2012, p. 319

(ii) Letter No 211, p.333, Selected Letters of Rabindranath Tagore, (eds) Krishna Dutta and Andrew Robinson, 1997

(iii) Letter No 209, p. 329, Ibid

(iv) Letter No 247, p. 394, Note 1, Ibid

(v) Mario Prayer, "On Tagore", Rabindranathviksha, Vol 39, p.39, Visva-Bharati, 2001, translated from Carlo Formichi's book 'India e Indian', published by Alps, Milan, 1939

(vi) Bikash Chakravarti, "Mussolinike Rabindranath : 21 November

1930'. pp.105-118. Chaturanga, Kolkata, 1415. Also, vide http ://gandhiking.ning.com/profiles/blogs/mussolini-and-mahatma-gandhi-1

(vii) Giuseppe Flora : Rabindranath Tagore and Italy : Facing History and Politics, p.281, Reclaiming a cultural Icon, Visva-Bharati, Calcutta, 2005

(viii) Letter No 247, p.394, Selected Letters of Rabindranath Tagore, (eds) Krishna Dutta and Andrew Robinson, 1997

(ix) last page of the chapter 'Post Trip'

APPENDIX

(ii)

National Anthem and Rabindranath Tagore

When the Constituent Assembly of India met on Tuesday 24 January, 1949 in the ConstitutionHall to sign the Constitution its President, Dr Rajendra Prasad, began the proceedings with a statement on the question of a National Anthem of India :

> The composition consisting of the words and music known as *janaganamana* is the National Anthem of India subject to such alteration in the words as Government may authorize as occasion arises; and the song *Vandemataram* which has played a historic part in the struggle for Indian freedom shall be honoured equally with *Janaganamana* and shall have equal status with it.

After the Members of the Assembly had signed the Constitutuion Shri Ananthasayanam Ayyangar asked the President if he would permit all Memebers of the House to sing *Janaganamana* and the President giving his assent Smt. Purnima Banerji with other members sang it for the first time after its formal adoption as our National Anthem.

This was however, not the first time that *Janaganamana* was sung in the Constituent Assembly. The proceedings of the historic session of the body at the midnight of 14 August 1947 ended with the song although it was then sung only as a national song following *Sare Jahan se Achcha Hindustan hamara.* The first item on the agenda for the session was the singing of *Vandemataram.* In fact, soon after independence it was provisionally recognized as India's National Anthem till a choice was formally made by the Constituent Assembly in 1949. Jawaharlal Nehru himself preferred *Janaganamana* and he gave his reason in a statement made in Parliament on 25th August 1948 and 10 days before on 15th August that year the Sikh Regiment Central struck the tune of the song at the hoisting of the National Flag at the first anniversary of Independence at the Red Fort in Delhi.

Janaganamana was composed by Rabindranath Tagore some-time towards the end of 1911 and was first sung on 29th December that year at the second day's sitting of the twenty-sixth session of the Indian National Congress held in Calcutta under the President ship of Bishan Naraya Dhar. The choir included Shri Amal Home and Smt. Chitralekkha Devi, wife of a former Vice-chancellor of the Calcutta University.

Reporting the proceedings of this session *Amrit Bazar Patrika* in the 28 December 1911 issue called *Janaganamana* a 'song of benediction' and *The Bengali,* a paper edited by Surendranath Banerjee who was one of the principal organizers of this session of the Congress, also in its issue of 28th December 1911 called it a 'patriotic song' and published an English version of it in its report.

The official report of the Indian National Congress covering this session says that 'the proceedings commenced with a patriotic song composed by Rabindranath Tagore' and that after that a 'song of welcome to their Imperial Majesties composed for the occasion was sung by the choir.' This song of welcome was in Hindi and was composed by Rambhuj Dutt Choudhuri, husband of Sarala Devi, a niece of the poet.

The Congress included it in the programme because it desired to be polite to King George V then visiting India after he had announced the annulment of the partition of Bengal against which it had agitated about six years.

Two Anglo-Indian newspapers of Calcutta, *The Englishmen* and

The Statesman in their issues of the same date and Reuter on 29 December 1911 deliberately or ignorantly reported that the song by Tagore was a song of welcome to the king.

The Englishman said : The proceedings open with a song of welcome to the King Emperor, specially composed for the occasion by the Babu Rabindranath Tagore... This was followed by a song of Hindi welcoming their Imperial Majesties.

The Statesman did not mention either the content or the author of the Bengali song but called the second song a hymn of welcome to the King specially composed for the occasion by Rabindranath Tagore, the Bengali poet. Reuter reported that 'when the Indian National Congress resumed its session on Wednesday Dec 27, a Bengali song, specially composed in honour of the Royal visit was sung. It may be noted that the three erroneous reports are inconsistent with each other.

How careless or irresponsible some reporters can be when the identity of Indian languages is involved is evident from a report published on 15th May 1949 in the *Sunday Times*, London in which *Vandemataram* is mentioned as a song written by Tagore and *Janaganamana* as song composed in modern Hindi. It is also surprising and puzzling that the same *Statesman* reporting on the thirty-second session of the Congress held in Calcutta in 1917 went against its previous reporting and said in its edition of 30th December 1917 that the Congress commenced with *Janaganamana* 'a national song composed by Rabindranath Tagore.

Such obvious errors in reporting would not deserve mention were it not for the fact that those who did not favour the adoption of *Janaganamana* as our National Anthem used them as an argument against the song. When in 1937 the Working Committee of the Congress appointed a sub-committee to consider the whole question of a national anthem for India with Abul Kalam Azad, Jawaharlal Nehru, Subhas Chandra Bose and Narendra Dev as its members there arose a controversy as to the relative claims of *Vandemataram* and *Janaganamana* on the distinction and the exponents of the first song sought to strengthen their case by fabricating a scandal about the second.

They knew that the scandal was utterly baseless but could not but take advantage of what they considered to be its tactical value in the controversy.

Presumably some of them thought it was effective reply to the poet's remark that parts of *Vandemataram* could offend Muslim sensibility. The poet had an occasion to say this when Jawaharlal Nehru asked him for his opinion on *Vandemataramin* in 1937. That the poet unhesitatingly approved of the adoption of the first two stanzas of *Vandemataram* as our national anthem was not enough for the exponents of Bankimchandra's song.

When Tagore was told about what was being said about the origin of *Janaganamana* he said in a letter to Pulinbihari Sen dated 20 November 1937, published in Vichitra, in the month of Paush, 1344 Bengali year i.e. January 1937 :

> A friend influential in the Government circles had importuned me to compose a song in praise of the King. His request had amazed me and the amazement was mingled with anger. It was under the stress of this violent reaction that I proclaimed in the *Janaganamana adhinayaka* song the victory of that Dispenser of India's destiny who chariots eternally the travellers through the ages along the path rugged with the rise and fall of nations,— of Him who dwells within the heart of man and leads the multitudes. That great Charioteer of man's destiny in age after age could not by any means be George V or George VI or any George. Even my 'loyal' friend realized this; because, however powerful his loyalty to the King, he was not wanting in intelligence.

In yet another letter written to Smt. Sudharani Devi dated 23 March 1939 Tagore said : "I should only insult myself if I cared to answer those who consider me capable of such unbounded stupidity as to sing in praise of George IV or George V as the Eternal Charioteer leading the pilgrims on their journey through the countless ages of the timeless history of mankind."

This silenced the detractors of *Janaganamana* for a time and when the song was finally adopted as our national anthem nobody repeated the fantastic view that it was an ode to an earthly king. But because of misinformation, lack of proper historical investigation by those who think that the song was an address to King George V and on top of it because of utter absence of poetic sensibility and understanding there are many who would repeat the old allegation against Tagore by quoting the same two Anglo- Indian newspapers and a foreign news agency that the song was, infact written in praise of the King of England. Here two points are worth mentioning;

There is no mention of a song of welcome to the King composed by Tagore in the elaborate report of the royal visit to India known as *The Historical Record of the Imperial Visit to India* , published by John Murrey in 1914. There is no mention either in John Fortesque, *Narrative of the Visit to India of Their Majesties King George V and Queen Mary, London 1912.*

Janaganamana was published under the title *'Bharat-Vidhata'* and sub-title *Brahmasangit,* in the *Tattvabodhini patrika,* the official organ of Adi Brahmo Samaj founded by the poet's father , and then edited by the poet himself. A song of welcome to an earthly king would never be included in the hymn-book of Brahmo Samaj.

Even those who are not acquainted with Tagore's political ideas atleast would have the common sense to realize that after the movement of 1921, 1930 and 1942 the political leadership of the country would never have accepted a song as national anthem when it was known to have been

composed as an ode to a British sovereign. In 1946 Mahatma Gandhi had said as quoted in the 19th May 1946 issue of *Harijan,* that the song has found a place in our national life. It is not only a song but it is like a devotional hymn. In 1961 Jawaharlal Nehru had said :" It was a great happiness to me when after the coming of Independence, we adopted *Janaganamana* as our national anthem."

There are many who suspect that the word *singhasan* meaning throne brings the idea too close to a king may remember that the throne of the Lord is a popular image for the power of the Deity in religious literature. In song 49 of *Gitanjali* The king comes down from his throne and stands at the cottage door of the poet is the

Deity who in the 3rd stanza of the song *Janaganamana* is addressed as *chirasarathi*, the eternal charioteer, who takes mankind along the right path in the midst of the terrific revolutions his voice reaching the human ear like the sound of a conch shell almost like the verse 1.14 of the *Bhagvadgita* where Lord Krishna brings Arjuna to the battlefield of Kurukshetra in his chariot and blows his conch shell *panchajanya*.

The forth stanza of the song is a praise for the Lord, who is addressed as the father in the beginning is now called mother— *sneha mai tumi mata*. This kind of an imagery will be unthinkable in the western perception for a British king but so common a feature of the Indian religious sensibility. In the *Bhagavadgita* in the verse ix.17 Lord Krishna says :

> *Pitamaham assya jagato mata dhata*
> "I am the Father Mother Sustainer of this world"

What is striking about this religious imagery in *Janaganamana* is that unlike Bankimchandra's *Vandemataram* and Tagore's own *Ayi bhuvanamanamohini* it does not hypostatize the country into a Divine Mother but presents it as a living human society moving towards the realization of its destiny under some Divine dispensation. It is a hymn celebrating the regeneration of the *janaganamana* collective mind of a people in a cosmic process which the poet views as the working of a Divine purpose of history.

❑❑